W9-ATH-327

FAITH & REASON

19-20

FAITH & REASON

Essays IN THE Philosophy OF Religion BY R. G. Collingwood

EDITED WITH AN INTRODUCTION BY
LIONEL RUBINOFF

Chicago Quadrangle Books 1968

 For information, address: Quadrangle Books, Inc., 12 East Delaware Place, Chicago 60611. Manufactured in the United States of America.

Library of Congress Catalog Card Number: 67-21641

Grateful acknowledgment is made to the following for permission to reprint copyrighted materials: Clarendon Press for selections from *Speculum Mentis;* George Allen and Unwin Ltd. for "Reason Is Faith Cultivating Itself" from the *Hibbert Journal; Theology* for "What Is the Problem of Evil?"; the Literary Executor of the late Canon B. F. Streeter for "The Devil"; and the Aristotelian Society for "Can the New Idealism Dispense with Mysticism?"

PREFACE

THIS book contains most of R. G. Collingwood's published writings in the philosophy of religion. It includes all of his published papers (exclusive of book reviews) as well as selections from *Religion and Philosophy* and *Speculum Mentis.* Although I consider these materials the most basic and most valuable of Collingwood's writings on religion, the student, in search of a more comprehensive picture of Collingwood's thought, should not overlook those sections in *An Essay on Philosophical Method* (Ch. VI, § 2) and *An Essay on Metaphysics* (Pt. iii.A) which deal with the ontological argument, as well as the relevant sections from *Religion and Philosophy* and *Speculum Mentis* not included in this collection.

The selections here are arranged to coincide with the particular interpretation of Collingwood's thought outlined in the introductions that precede each part. I genuinely trust, however, that this will not discourage the reader from viewing these writings against the background of his own interpretation. And, above all, I hope that my own interpretation will not prevent the reader from encountering the power of Collingwood's thought as it exists in its own right. For while the arrangement of materials clearly follows a particular interpretation, none of the selections included has been expurgated. This will, I trust, facilitate any number of fresh interpretations that may be suggested by the texts themselves. And no doubt almost every reader will be able to detect inconsistencies between the editor's interpretation and what Collingwood actually says. But this is as it should be, for philosophy thrives on such dialectical encounters.

The preparation of any book is a difficult and, at times, thankless task. It is therefore with gratitude that I acknowledge the contributions of those whose efforts and sympathies have made this task a little more bearable. Although no amount of gratitude can ever compensate for the sympathy and tolerance extended by a wife to a husband wedded to the production of a book, it is only just that recognition be extended first to this most precious of all gifts. Years of discussion with Professors W. H. Dray and E. L. Fackenheim of the University of Toronto have greatly helped to shape the intellectual atmosphere in which my approach to Collingwood's thought has grown. Professor James Edie of Northwestern University played a helpful role in getting the manuscript into print and made many suggestions concerning the organization of materials. I am also indebted to Ivan Dee, managing editor of Quadrangle Books, for his valuable help throughout the production of the book. Professor John O'Neil of York University read the introductions in their entirety and is responsible for many improvements. A series of grants made available during the years 1966-1967 by The Canada Council and the committee on minor research grants of York University has covered many of the expenses incurred in the preparation of the manuscript.

LIONEL RUBINOFF

Toronto, June 1967

ABBREVIATIONS

The titles of Collingwood's works are abbreviated in the text as follows:

BOOKS

A	*An Autobiography* (1939)
EM	*An Essay on Metaphysics* (1940)
EPM	*An Essay on Philosophical Method* (1933)
FML	*The First Mate's Log* (1940)
IH	*The Idea of History* (1946)
NL	*The New Leviathan* (1942)
OPA	*Outlines of a Philosophy of Art* (1925)
PA	*The Principles of Art* (1938)
RP	*Religion and Philosophy* (1916)
SM	*Speculum Mentis* (1924)

ARTICLES

CNI	"Can the New Idealism Dispense with Mysticism?" (1923)
D	"The Devil" (1916)
FR	"Faith and Reason" (1928)
PE	"What Is the Problem of Evil?" (1922)
RFCI	"Religion Is Faith Cultivating Itself" (1927)
RSP	"Religion, Science, and Philosophy" (1926)

CONTENTS

Part Four. Religion and Absolute Spirit: The Metaphysisc of Absolute Self-Making

EDITOR'S INTRODUCTION

1. RELIGION AND THE RAPPROCHEMENT BETWEEN FAITH AND REASON

Although Collingwood has been known chiefly for his philosophy of history, his concern with and contribution to the philosophy of religion was no less profound. His first publication was called *Religion and Philosophy,*[1] and it was in this book that he formulated the problems to whose solution the rest of his writings were devoted. *Religion and Philosophy* rests on the presupposition that "the form of consciousness called religion really does exist" (3; 43) [2] not simply as ritual, custom, or emotion but as genuine knowledge. Just as in the *Idea of History* and other works Collingwood sought to free history from the domination of the natural sciences, so in *Religion and Philosophy* he sought to remove religion from the charge of irrationalism by grounding it in a rapprochement between faith and reason.

By irrationalism Collingwood meant not only mysticism, and what logical positivists were later to call the emotive theory of religion,[3] but any attempt to reduce religion to purely sociological and psychological grounds, such as William James's *Varieties of Religious Experience.* In *Religion and Philosophy* Collingwood attacked any and every socio-psychological treatment of religious

1. London: Macmillan & Co., 1916.

2. References to the original texts appear first, followed (where applicable) by cross references to the same material as reprinted in this volume.

3. For example, A. J. Ayer writes in *Language, Truth and Logic* (London: 1936; 1946): "We conclude, therefore that the argument from religious experience is altogether fallacious. The fact that people have religious experience is interesting from the psychological point of view, but it does not in any way imply that there is such a thing as religious knowledge, any more than our having moral experiences implies that there is such a thing as moral knowledge. The theist, like the moralist, may believe that his experiences are cognitive experiences, but, unless he can formulate his "knowledge" in propositions that are empirically verifiable, we may be sure that he is deceiving himself. It follows that those philosophers who fill their books with assertions

experience. "The mind regarded in this way," he declared, "ceases to be a mind at all" (RP, 42; 77; Cf. A, 93).[4]

Collingwood sought to demonstrate throughout his writings that religion was just as philosophical as science or history and just as necessary to the integrity and health of life as any other form of knowledge. Religion is a form of human self-making which in its highest moments becomes an experience through which the finite, historical self transcends its finitude and celebrates in the transcendental experience of absolute truth. Thus religion, he argued, is a necessary and permanent part of the life upon which the other forms (science, history, philosophy, and art) are built, and without which there can be no genuine exercise of imagination and no proper employment of reason.

It was Collingwood's lifelong belief that the goal of philosophy is and always has been to unify the forms of life and thought. But the world of the twentieth century has presented a philosophical crisis by becoming an age of intense specialization. Collingwood regarded the detachment of the forms of experience resulting from specialization as not simply an intellectual problem but as a source of social and cultural alienation as well, which unless corrected will lead to the downfall of culture and the return of barbarism.

Collingwood's response to this crisis was a philosophy of rap-

---

that they intuitively "know" this or that moral or religious "truth" are merely providing material for the psychoanalyst. For no act of intuition can be said to reveal a truth about any matter of fact unless it issues in verifiable propositions. And all such propositions are to be incorporated in the system of empirical propositions which constitutes science" (pp. 119-120).

4. But not only does Collingwood reject this positivist approach to religion; he would be just as unhappy with those attempts to restore the meaning of religious statements by subsuming them under the principle of use, such as R. B. Braithwaite's *An Empiricist's View of Religious Belief* (Cambridge, 1955) which makes the primary use of religious assertions that of expressing the intention of the asserter to act in a specific sort of way specified in the assertion (which in the case of a Christian would be the agapeistic way of life). Collingwood would no doubt have argued, in sympathy with Austin, that while use may define the meaning of a religious assertion the force of that assertion lies in its truthfulness, which for Collingwood derives from the contribution of such beliefs to the self-making processes of finite and absolute mind.

prochement which sought to bring together the various forms of thought and experience which since the Renaissance had been rent asunder. He sought, therefore, to break down the dogma of specialization by showing how the forms interpenetrate and feed each other's integrity and by warning that corruption in one form of life means a deterioration in each of the other forms. Collingwood made this point in the *Principles of Art* (1939). Good art, he argued, is possible only in a healthy society which is founded on a "truthful" consciousness. But if the self as revealed in one sphere of activity is corrupt, then it is just as corrupt when revealed in all the other spheres. Corruption of consciousness is the same thing as bad art and bad art is the same thing as corruption of consciousness. "Just as the life of a community," wrote Collingwood, "depends for its very existence on honest dealing between man and man, the guardianship of this honesty being vested not in any one class or section, but in all and sundry, so the effort towards expression of emotions, the effort to overcome corruption of consciousness, is an effort that has to be made not by specialists only but by everyone who uses language, whenever he uses it." Collingwood declared further that, "Every utterance and every gesture that each one of us makes is a work of art" (PA, 285). Religion, no less than art, is also a *conditio sine qua non* of the very possibility of consciousness, and a society which has lost its religious integrity lives in what Sartre would call bad faith if it deceives itself into believing that it can nevertheless remain true to the requirements of reason and science:

> Every man has his own duties, and every class of men has duties proper to itself as a class; but just as the "man of action" is not freed from the obligation to truth, nor the "man of contemplation" from the obligation to morality, so the layman is as much bound as the priest by the ideals of the religion which in some form or other he cannot help professing (RP, 36; 72).

But once corruption has entered the fabric of consciousness the only antidote is philosophy in the form of metaphysics which seeks to restore the authenticity of consciousness through a critical examination of presuppositions. Collingwood's philosophy of religion is, therefore, an exercise in the metaphysics of experience, an attempt to locate and define the presuppositions of consciousness insofar as it assumes the shape of religion. But Collingwood wrote, "If we really try to discover what is the inward heart and essence of the thing called religion, we must not be alarmed if we find that our practiced vision sees it in places where, till now, we had not expected to find it" (RP, xvii).

2. PHILOSOPHY AND THE RAPPROCHEMENT BETWEEN THEORY AND PRACTICE

Collingwood believed that philosophy has important practical effects which no genuine philosopher can afford to ignore. He contended that this emphasis on the relation between philosophy and life lies at the very heart of the classical tradition of philosophy which, during his own lifetime, was being undermined by an entirely different attitude. "The philosophers of the classical tradition," wrote Collingwood, "were men who used their trained faculties of thinking in order to think about facts, and primarily of facts of practical importance in relation to the lives of their fellow men" (FML, 176). Indeed, Collingwood declared, the philosopher is the organ by which the corporate consciousness of society examines and criticizes itself. As the organ of his own society's self-criticism the philosopher finds himself called to follow Socrates in the calling that led Socrates to condemnation and death:

> That call came from Delphi; and the philosopher who makes his pilgrimage to Delphi sees there, not merely the place where long ago an event happened which was important in its time and may still interest the historian but the place whence issued the call he still hears: a call which, to one who can still hear it, is still being uttered among the fallen stones of the temple and is still echoing from the "pathless peaks of the daughters of Parnassus" (FML, 68).

But philosophy is no longer following the call from Delphi. According to the new outlook, which Collingwood characterized as the dogma of philosophical realism (A, 44 ff.), *knowing makes no difference to the object known:* from which it follows that the philosophical study of moral, religious, political, and economic phenomena can have no practical effect on the actual conduct of living. Thus the realists declared to their generation: "If it interests you to study politics, ethics, and religion do so; but don't think it will be of any use to you. Remember the great principle of realism, that nothing is affected by being known. That is as true of human action as of anything else."

It would be no exaggeration to say that Collingwood dedicated his entire philosophical career to the refutation of philosophical realism which he described as "the undischarged bankrupt of modern philosophy" (A, 45), engaged in "building card-houses out of a pack of lies" (A, 52). For it seemed to Collingwood that the very opposite of realism was not only a truth, but a truth which for the sake of one's integrity and efficiency as a practical agent ought to be familiar to every human being: namely, that in our capacity as moral, political, or economic agents we live not in a world of hard facts to which thoughts make no difference but in a world which is *essentially* one of thought. In other words, a change in the moral, political, and economic theories generally accepted by society will result in a change in the very structure of that society itself, while a change in one's own personal theories will result in a change in one's relation to that society. In either case the end result will be a change in the way we act. Collingwood's thought may therefore be seen as a conscious effort to supply the philosophical basis for a rapprochement between theory and practice.

Collingwood argued that the destruction of the relationship between theory and practice implied by the principles of philosophical realism was one of the consequences of the disruption of the unity of the sciences which derived from the Renaissance concept of specialization. In regard to the relationship of the sciences, the motto of the Renaissance was that the secret of the well-being of each discipline lay in mutual separation (SM, 34). Each science in its search for freedom demanded a complete separation from every other form of life; art for art's sake, and so on. The result of this trend of thought was that each science. insofar as it was cut off from the others, tended more and more to lead its followers into a desert where the world of human life was lost, until finally the very motive for going on seemed to have disappeared altogether. Each discipline tended to become an activity pursued by specialists for the applause of specialists, useless to the rest of mankind, and unsatisfying even to the specialist when he turned upon himself and asked himself why he was following it.

This was the state of affairs which Collingwood believed his own generation to have reached: a state in which scholars, scientists, artists, and even philosophers "work only for themselves and their own kind in a vicious circle of academicism," with the result that they had lost contact not only with each other but with the public as well. "The producers and the consumers of spiritual wealth," he wrote, "are out of touch" (SM, 20). Thus the Renaissance search for abstract freedom had come home to roost in the form of a complete disruption of life. Collingwood wrote, "[today] we can be as artistic, we can be as philosophical, we can be as religious as we please, but we cannot ever be men at all; we are wrecks and fragments of men, and we do not know where to take hold of life and how to begin looking for that happiness which we know we do not possess" (SM, 35).

Contrary to the radical pluralism of Renaissance thought, Collingwood contended that the various forms of human activity were identical, that the theoretical moment of any experience had practical effects on that experience itself and, in view of the unity of experience, on every other form of experience as well. He describes in his *Autobiography* how he set out to reconsider all the familiar topics and problems of morals, politics, and economics (A, 148). There are, he held, no merely moral actions, no merely political actions, and no merely economic actions. Every action is moral, political, and economic (A, 149). He argued with equal conviction that scientific, historical, or philosophical thinking depends quite as much on moral qualities as on intellectual ones and that moral difficulties are to be overcome not by moral force alone but by clear thinking (A, 150).

At the same time Collingwood realized that, while the various forms of human activity could not be separated, neither is their identity a night in which all cows are black, a blind abstract identity which is indifferent to differences. "All such identities," he wrote, "are barren abstractions" (SM, 246). On the contrary, he argued, the basis of the unity of the forms of experience is a concrete dialectical identity to which difference is essential and organic. "To assert the identity without the difference," he charged, "or the difference without the identity is to turn one's back on reality and amuse oneself with paradoxes" (SM, 246). It was to the task of establishing the basis of such an identity that Collingwood devoted a great deal of his philosophical career, and it was with the faith that this task could be accomplished that he proposed his remedy for the disease of his age:

> For we now recognize the nature of our disease. What is wrong with us is precisely the detachment of those forms of experience—art, religion, and the rest—from one another; and our cure can only be their reunion in a complete and undivided life. Our task is to seek for that life, to build up the conception of an activity which is at once art, and religion, and science, and the rest (SM, 36).

Collingwood believed that to restore the unity of life in this way is simply to fulfill the fundamental principle of Christianity, according to which "the only life worth living is the life of the whole man, every faculty of body and soul unified into a single organic system" (SM, 36). Christianity teaches that the individual is nothing without his fellow men, that the Holy Spirit lives not in this man or that but in the church as the unity of all faithful people (SM, 37). Thus philosophy finds in Christianity the touchstone by which to test its power of explanation (RP, xiii). Religion can both illustrate and demonstrate the philosopher's conception of absolute mind. At the conclusion of *Speculum Mentis,* Collingwood declares that the dialectic of absolute mind can never be more profoundly or impressively pictured than in the religious drama of the fall and redemption of man (SM, 303; 303). The Christian solution to the problems of philosophy is to destroy the illusion that each form of knowledge exists independently of every other and that truth resides exclusively in one or the other of these forms. The practical unification of the forms of life depends therefore upon a new theoretical understanding of the relations which obtain among the forms. The Christian solution is represented by this very understanding and is worked out by Collingwood in his theory of knowledge as a scale of forms, the dialectic of which is exemplified in *Speculum Mentis* and the logic of which is found worked out in *An Essay on Philosophical Method.*

3. PHILOSOPHY AND THE METAPHYSICS OF EXPERIENCE

Collingwood defines philosophy as the theoretical or reflective moment of any given form of experience, including its own activity of reflecting upon the structure of all other activities. There is, in other words, a philosophy of philosophy, as well as a philosophy of art, religion, science, and history.

The task of philosophy is to render explicit what is implicit in any given form of experience. There are certain principles and distinctions in every experience which are consciously known to the person having the experience. Collingwood calls these the "explicit features of the experience in question" (SM, 85). Thus, for example, a moral agent *qua* moral agent is necessarily and explicitly aware of the distinction between right and wrong in the same sense that every religious person *qua* religious is explicitly aware of the distinction between faith and reason, and between sin and redemption. An observer, however, studying a certain form of experience often finds it impossible to give a rational account of it without stating certain principles and distinctions, whether or not they are consciously made by the person whose experience he is studying. Thus, to cite an example, if you wish to describe the world view of primitive man, you must first point out that to the primitive mind "all things are full of gods" (the principle of polytheistic animism) and that for this reason the epistemological relation which best characterizes man's attitude to nature is not the relation of subject to object (I-it) but the relation of subject to subject (I-thou). Only by means of such principles can the experience of primitive man be rendered intelligible. Collingwood holds that such principles are "unconscious," by which he means that they are *implicit in the experience in question* (SM, 85 and 93). Translated into the language of his later philosophy, Collingwood is saying that the observer or historian of any given form of experience can give an account of this experience only in terms of the "absolute presuppositions" which are implicit in the experience in question.

4. PHILOSOPHY AND THE CLASSIFICATION OF THE SCIENCES

From the very outset Collingwood was intent upon establishing a new basis for the classification of the sciences which would demonstrate, against popular conceptions, that all distinctions among ways of knowing are illusory and abstract. Of central importance both in his early and later writings is a rejection of the mythology of dualism—the claim that there are two separate worlds, the one unchanging and self-identical known only to philosophy and science, and the other subject to change and development known only to history. This bifurcation of reality leads, in Collingwood's opinion, to serious difficulties, particularly when applied to human nature. Ultimately it leads either to radical scepticism or rigid dogmatism. Scepticism arises not only from failure to bridge the gap between appearance and reality, permanence and change, but also from the tendency to bridge this gap by postulating change as the only reality. Dogmatism is a consequence of denying altogether the reality of change and postulating the world of permanent and unchanging truths as the only reality. Collingwood was therefore dedicated to the abolition of all such false distinctions.

This does not mean, of course, that he recognized no differences at all. On the contrary, it was clear to him from the very beginning that the problem of the unity of science could not be solved by postulating some kind of Parmenidean self-identity. A world of "mere self-identity," he writes in *Religion and Philosophy*, "would be as inconceivable as a world of mere change" (RP, 51; 84). Indeed, Collingwood clearly recognized that all abstract distinctions have a tendency to turn into their logical opposites. The very notions of abstract separation and abstract identity are internally related by an inescapable dialectic which continually reduces the one to the other. He therefore postulated, as the metaphysical basis of his new classification of the sciences, a synthesis of permanence and change in which reality was defined, after the fashion of Bradley, as the totality of its appearances. In short, according to Collingwood, the doctrine of the unity of science can be derived only from the metaphysical doctrine of identity in difference.

In *Religion and Philosophy,* where philosophy is defined as the basis through which the unity of Christianity may be restored, the concept of identity in difference is presented as an activity of concrete self-identity which necessarily presents itself under the aspect of innumerable differences and which through a process intrinsic to the very nature of this activity overcomes these differences without totally abolishing them (RP, 104 ff; 176 ff). "Christianity," Collingwood writes, "is approached as a philosophy, and its various doctrines are regarded as varying aspects of a single idea which, according to the language in which it is expressed, may be called a metaphysics, an ethic, or a theology" (RP, xiii). Thus any particular form of life, whether it be religion, science, art, or history, "which comes to reflect upon itself will recognize itself as a necessary part of the life of philosophy" (RSP, 2; 91). Philosophy, in other words, is the basis from which all diversity in knowledge both proceeds and returns. It is, to borrow a phrase of Aristotle's, the act to which all other form of knowledge are related *pros hen legomena* (i.e., as things directed towards a single end).

In *Speculum Mentis* this concept of identity is further explicated by dialectical logic, and subsequently applied to the organization of the various sciences into a concrete system. In the language of *An Essay on Philosophical Method,* which expounds in masterly detail the terms of the new dialectical logic, the various sciences are seen to constitute a "scale of overlapping forms" rather than either a series of mutually exclusive classes conceived as coordinate species of a common genus, or even (as *Religion and Philosophy* tends to suggest) a system of distinct but identical sciences each treating different aspects of the same subject matter (EPM, 188-189). Collingwood argues that the various forms of life (and hence the sciences) form a natural or "serial" order of their own (SM, 50-57; NL, 63), such that each logically renders explicit what is implicit in all previous standpoints, i.e., resolves the inherent contradiction between what each previous standpoint claims to be and what it really is. But in so doing a further error is committed and a new contradiction emerges which requires resolution at a higher level. And the new error leads to the creation of a new standpoint. Since for Collingwood there is no such thing as a pure or total error—the truth being to some degree present even in the most egregious error (EPM, 83)—the basis of this new standpoint is therefore already implicit in the old standpoint which it supersedes. Thus religion renders explicit what is implicit in art, science what is implicit in religion, history what is implicit in philosophy, and philosophy what is implicit in all the rest (SM, 108). But *Speculum Mentis* declares that while implicitly all of the sciences have the same object (in which case they may be regarded as identical) this identity becomes explicit only through the logical and phenomenological development of consciousness in the course of which philosophy gradually emerges. Again the principle is repeated that philosophy is not just one among the variety of sciences but is the very ground of the unity of this variety.

5. THE TRIPARTITE ONTOLOGICAL STRUCTURE OF CONSCIOUSNESS AND EXPERIENCE

Collingwood stresses in *Speculum Mentis* that the act of knowing is conceived as a "concrete universal," expressing itself through a variety of distinct but dialectically related forms, and the task of philosophy is explicitly defined as the systematic attempt to locate and expound the presuppositions which define the various forms of thought. This task has the twofold purpose of vindicating the autonomy of the separate standpoints, on the one hand, and of exposing their interconnections and concrete identity on the other.

According to the theory of philosophy which Collingwood expounds in various places there appear to be at least three levels of philosophical activity which in turn are grounded in the tripartite structure of experience itself.[5] Experience, in other words,

5. The interpretation of Collingwood's thought which underlies the organization and presentation of the selections included in this volume differs sharply from those interpretations currently supported by the majority of Collingwood's critics, such as T. M. Knox and Alan Donagan. Most critics support

undergoes a logical and dialectical development not only from one form to another (from art to religion, for example) but also within each form from one ontological level to another.

At the first ontological level each of the particular forms makes an unequivocal and dogmatic interpretation of its own essential nature. This interpretation turns out, when criticized, to be based on a false and arbitrary distinction. For example, the essence of art is defined *ab intra* as pure imagination, or imagination without assertion. When criticized *ab extra* from the absolute standpoint, it is shown to rest on an erroneous and arbitrary distinction between imagination and reason. Religion is defined *ab intra* as pure faith. *Ab extra* it is described as metaphor mistaking itself for literal assertion, and its claim to autonomy turns out to rest upon a false distinction between faith and reason. Science, meanwhile, is an affirmation of the abstract universal conceived as the whole of reality. *Ab extra* this is shown to presuppose a false distinction between appearance and reality. And so on.

First-level dogmatism rests on two fundamental presuppositions. The first is that each form has a fixed and given self-identical nature. The second is that the particular conception of reality implied by any given standpoint is the only true and valid one, which itself presupposes that there is only one true view of reality (SM, 41). The theoretical moment of each standpoint, in other words,

---

some version of what I have called "The Radical Conversion hypothesis," the thesis, namely, that Collingwood's thought is subject to radical discontinuities and that such differences in outlook as are reflected by his various writings are due to radical changes of outlook. According to my interpretation, however, Collingwood's thought should be regarded as a gradually developing scale of forms which admits of differences as well as similarities. And such differences as may appear either as a series of irreconcilable inconsistencies or as evidence of significant changes of outlook will emerge, when so regarded, as systematic differences which perform a dialectical function in the system as a whole. This present volume is an attempt to organize Collingwood's papers in the philosophy of religion into such a scale of forms. For other discussions of this interpretation see my "Collingwood and the Radical Conversion Hypothesis," *Dialogue,* V, 1, 1966, pp. 71-83; reviews of Collingwood's *Essays in the Philosophy of Art* (ed. by A. Donagan) and *Essays in the Philosophy of History* (ed. by W. Debbins), *Dialogue,* V, 3, 1966, pp. 467-475; and "Collingwood's Theory of the Relation Between Philosophy and History: A New Interpretation," *Journal of the History of Philosophy,* forthcoming.

presents itself not simply as a dogmatic *Weltanschauung* but as a *Weltanschauungslehre.* Religion, for example, not only asserts itself as pure faith, but the qualities which define the objects of faith are extended to the entire world of reality. Hence religion gives rise to theology and religious philosophy which attempt to vindicate religion's claim to be absolute truth. It is not surprising, then, that such philosophies as exist at this level tend to assume an attitude of total indifference, if not intolerance, to any other interpretation of reality.

As a consequence of the dialectical interplay between the *ab intra* and *ab extra* approaches, however, consciousness is forced to the recognition that the absolute presuppositions of the first level of criticism are inconsistent. Once it is realized that each standpoint, as defined at the first level, rests upon a false distinction, consciousness is obliged to redefine the nature of each standpoint and start anew. Each standpoint will now conceive of itself as only one of a number of equally valid standpoints and proceed to define itself accordingly. Thus religion, for example, which at the first level posits itself as the only fundamental mode of existence, coexists at the second level with other forms whose validity and claims to knowledge it no longer denies. Likewise, each of the other forms conceives of itself as one of a number of equally valid and true standpoints which arise as a result of the various ways in which the mind views what is essentially the same object. At the same time each form recognizes that it has a history which to some extent reflects the influence which the other forms have had upon it.

But the philosophy or reflective-theoretical moment which seeks to justify this point of view is characterized by two peculiarities which set it apart from the third level. In the first place, at the second level, consciousness has not yet overcome the subject-object distinction—the negation of which is the differentia of absolute philosophy. It therefore continues to posit the object of each form as an independently existing entity. In the second place, second-level consciousness treats each form as if it were the species of a genus, and any overlap which exists is therefore treated as a mere overlap of extension between classes—i.e., the forms are externally related through the simple mediation of the universal genus.

But again, as a result of the dialectical interplay between the *ab intra* and the *ab extra,* consciousness transcends itself. The relation between subject and object becomes one of dialectical identity, while the relation among the forms becomes one of rapprochement. The result is the discovery of a new and higher level of existence in which philosophy treats each form not as the species of a genus, but as a member of a scale of forms whose overlap is an overlap of "intension" between concepts or categories rather than an overlap of "extension" between classes. As Collingwood himself puts it in *An Essay on Philosophical Method,* each category in its degree specifies its "generic" essence but each embodies it more adequately than the one below. Or, to put it another way, whereas according to the logic of genus and coordinate species the generic essence totally transcends the variable element (as represented by the species), according to the logic of the overlap of classes the generic essence is immanent in or identical with the variable element (EPM, 92-103). This, in effect, is the principle of rapprochement philosophy, which Collingwood elsewhere describes as the principle

> that our five forms of experience are not five abstractly self-identical types of event which, by their recurrence in a fixed or changing order, constitute human experience; but types whose recurrence perpetually modifies them, so that they shade off into one another and give rise to new determinations at every turn (SM, 86).

And this means, among other things, that each particular form within the total system of forms is itself a scale of forms, having its own logical and historical development. In the case of religion, for example, there will be an esthetic, a strictly religious, a scientific, a historical, and even a philosophical form of religion. The same applies to each of the other forms. Thus the third level introduces for the first time the possibility of a genuine rapprochement between reason and imagination, faith and reason, philosophy and history, mind and nature, and so on. What is more, it is the level at which morality and social relations in general may finally transcend both the vicious dogmatism of prejudice and intolerance, on the one hand, and the pseudo-liberal-humanism of "toleration," on the other, for a genuine community of persons.

6. TOWARD A REINTERPRETATION OF COLLINGWOOD'S THOUGHT

The tripartite dialectic of experience outlined above provides a new conceptual framework for the interpretation of Collingwood's thought in general and for his philosophy of religion in particular. On the basis of this conceptual framework, for example, the following conclusions concerning the structure of the argument in *Speculum Mentis* can be drawn. In the first place, while the main purpose of *Speculum Mentis* is to explicate the structure of the first and most primitive level of consciousness, there is nevertheless implied by this analysis the need for the further critiques of second- and third-level consciousness. Thus *Speculum Mentis* must be treated not simply as a piece of juvenilia which has been rendered obsolete by the later and more mature writings, but as a necessary prolegomenon to the various critiques of second- and third-level consciousness exemplified by Collingwood's other philosophical writings. From this hypothesis it follows that the apparent inconsistencies between *Speculum Mentis* and the later writings have in fact already been anticipated by the plan of *Speculum Mentis* and are due therefore not so much to the fact that Collingwood changed his mind as to the fact that his own philosophical development obeys the very rules laid down for philosophy by the theory of *Speculum Mentis;* the theory, namely, that philosophy consists of a scale of overlapping forms which permit discontinuities as well as continuities. Thus such differences as may appear as either a series of irreconcilable inconsistencies or as evidence of significant changes of outlook will emerge, when regarded from the standpoint of the logic of the overlap of classes, as forms on a scale—i.e., as systematic differences (or errors) which not only have been anticipated from the start but which perform a dialectical function in the system as a whole.

This claim may be tentatively explained as follows. *Speculum*

Mentis is a general phenomenology of the mind, conducted from the absolute standpoint. As such, its task is to organize and relate the various categories or habits through which the mind expresses its universal or generic essence. At the same time, with a single exception, it is a third-level critique of a series of first-level standpoints. The exception is philosophy, which is described not only as a series of first-level dogmatisms but also as a third-level activity, the philosophical examination of its own presuppositions. The latter discloses the presuppositions according to which the third-level critique of the first-level dogmatisms is conducted. Each of the main categories of mind gives rise to a series of first-level dogmatisms which are expounded *ab intra* and then criticized *ab extra,* so that developments within each single form, from level to level, while not explicitly described, are at least implicit. Thus, the clue to the future development of religion, from the first to the third levels, is provided by the phenomenological transitions within mind itself from imagination (esthetic consciousness) to faith (religious consciousness) to understanding (scientific consciousness) to reason (historical and philosophical consciousness). And, third-level religion, while not explicitly expounded, is nevertheless implicit in philosophy's third-level account of itself which runs throughout the whole of the book. The same considerations apply also to each of the other standpoints.

Speculum Mentis confronts us, therefore, with a dramatic portrayal of the conflict between the presuppositions of the third level and the presuppositions of the first level: a conflict which is further exemplified by the differences between the first-level accounts of art, religion, science, and history in *Speculum Mentis,* and their third-level accounts in the latter writings, so that (as I have already suggested) the so-called discrepancies between the early and the later writings turn out to have been clearly anticipated by the phenomenological structure of *Speculum Mentis.*

7. THE DIALECTIC OF RELIGION

In the case of religion the dialectic of development may be briefly summarized as follows. The first stage in the growth of consciousness is the dogmatism which treats religion as a separate and exclusive form of life and then makes a claim to absolute truth. From the dogmatic standpoint religion is identified with feeling and emotion, not reason. It is metaphor mistaking itself for literal assertion. Feeling is accordingly elevated into a position of superiority over the other forms. The critical examination of this attitude is found in *Speculum Mentis* (108-153 and 264-270), the main purpose of which (with respect to religion) is to show how the abstract separateness of religion is overcome when it is superseded by science, history, and philosophy—i.e., when it is shown, for example, that implicit in religion are problems which can be solved only by the other forms and that religion therefore requires these forms in order to fulfill its explicit aims. Most readers of *Speculum Mentis* have failed to realize that the dialectical transformation of religion into science and philosophy does not mean the end of religion. Religion is not annihilated or rendered obsolete by the other forms. The dialectical process is a creative one. Rather than being annihilated, religion is reborn. The transition from religion (faith) to science (reason), for example, is the occasion for a new scientific approach to religion; rather than standing against the other forms, religion now regards itself as an application of the same "scientific" method that informs the other disciplines. While the account of religion in *Speculum Mentis* is not reprinted in this volume, a summary of the dialectic of the transition from religion as pure faith to religion as reason is provided in the introduction to Part One, which deals with the first stage of the dialectic of religion as reason.

The transition in *Speculum Mentis* from religion as pure faith to religion as reason introduces the possibility of a philosophical rapprochement between faith and reason. For example, implicit in this transition is the conception of the various disciplines as equally valid and equally true coordinate species of the single act of knowing. Religion is just as much an exercise of imagination as art (which dialectically precedes it) and just as much an act of assertion as science (which dialectically supersedes it). And finally it is shown to be just as much a form of self-knowledge and self-making as philosophy. In short, art, religion, and philosophy turn out to have the same object and are, therefore, declared to be the same thing. They are all equally valid forms of mind knowing itself, and we are thus brought to the second level in the dialectical scale of progression, the level at which rapprochement is achieved according to a logic of genus and species. This attitude, which I characterize as the *abstract theory of rapprochement,* is found in such writings as *Religion and Philosophy* (Part One), and "Religion, Science, and Philosophy" (1926), which are therefore grouped together in Part One as the first critical response to the dogmatism of the religion of pure faith. In these writings religion is shown to be just as philosophical as science and history. It has the same object, deals with the same problems, and is a species of the same act of judgment.

The weakness of second-level dogmatic philosophy, however, is that it achieves identity at the expense of difference. A more adequate rapprochement should establish identity while yet preserving the important concrete differences without which the particular forms lose their autonomy. The disciplines, in other words, must be shown to be distinct but not separate. Such an outlook is made possible by the development within philosophy itself from the scientific to the dialectical phase, from the philosophical view of reality as a collection of univocally related classes or species of being (the theory of the abstract universal) to the theory of reality as a dialectical system of overlapping modes of being (the theory of the concrete universal). This development is worked out first in *Speculum Mentis* and later in *An Essay in Philosophical Method.* Such a philosophical revolution, once achieved, gives birth to the possibility of a more adequate rapprochement between religion and reason, a rapprochement which exhibits these acts as overlapping forms on a scale.[6]

Thus arises the third level of philosophical religion in which the rapprochement between faith and reason is finally grounded in a dialectical theory of truth and reality. This level of rapproche-

6. The dialectic of the transition from second to third level religious philosophy is summarized in the introduction to Part Two.

ment is revealed in such writings as "Faith and Reason" (1927), "Reason Is Faith Cultivating Itself" (1928), and "What Is the Problem of Evil?" (1926), which are here grouped together as Part Two.[7]

According to the rules governing rapprochement philosophy, the various disciplines form a scale in the sense that they are all forms of self-knowledge and self-making. The thought which constitutes itself into a scale of forms makes itself at the same time—that is to say, it endows itself with a character and essence, not only as finite but as infinite thought.[8] As a form of finite self-knowledge, religion may therefore be regarded as an experience through which the self constitutes itself as a self, so that philosophy of religion emerges as a philosophical anthropology. The contribution of religion to self-making is discussed in such writings as *Religion and Philosophy* (Part Two and Part Three) and "The Devil" (1916) which are here grouped together as Part Three, *Religion and Philosophical Anthropology: The Metaphysics of Human Self-Making.*

Finally, religion may be regarded as a form of absolute self-making, and philosophy of religion becomes a type of absolute philosophy. According to the dialectic of salvation man is redeemed through the revelation of God in the form of self-knowledge: "Human nature sunk in error is confronted by the confutation of its own error, and thus, though a fresh dialectical process, redeemed" (SM, 303; 303). But while the redemption of man depends upon his encounter with the transcendence of God, God's transcendence is not separate, aloof from the drama of human sin and redemption, but immanent in the very process of finite self-making itself. "It is God who accepts the burden of error, takes upon himself the moral responsibility for the fall, and so redeems not his creature but himself" (SM, 303; 303). Collingwood's discussion of the dialectic of absolute self-making is contained in

7. A more detailed discussion of the contents of these papers will be found in the introduction to Part Two.

8. The dialectic of finite self-making is further discussed in the introduction to Part Three while the dialectic of infinite self-making is discussed in the introduction to Part Four.

chapters VII and VIII of *Speculum Mentis, Religion and Philosophy* (Part Two and Part Three) and "Can the New Idealism Dispense with Mysticism?" (1923). Representative selections from these writings are here grouped together as Part Four, *Religion and Absolute Spirit: The Metaphysics of Absolute Self-Making.*

Part One. Religion as Reason: The Abstract Theory of Rapprochement

INTRODUCTION

I. THE PHENOMENOLOGY OF RELIGIOUS EXPERIENCE

In order to appreciate fully Collingwood's theory of religion as a form of reason, it is necessary to understand how religion arises in the first place, not as a sociological and psychological phenomenon but as a necessary mode of human consciousness. In *Speculum Mentis* Collingwood treats faith as a fundamental category or habit of mind which commits the error of conceiving itself as absolute and thus elevates itself to the rank of a dogma. This elevation of faith to the rank of a dogma is the source of religion as a separate and autonomous discipline which seeks to vindicate its autonomy by asserting itself against all other standpoints as the only valid claim to truth. Collingwood's account of the birth of religion and first-level religious dogmatism may be summarized as follows:

The birth of religion as a distinct form of consciousness lies in the failure of art (the specialized form of imagination) to achieve its goal, which is to express reality as truth. The essence of art lies in its claim to be pure imagination—a claim which rests on the presupposition that all knowing is intuitive. At the same time, however, the products of imagination are expressed as meaningful truths. But if all knowing is intuitive, the meaning which art expresses cannot be known conceptually, and hence cannot be asserted; for to *express* the products of the imagination is one thing while to *assert them as truths* is quite another matter. Thus art is forced to locate its meaning in the experience of beauty (which is then surreptitiously defined as truth). But beauty is an object of intuition, and the implicit meaning of art, while expressed, has not yet been asserted. Art is therefore faced with the predicament of expressing a meaning which it cannot itself grasp *qua* meaning. Art, in other words, *says* what it means but it cannot *know* what it means; for when you know what you mean, says Collingwood, you have achieved philosophy, while when you know *that* you mean something and cannot tell what, you have achieved art (SM, 89-90).

Thus art is pregnant with a message which it cannot deliver (SM, 110). The problem which arises when art (in the form of philosophy) reflects upon its own intrinsic limitations is one of satisfying the requirement of consciousness to assert, in the form of truth, what is only imagined. This inability on the part of consciousness to assert as truth what is imagined creates tensions which can be resolved only by reuniting the activities which art itself has separated. And this reunion is achieved when consciousness not only asserts what it imagines but believes in the reality or truth of this assertion as well. To assert the products of the imagination in the form of truths to be believed is the function of religion; and in the revelation which religion brings, the distinction between truth and falsehood becomes explicit for the first time.

But while religion is explicit assertion, it is assertion which absolutely refuses the responsibility of justifying itself against criticism. The attitude which accompanies this form of assertion is "faith" (SM, 132), and the differentia of religion is therefore the distinction between faith and reason. Accordingly, the history of religion is the history of the various ways in which consciousness tries to assert truth as an object of faith. The interpretation may vary from age to age but the basic distinction between faith and reason remains permanent. At the same time, of course, the distinction becomes more and more concrete until what began at the first level of consciousness as a basic antithesis becomes at the third level a rapprochement.

Judged from the absolute standpoint the theory of pure faith, like the theory of pure imagination, is shown to be illusory. As in the case of art there is at the basis of religion a contradiction between what is said and what is meant. The explicitly affirmed distinction between faith and reason is implicitly denied. This is evident in the fact that religion not only asserts a truth but implicitly claims to defend it as well. God the holy, the object of faith, becomes God the concept, the object of reason. Thus we pass from the realm of the "holy" to the realm of "reality." When this implicit interpretation of God as "reality," the object of thought, is rendered explicit, we pass from religion as such to theology, which as a form of criticism is essentially philosophical. Theology is, in fact, the science of the presuppositions of the religious experience and exists therefore on three levels. At the first level it is the dogmatic religious philosophy which recognizes no other form of knowledge. At the second level it is the analysis of faith as one of a number of possible attitudes which the mind takes toward reality. At the third level it seeks to establish a rapprochement between faith and reason and becomes philosophical theology.

The failure on the part of religion to maintain the separation of faith and reason, which religious consciousness claims *ab intra* to be its differentia, lies in a confusion between symbolic and literal thinking. Religion makes claims about the nature of reality which it expresses by means of symbols and metaphors. But religion *qua* religion confuses the two, with the consequence that there is a contradiction between what religion claims to be and what it really is. In reality religion is metaphor mistaking itself for literal assertion. It asserts the reality of what is only a symbol and thereby treats the symbol as though it were a concept (SM, 153). The differentia of first-level religion, then, is the philosophical error of treating symbol and meaning as though they were identical.

Collingwood cites the example of the church, a symbol whose meaning, "worship," can be expressed in a variety of different ways. From the point of view of religion the church is not just a symbol of worship but the *only form* of worship. The church, in other words, becomes the very meaning which it ostensibly seeks only to symbolize and thereby makes a mistake in categorization of the same order as the defining of the genus in terms of only one of its species. Since the distinction between symbol and meaning is the basis of the distinction between faith and reason, the kind of confusion between symbol and meaning which results in their identification has the consequence of denying the more general distinction between faith and reason. The argument of religion is: "You cannot criticize my assertions because what I assert is an image, not a concept, and criticism applies only to concepts." But at the same time, religious language demonstrates the contrary position by treating the images it asserts as though they were concepts, and in this way the language of religion becomes a rational language seeking not only to disclose an interpretation of truth but to defend it as well.

But the language and categories of justification must lie outside of religion. The very existence of religion, in other words, implies the existence of a nonreligious truth. To recognize this would mean to pass beyond metaphor and symbol and concentrate on meaning, which involves treating the language of expression for what it really is, mere metaphor or symbol, and creating another language with which to describe meaning. This, in effect, is what theology does when it seeks to explain the entire mass of religious imagery in terms of the concept of God. This procedure of explaining imagery in terms of concepts, while it is the very negation of the religious outlook, is at the same time the basis of a new standpoint which is called natural science. The latter is founded on the explicit recognition of a distinction between language and meaning —a distinction which expresses itself for science by making the distinction between particular and universal, appearance and reality, events and their causes, phenomena and the laws of their behavior. When this distinction is rendered abstract and absolute (that is to say, elevated to the rank of a dogma), science as an autonomous form of life emerges, and we reach the first stage in the life of pure thought.

The breakdown of first-level religious consciousness then is due to an implicit and unresolved contradiction between meaning and symbol. *Ab intra* religion is the active worship of a "truth" which is ostensibly an object of faith only. The experience of worshiping such an object finds expression in symbols and metaphors which religion will therefore employ only as a means toward celebrating in this faith. In its actual behavior, however, the symbol is not only identified with its meaning, but the meaning itself is treated as a concept rather than as an object of faith and, moreover, defended by reason. This contradiction is resolved when the principle implicit in the behavior of religion is rendered explicit and made the basis of the scientific standpoint in which the tension between symbol and meaning is resolved into the distinction between appearance and reality, and the attitude of devotion which formerly characterized religious consciousness is now recognized to be an explicit affirmative judgment.

The birth of science does not, of course, mean the death of religion in any absolute sense of the term. But it does, together with the birth of history and philosophy (both of which are implicit in science), seriously affect the basic structure of the religious consciousness which must now reconstitute itself in terms of a rapprochement between faith and reason. The birth of science, in other words, is the occasion upon which religious consciousness advances toward the second and third levels of experience, an advance which cannot be completed, of course, until the appearance of history and philosophy. The history of religion may therefore be viewed as a scale of forms developing on three levels, each exemplifying to a degree the rapprochement between faith and reason which is the ideal limit toward which religious consciousness aims.

Collingwood's interest in a rapprochement between faith and reason begins with *Religion and Philosophy,* which I have already characterized as an examination of second-level religious consciousness on its way to becoming a third-level experience. Collingwood's purpose in *Religion and Philosophy* is to treat religion, particularly Christianity, "not as dogma [this is the mark of a first-level experience] but as a critical solution of a philosophical problem [which is the mark of the second and third levels]" (RP, xiii). He is also intent upon demonstrating, contrary to popular conceptions, that the essence of religion does not lie in emotion or even in the performance of ritual acts. He therefore denies the legitimacy of contrasting religion conceived as an irrational and therefore inferior form of knowledge with science conceived as a superior form which is grounded in cognitive certainty. This contrast, he argues, is in fact founded on false premises. Accordingly he sets out to demonstrate that religion is much more like philosophy insofar as its status as a form of knowledge is concerned and that it should be regarded not as "the activity of one faculty alone," but as "a combined activity of all elements in the mind" (RP, xvi). This is accomplished in the selections reprinted below by showing that religion can be identified with such admittedly rational activities as science, morality, history, and philosophy.

There are, according to Collingwood, three types of argument which locate the origin of religion in some disposition or faculty other than thought, thereby excluding thought from the definition of the religious consciousness. The first is the theory that religion consists solely in the performance of ritual acts. The second is the theory that religion is neither more nor less than a system of moral conduct. Finally, there is the theory that religion is an expression of sheer feeling or emotion.

Against the view that religion consists in ritual alone Collingwood offers the following objections. First he points out that the argument is based almost exclusively on a study of the religions of primitive or savage societies. But, he adds, it is a mistake to assume that the religions of the more developed societies are no different from those of a primitive society. The very essence of religions like Judaism and Christianity lies precisely in their liberation from the bondage of ritual.

Collingwood then says that the argument rests on too superficial a view of primitive religion. To draw attention to the importance of ritual in primitive religion is not to explain the reasons why the savage practices these rituals in the first place. Ritual is not mere motiveless play. Its very character as ritual is grounded in the importance which is attached to it, in the fact that it is felt to have a value and to be obligatory and necessary. This is not, of course, a mere feeling of the importance of ritual but an assertion which presupposes certain beliefs about the nature of the universe. The savage, in other words, performs certain rituals because he believes that it pleases the gods and induces or compels them to make rain, grow crops, ensure fertility, and ward off evil spirits, thus ensuring a variety of desirable benefits. These beliefs constitute the savages' creed and, whatever particular form this creed takes, it is always creed and nothing but creed that impels the savage to ritual. If this be granted, Collingwood argues, we can hardly continue to regard even primitive religion as totally irrational or nonintellectual (RP, 4-7; 44-46).

Collingwood makes much the same point against those who argue that religion is exclusively a matter of moral conduct. The theory under attack closely resembles the popular view that the sources of religious conduct are largely environmental. It claims that a person is caused to believe and to act as he does as a result of the interaction of certain psychological and sociological forces. But Collingwood denies that the *whole* meaning of conduct can be explained only as a reaction to causes. The rationality of human behavior lies not in its *causes* but in the agent's *reasons* for doing what he does. *Explaining the causes of behavior* is one thing. *Understanding the force or meaning* of that behavior is quite another matter. The latter is made possible only through a conceptual analysis of conduct which identifies the reasons according to which the agent acts, and these reasons are logically independent of whatever causes may be relevant to the explanation of that conduct.

Collingwood is saying, in effect, that human conduct is intentional. But the logic of intentionality requires that I intend to do only what I believe to be right or true. My intentions, in other words, presuppose a system of beliefs—a creed. Thus the moralistic theory of religion, no less than the ritualistic theory, comes to grief over the fact that there is such a thing as a creed; for a morality assisted by creed is a morality founded upon intellect (RP, 7-10; 46-49).

The recognition of religion as having an intellectual content, however, throws it open to intellectual criticism, and in order to escape from such criticism it has sometimes been assigned to that faculty of mind whose function is feeling. But, Collingwood contends, even if religion does involve the expression of emotion, which cannot be denied, it must be remembered that there is no emotion that does not entail the activities of the other so-called faculties of mind. For example, the chief religious emotion is love of God. And the successful expression of this emotion presupposes an intellectual context of assertions. For the love of God implies both *knowing* God, on the one hand, and *knowing how* to do his will, on the other. Collingwood is therefore affirming the famous doctrine of Spinoza that the love of God is an *intellectualis amor Dei.*[1]

Thus, according to Collingwood, all such attempts to deny the

1. In the *Principles of Art* (1938) Collingwood makes precisely the same point about the theory of art as the expression of emotion, which is that the successful expression of emotion in art presupposes criteria of an intellectual nature, and a genuine theory of art must therefore presuppose a rapprochement between imagination and reason.

rationality of religion fail through their common dependence upon the necessity of creed. The most crucial element of this creed is, of course, a system of definite beliefs concerning the existence and nature of God—beliefs about the relation of God to man and to the universe as a whole. Such beliefs are of a theological-philosophical nature and may therefore be regarded as constituting the intellectual content of religion (RP, 10-15; 49-53).

If this be granted, then religion clearly overlaps philosophy in the sense that they are both theories of the universe. Religion and philosophy are therefore the same thing differing only in the vocabularies with which they express the same facts (RP, 15-20; 53-58).

But having arrived at the conclusion that all religion has an intellectual element, that this element is a creed or theology and at the same time a cosmology or philosophical theory of the world, Collingwood goes on to explore other dimensions of religion, such as its practical and historical nature. For example, not only does religion prescribe certain definite convictions, but it also inculcates certain definite modes of action. But the important thing about the relationship of religion to conduct is that it is the source of the truthfulness of conduct: "whereas a good religion teaches good conduct, a bad religion teaches bad" (RP, 29; 66).

Thus morality, properly understood, turns out to be grounded in religious faith so that a corruption at the level of religion necessarily leads to a corruption at the level of morality.

Collingwood further argues that the doctrines of religion, like some philosophical beliefs and doctrines, are historical facts. Collingwood shows, in various places throughout his writings, that a philosophical theory of ethics, for example, like utilitarianism, is a theory about what certain persons at a certain period of time believed to be true, and the fact of its being so believed at a certain historical time is an integral part of its meaning (PH, 12-13, and IH, 195). Likewise, Collingwood argues in *Religion and Philosophy,* philosophical-theological speculations upon the meaning of the Christian faith presuppose the existence and reality of the historical facts they are about. It makes a difference, in other words, whether Christ really lived and acted as he is described (RP, 52-54; 86-87).

Finally Collingwood attacks the theory that religion has been discredited by the advance of science by showing that religion is the same thing as science. He mounts his attack by applying the same criterion he used to establish a rapprochement between religion and philosophy. He states that religion, philosophy, and science are all concerned with the same object:

> Philosophy is the knowledge of ultimate reality: and both religion and science are just enough concerned with ultimate reality to facilitate a hasty identification of both with philosophy and therefore with each other (RSP, 2; 91).

But whereas science knows reality in its fragments (analyzing it, dissecting it into features each of which is by itself an abstraction) in religion we seek not so much to grasp this reality in an act of knowledge as to achieve a living unity with it.

In the end, then, Collingwood achieves his goal by demonstrating that religion is the same thing as science, history, and philosophy in the sense that (a) each depends upon and presupposes the other and (b) they cannot be distinguished either by their activities or their objects. Each is an act of judgment, each is concerned with the same object, which is mind or reality, and each is, therefore, concerned with the same problems concerning the nature of reality and the conditions under which this reality can become an object of knowledge.

The rapprochement at this level is achieved by stressing the similarities which relate religion to the other forms. But, as we have already noted, and as we shall see demonstrated in Part Three, when Collingwood realized that this approach achieves identity at the expense of differences, he reconsidered his position and stressed the differences as well as the similarities which obtain among the forms. This higher level of rapprochement is made possible through the development of philosophy which knows reality not in its fragments, nor in living unity with it, but in its wholeness, as *totum in toto et totum in qualibet parte.* And in this knowledge, which is philosophy, we see for the first time that religion, science, and philosophy are not simply identical with each other, but that each is a necessary part of that life which, when it comes to reflect upon itself, recognizes itself as the life of philosophy conceived no longer as simply one of a number of equally valid standpoints but as a concrete dialectical synthesis of opposites (RSP, 2; 91). The progressive reduction of religion, science, and history to philosophy means nothing more than the exposition of the life of philosophy as the lives of religion, science, and history. In a sense, then, each one of these lives disappears. But in another sense they disappear only to reappear. They disappear as identical but separate coordinate species of a genus and reappear as distinct but overlapping forms on a scale (SM, 293; 295).

RELIGION AND PHILOSOPHY

To determine the relation in which religion stands to the other activities of the mind, philosophy, conduct, and so on, might seem impossible without previously defining both religion itself and the other activities or forms of consciousness. But we cannot frame a definition until we have investigated these relations; and to offer it dogmatically at the outset would be to beg the very question we wish to solve. This is a difficulty common to all philosophical, and indeed in the last resort to all other, investigations. No science is really in a position to define its subject-matter until it has brought its discoveries to a close.

Consequently we offer no definition of religion at the beginning, but hope to arrive at one in the course of our inquiry. In fact, these introductory chapters are intended to lead to a general conception of religion; abstract indeed, because its content will only be examined in the latter part of this book, but sufficient for the purpose of preliminary definition. We start here with only one presupposition: namely, that the form of consciousness called religion really does exist. What it is, and of what it is the consciousness, are questions we shall try to answer in the course of our inquiry.

1. The first relation to be examined is that between religion and the intellect, that activity of the mind by which we think and know. The question before us is whether religion involves this activity or not, whether or not the intellect has a part in the religious life. At present we do not ask whether it constitutes the whole of religion, and whether religion contains also non-intellectual elements. We only wish to determine whether it has an intellectual element; and if so, what is the general nature of this element.

This question naturally leads us to investigate certain views of religion which place its essence in something other than thought and exclude that faculty from the definition of the religious con-

Reprinted from *Religion and Philosophy* (London: Macmillan & Co., 1916), pp. 3-20.

sciousness. It has, for instance, been held that religion consists in the performance of ritual acts, and that all else is secondary and irrelevant; or that it is neither more nor less than a system of practice or morals; or again that it is a function of a mental faculty neither intellectual nor moral, known as feeling. We shall examine these views as mere types, in the abstract, not criticizing any particular exposition of them, but rather treating them on general grounds as alternative possible theories.

(*a*) The view that religion consists in ritual alone does not result from a study of the more highly developed religions. In these ritual may be very important and have a prominent place; but no one, probably, would maintain that they ever make ritual their sole content to the exclusion of creed. The theory springs rather from an examination of the religions of the lower culture: the evidence for it is "anthropological" in the common sense of that word. Anthropologists sometimes lay down the principle that the beliefs of primitive peoples are less worth studying than their practices. All ceremonial, whether of primitive or advanced religion, is definite and instructive; but to question a savage as to his creed is at best a waste of time, since his powers alike of self-analysis and of self-expression are rudimentary, and at worst, for the same reasons, positively misleading. How valuable this principle is everyone must recognize who has compared its practical results with those of the old-fashioned catechizing method. But in order to explain its value, anthropologists have sometimes been led to assert that religion primarily consists in ritual alone, and that dogma or creed is at first non-existent, and only arises later through the invention of "etiological myth." The important thing, we are told, is that a savage does such and such actions at such and such times; the story he tells, when pressed by an inquiring neophyte or a privileged stranger to explain why he does them, is a subsequent accretion and no part of the real religious impulse. Now this explanatory story or etiological myth is supposed to be the germ which develops into creed; and therefore it follows that creed, with all its theological and philosophical developments, is not an integral part of any religion at all.

Such a position, however plausible it may seem at first sight, involves a host of difficulties. To begin with, it is at least unsafe to assume that religion in us is essentially the same as religion in the savage. No proof of this is forthcoming. It may well be the case that the emphasis we lay on creed has quite transformed religion, so that it is to us a different thing, incapable of explanation by analogy with that of the savage. Thus anthropologists tell us that the purpose of clothing, in the most primitive culture, is to attract the eye, evil or otherwise, of the spectator, not to keep out the weather. Am I therefore to resist the inclination to wear a greatcoat when I go to the post on a wet night, on the ground that it is a mere freak of vanity and useless because no one will see me?

Even if the account of savage religion is true, it does not follow that it is a true account of the religion of other cultures. It is useless to appeal to the principle, if principle it is, that to understand a thing we must know its history and origin; for if religion has really undergone a radical change, that principle is a mere cloak for giving irrelevant information: the history offered is the story of something else.

Secondly, such an account of savage religion itself seems to be incomplete. It fails to give any reason why the savage practices his ritual, for *ex hypothesi* the etiological myth only gives a fictitious reason. No doubt it is possible to say that there is no reason at all, that he has no motive, no special feelings, impelling him to these ceremonies. And it may be true that the accounts given by savages of their motive in ritual are unsatisfactory and inconsistent. But ritual is not mere motiveless play. If it is ritual at all, some definite importance is attached to it; it is felt to have a value and to be obligatory or necessary. What is the nature of this importance which the savage attaches to his ritual? It cannot be a mere "feeling of importance" in the abstract; such a feeling is not a possibility. However difficult it may be to explain *why* we feel something to be important, there must be an expressible reason for our feeling; for instance, the belief that this ritual averts evil consequences of actions done, or ensures benefits of some kind. It is not necessary that the conception be very sharply defined; but some such conception necessarily underlies every ritual action, and indeed every other action that is not regarded as an end in itself. Ritual is not in this sense an end in itself; it is not performed as a pleasure but as a necessity;

often as practiced by savages a most painful and expensive necessity.

If we could get at the savage's real mind, he would surely reply, when we asked him why he performed certain ceremonies, that otherwise crops would fail, rain would not fall, the spirits which surround his path and his bed would turn against him. These fears constitute, or rather imply and express, the savage's creed. They, and not etiological myth, are the germ which develops into creed as we know it. They differ from etiological myth precisely in this, that whereas they are the real motive of ritual, the latter expresses not the real motive but a fanciful motive, invented when the self-analysis of the primitive mind has failed to discover the real one. That it should try to discover its motive is inevitable; that it should fail to do so is not surprising. Nothing is more difficult than to give a reasonable answer to the question why we behave as we do. And the anthropologist is right in refusing to take such myths as really accounting for ritual; he is only wrong if his dissatisfaction with fanciful accounts makes him doubt the possibility of a true and adequate account.

The point, then, which is independent of any view as to the relation of magic and religion, because it applies to both alike, is that ceremonial is based on creed. It is not the foundation of creed; it depends upon it. The word creed is here used in a quite rudimentary sense, as indicating any theory of the nature of the power which governs the universe. You perform a ritual act *because* you believe that it pleases that power and induces it to make rain, or compels it to make rain, or simply makes rain come automatically; whatever particular form your creed takes, it is always creed and nothing but creed that impels you to ritual.

The principle of the centrality of ritual and the secondary nature of belief seems thus to be a result of insufficient analysis; and though we have examined it only in its relation to savage religion, it is equally true of all religion that ritual is explicable by, and founded in, positive creed; and that apart from creed ritual would always be meaningless and unmotived.

(*b*) The second anti-intellectual view of religion asserts that it is exclusively a matter of conduct, and that doctrine, so far as it does not immediately bear upon conduct, is no true part of religion at all. Now we may grant at once that religion has much to do with conduct; we may even say that no part of it is irrelevant to conduct; and yet we may be right in refusing to expel the intellectual element from it. For truth and conduct are not absolutely unrelated. Every piece of conduct depends on the realization of some truth, since we could not act efficiently, or indeed at all, without some knowledge of the situation with which we are dealing. The problem "How am I to act?" is only soluble in the light of knowledge. And conversely there is no piece of knowledge which has not some practical corollary; either it supplies us with the solution of a practical problem, or it suggests a new problem for future solution. There is no such thing as conduct divorced from knowledge or knowledge divorced from conduct.

The view we are considering seems to depend upon a form of skepticism. It admits (and we should agree) that one action is better than another and that there is a duty to promote good actions; and it asserts that the best religion is that which promotes the best life. But it goes on to maintain that the doctrines of religion have no other value except their moral value; that to describe one religion as true and another as false is meaningless. This implies that the intellectual problems of religion are insoluble and that no one answer to them is truer than any other; whereas the practical difficulties of the moral life are real and can be overcome or alleviated by religious means. Or if it is not maintained that the problems are insoluble, it is denied that religions solve them; it is perhaps supposed that they are soluble by means of another kind of thinking: by science or philosophy.

Empirical difficulties against this purely moral view of religion arise from the fact that atheists and persons who differ from their neighbors in religion do not necessarily differ in morality. If a man living in a Christian society rejects Christianity, on this theory the only possible meaning of his action is that he rejects the Christian morality, for Christianity is defined as being precisely the Christian morality. But in practice this does not necessarily follow; his morality may remain what it was before. The theory can only deal with such a case in two ways. Either it must say that he rejects Christianity in name only, while unwilling to uproot it out of his heart; or else it must maintain that he rejects not the real Christianity (the morality) but Christianity falsely so called, the intellectual system which is arbitrarily annexed to it. Both these are unsatisfactory; the first, because it makes a virtuous atheist into a mere hypocrite, and the second because the "arbitrary" connection of an intellectual system with a moral one is precisely the fact that requires explanation.

If the intellectual system (though false) is really necessary as a psychological basis for morals,[1] how can the former be rejected and the latter kept? If not, why should the two ever be united at all? The moralistic theory of religion comes to grief over the fact that there is such a thing as creed. On the theory, there ought not to be; but, nevertheless, it is there. Why is it there? Because—we cannot evade the answer—it is believed to be true. Creed may be, among other things, a means to morality; but it cannot be a means to anything unless it is first held as true. For a belief that no one believes can have no influence on anyone's conduct. A morality assisted by creed is a morality founded upon the intellect, for to judge something as true is the characteristic function of the intellect.

Further, if the action induced by a belief is to be really good as well as really due to the belief, then the belief must be true. We may stimulate our moral consciousness by fictions, as that this day is our last on earth; but the resulting action, so far as it is good, is due not to the belief but to the reawakened moral consciousness. Any action really due to the belief, such as taking farewell of our families and making arrangements for the funeral next day, would be merely silly. So, if our creeds are not truths but only means to good action, those actions which are good are not really due to them, and those which are due to them are a waste of labor. That is to say, they are a hindrance, rather than a help, to right conduct.

This form of skepticism, like most other forms of the same thing, is in fact less a philosophy than a propaganda. It is not a

1. "It is necessary to most people, but not to everyone" is a useless answer, not only because it implies that different people's minds may be constructed on absolutely and radically divergent lines—an assumption which anyone is at liberty to make if he likes, and if he will take the trouble to see where it leads him—but because it begs the question. Necessary for some people but not for others, as regular exercise, or a nap after lunch, or a thousand a year, means, as we are using terms, not necessary.

theory of what religion is; it is a proposal to reconstitute it on the principle of leaving out the creed and only keeping the commandments. There might, perhaps, be such a thing as non-religious moral teaching. We will not at present deny that. But it would not be religion. And we are not asking what improvements might be made in religion, or what better thing might be substituted for it; we only want to discover what it is. This humbler inquiry may possibly be of value even to those who, without asking what it is, have decided to abolish or reform it.

(*c*) The recognition of religion as having an intellectual content throws it open to intellectual criticism; and in order to withdraw it from such criticism it has sometimes been placed in that faculty of the mind whose function is feeling.

The term feeling seems to be distinctively applied by psychologists to pleasure, pain, and emotions in general. But emotion is not a totally separate function of the mind, independent of thinking and willing; it includes both these at once. If I feel pleasure, that is will in that it involves an appetition toward the pleasant thing; and it is also knowledge of the pleasant thing and of my own state. There is no emotion which does not entail the activity of the other so-called faculties of the mind. Religion is doubtless an emotion, or rather involves emotions; but it is not emotion in the abstract apart from other activities. It involves, for instance, the love of God. But the love of God implies knowing God on the one hand and doing his will on the other.

Moreover, the term itself is ambiguous. The word feeling as we use it in ordinary speech generally denotes not a particular kind of activity but any state of mind of a somewhat vague, indefinite, or indistinct character. Thus we have a feeling of the truth of something when we can hardly say yet that we are convinced of its truth; a feeling of the right treatment of a recalcitrant picture or sonnet, when we are not quite convinced of the right treatment; a feeling that we ought to do something when we are not really sure. In this sense religion is decidedly not a matter of feeling. Some people's religion is doubtless very nebulous; but religion as a whole is not distinguished from other things by its vagueness and indefiniteness. Religion is sometimes said to be a "low" degree of thought in the sense that it contains half-truths only, which are in time superseded by the complete truths of philosophy or science; but in the meantime it errs (if the description is true) not by being vague but by being much more definite than it has any right to be. To define religion as mere feeling in this sense would amount to complaining that it is not sufficiently dogmatic.

In another commonly used sense of the word, feeling implies absolute and positive conviction coupled with inability to offer proof or explanation of the conviction. In that case, to "feel" the truth of a statement would merely mean the same as to know it; and this use of the word therefore already asserts the intellectual content of religion. . . .

2. These types of theory all seem to fail through the same fault, namely, their common denial of the necessity of creed in religion. They describe characteristics which religion does undoubtedly often or always possess; but they try to explain it as consisting chiefly or only of these characteristics, and to avoid admitting its basis in positive creed. Without examining further theories of the same kind, therefore, we may venture to assert that religion cannot exist without a definite belief as to the nature of God. This contention would probably be borne out by any careful investigation of actual religions; every religion claims to present as true and intellectually sound a doctrine which may be described as a theory of God.

This statement of belief as to the nature of God, which of course includes beliefs as to the relations of God and the world, God and man, and so forth, is the intellectual content of religion; and it is not a thing outside or different from the religion itself. It may be only one aspect or element of religion; but at least it is an element, and an indispensable element. I call it intellectual, even if it has not been reached by "scientific" processes, because the intellect is the name of that activity by which we think, know, hold convictions, or draw inferences; and a non-intellectual conviction would be a contradiction in terms.[2]

2. The word intellect is sometimes used to distinguish one type of cognition from other types called reason, intuition, and so on. Such distinctions are, in my belief, based on mistaken psychology; and accordingly I use the various words indiscriminately to cover the whole of the facts of knowing.

Now the Doctrine of God is of course theology; it is in fact the translation of that word. Accordingly, a creed is a theology, and there is no distinction whatever between theology and religion, so far as the intellectual aspect of religion is concerned. My theology is the beliefs I hold about God, that is to say, my creed, the intellectual element of my religion.

This identification is often controverted. In the first place, a distinction is sometimes made between religion and theology with a view to reconciling the claims of criticism with those of ecclesiastical authority. Criticism (it is supposed) merely affects theology; orthodoxy is a matter of religion and is untouched by critical arguments. Such a distinction enables us to make two promises: first, to believe whatever the church believes; and secondly, to accept whatever criticism proves. But the two spheres cannot be separated in this way. There is an abstract possibility that criticism should prove the Gospel a forgery and that philosophy should demonstrate God to be an illusion; and the second promise involves readiness to accept these results as promptly as any others. But this implication already denies any weight to the authority of the church; for no church would allow its members to accept such conclusions. The proposed *modus vivendi* is as valueless in practice as it is indefensible in theory.

Some writers, again, distinguish theology, as the thought which takes religion as its starting-point and builds a superstructure upon it, from the religion upon which it builds. But this is no distinction at all; for if religion supplies the premises from which theology infers other new truths, the two are only related as premises and conclusion in one syllogism, and one and the same syllogism cannot be split up into two distinct kinds of thought. Rather, this argument would prove the identity of the two; for there is no difference between putting together the premises and drawing the conclusion. It is only in the abstractions of formal logic that they are separated. The distinction therefore would be an entirely abstract one; we could never point to two different concrete things and say "this is religion and that theology."

The same objection would apply to the opposite distinction, according to which theology, instead of using religion as its starting-point, takes its pronouncements as conclusions, and endeavors to provide proofs for them. This does seem to be a way in which the word theology is sometimes used; thus the conviction of the existence of God might be described as religion, and the proofs of his existence as theology. But in that case theology would include the whole intellectual side of religion in itself, and religion would be merely the name for an incomplete and mutilated fragment of theology—the conclusion without the evidence—which when its deficiencies were made good would coincide with theology.

A somewhat similar distinction is that between religion as the personal experience of the individual and theology as the systematic statement of religious experience as a whole. If religion means "that fragment of theology of whose truth I have had personal experience," the distinction between the two can never be made at all. Theology is the whole, religion my particular part of it. *For me*—within my knowledge—the two are in every way identical. Whatever theology I know is to me religion, and the rest I do not know.

There is certainly a kind of thought which takes religious dogmas and tries to discover their logical result, and one which tries to prove their truth, and one which arranges and expresses them all in a systematic way. And if we like to call any or all of these theology, we have no doubt a right to do so. But we must remember, if we use the term, that theology so described is not different from religion. A religious truth does not cease to be religious truth and turn into theological truth because it is proved, or arranged in a system, or reflected upon.

In general, then, it does not seem that we can distinguish religion as creed from theology at all. Each of the above distinctions, as we have said, does correspond to a real difference in the way in which we use the words; and they may be summed up by saying that in ordinary language religion means something less deliberate, less consciously logical, than theology. Religious experience gives us a number of truths arranged anyhow, just as they come to the surface; all is knowledge, all the fruit of intellectual activity, since intellect means nothing but the attainment of knowledge; but it is knowledge unsystematized. Theology then, according to this view, arranges and classifies the truths already given in religion; it creates nothing new, but rather, so to speak, tidies up the workshop where religion has finished work for the day. But even this simile overstates the difference, for in the apparent chaos of the unsystematized experience, system is in fact already present. The work of co-ordination which we have ascribed to theology is already characteristic of religion itself; it supplies us not with a number of disconnected conceptions of the nature of God, but with *a* conception.

3. (*a*) If religion as creed is identical with theology, it remains to consider the further conception of the philosophy of religion. The philosophy of any subject means careful reflection upon that subject; thus we have the philosophy of art, of conduct, of science, and so on. To do a thing, and to understand what one is doing and how one does it, seem to be different things; and this distinction, it is thought, can be applied to intellectual as well as practical processes. To commit a crime is action; to reflect upon one's crime is ethics. Similarly, to conduct an argument is science, to reflect upon it is logic; to be conscious of God is religion, to analyze that consciousness is the philosophy of religion. Such is the common doctrine, but it does not not seem to provide us with a basis for distinguishing the philosophy of religion from other philosophies. Consciousness of truths is common to religion and all other kinds of thought; the only distinction between religious and other knowledge would be that they were concerned with different objects. But the theory of knowledge or logic does not consider differences of the object, but only processes of the subject; and therefore there is no distinction between the philosophy of religion (as theory of religious knowledge) and the theory of knowledge in general. If there is a general philosophy of knowing, it includes religious knowledge as well as all other kinds; no separate philosophy is required.

Similarly, if religion involves certain types of conduct, the whole theory of conduct in general is treated by ethics. That side of the philosophy of religion merges in ethics precisely as the intellectual side merges in the general theory of knowledge or logic. There can only be a distinct philosophy of religion if religion is a quite separate function of the mind involving neither knowledge, volition, or any other specifiable activity. But unless this hypothesis can be maintained (and we know already that it cannot), we must give up the idea of a special departmental philosophy, the philosophy of religion, and hand over the study of religion to philosophy in general.

(*b*) If the philosophy of religion is indistinguishable from philosophy as a whole, what is the relation of philosophy as a whole to religion or theology? Philosophy is the theory of existence, not of existence in the abstract but of existence in the concrete, the theory of all that exists, the theory of the universe. This is frequently denied; it is said that philosophy has problems of its own, and science has problems of its own, that they progress by attending each to its own business and using its methods where they are suitable, and that when philosophy tries to answer the questions proper to science the result is chaos. The example of natural science under the domination of Aristotelian philosophy in the latter middle ages is quoted as a warning to philosophy to confine its activities within its own province. Such a view seems to depend on a misconception as to the nature of philosophy. Sciences live by the discovery and employment of methods which facilitate their particular operations and are inapplicable to other kinds of research. Differentiation of problems and methods is the very essence of the natural sciences. It is important to realize that philosophy has in this sense no methods of its own at all, that it is through and through homogeneous, straightforward thinking where formulae and labor-saving devices are not used. This absence of definite and ready-made method is at once the strength and the weakness of philosophy: its weakness, because it makes philosophy much more difficult than any of the sciences; its strength, because failure through defects in the apparatus is avoided, and there is no limitation to one particular subject such as is necessarily entailed by a fixed method. Philosophy is the free activity of critical thought, and is applicable to any problem which thought can raise. The chaos of which the scientist complains is partly his own feeling of helplessness when confronted by philosophical questions to which his methods supply no answer, and partly real blunders like those of medieval science whose cause he imagines to be the invasion of science by Aristotelian philosophy, whereas they are really due not to the overbearingness of Aristotelian philosophy but to the defects of Aristotelian science.

Now if philosophy is the theory of the universe, what is religion? We have said that it was the theory [3] of God, and of God's relations to the world and man. But the latter is surely nothing more nor less than a view of the universe. Indeed religion is quite as comprehensive as philosophy. For the religious consciousness in its true and complete form nothing is irrelevant, nothing is without its own unique and individual value. Religion and philosophy alike are views of the whole universe.

But are they therefore (it may be asked) identical? May they not be views, but conflicting views? Or views from different points of view? Not the latter, because it is the aim of each alike to transcend particular points of view, to overcome the limitations of individual interest. And to ask whether religion and philosophy may not disagree is to assume a general agreement among religions, which certainly does not exist, and the same among philosophies, which exists if possible even less. No doubt this or that philosophy would conflict with this or that religion. The religion of Homer is inconsistent with the philosophy of Auguste Comte, but Comte's own religion and his philosophy are fully consistent with one another; they are indeed identical. If religion and philosophy are views of the same thing—the ultimate nature of the universe—then the true religion and the true philosophy must coincide, though they may differ in the vocabulary which they use to express the same facts.

But, it may be insisted, we have at least by this enforced agreement condemned unheard all philosophies but those which believe in a God; for we have defined religion as the theory of God, and many philosophies deny or doubt or never mention God. This difficulty may perhaps be cleared up by recollecting that we have not assumed the "existence of God" hitherto in any definite and

3. It is possibly worthwhile to guard against a verbal pitfall. "Philosophy is theory, but religion is not; it is fact." This common—and wrong—use of the word seems to imply that a theory ceases to be a theory when it is true, or when it is a matter of vital interest or strong conviction. It was Mephistopheles who said, *"Grau, theurer Freund, ist alle Theorie, und grün des Lebens goldner Baum."*

concrete sense; we have not, for instance, assumed a personal God. The God of whom we have been speaking was a purely abstract one, a mere name for the philosophical Absolute, the solution of the cosmological problem. Thus we said that savage ritual (religious or magical) implies a creed; but it may not imply anything we should call a theistic creed. The savage may believe that his ritual operates directly on the rain without any intervention on the part of a single supreme will. This is his "theory of God"; his "God" is not a person but a principle. The Buddhist believes in no personal God at all, but he has a definite scheme of the universe and doctrine of salvation; he believes in certain eternal principles; that is his "theory of God." Atheism itself, if it is a positive theory and not mere scepticism, is in this abstract sense a "theory of God"; the only thing that is not a theory of God is skepticism, that is to say, the refusal to deal with the problem at all. God, so far as our conception has traveled, is merely at present a name for the unifying principle of the world, however that principle is regarded. Every philosophy has a God in this sense, just in so far as it is a philosophy and not a mere collocation of disconnected doctrines, in which case it has a number of different Gods whose relations it has not yet determined. And this is the only sense in which some religions (such as Buddhism) have a God. In the sense, then, in which all religions require a God, one is equally required by all philosophy.

(*c*) Since religion, on its intellectual side, is a theory of the world as a whole, it is the same thing as philosophy; the ultimate questions of philosophy are those of religion too. But can we say the same of science? Is not science, at least as interpreted by many of its exponents, anti-religious in its materialism and its frequent atheism; and even if these characteristics were not present, does it not differ necessarily from both religion and philosophy in being a view of the universe not as a whole but in minute particular details only?

To the first question it must be replied that, paradoxical though it may seem, materialism and atheism are not necessarily irreligious. Philosophy, as well as science, may be both materialist and atheist; indeed there may be, as we have said, religions which show the same features. We may even be so bold as to assert that atheism and materialism are necessarily religions of a kind; for not only do they spring from the impulse to solve the intellectual problem of the universe, but they owe their form to an essentially religious dissatisfaction with existing solutions. Thus an atheist may well be an atheist because he has a conception of God which he cannot reconcile with the creeds of other people, because he feels that the ground of the universe is too mysterious, too august to be described in terms of human personality and encumbered with mythological impertinences. The materialist, again, may find in matter a real object of worship, a thing more worthy of admiration than the God of popular religion. The materialist Lucretius adores not the careless gods of the interstellar space, but the "alma Venus," the immanent principle of nature itself. And can we deny that such materialism or atheism is more truly religious, does more honor to the true God, than many theistic superstitions?

The materialism and atheism of modern science—if indeed these qualities are rightly ascribed to it, which is very doubtful—may or may not be preferable, considered as a view of the universe, to that offered by traditional Christianity. But whichever is right, each alike is a religion, and it is only because of this fact that they can ever come into conflict.

In reply to the second question, the suggestion that science, as the knowledge of detail, is irrelevant to philosophy, the knowledge of the whole, and therefore not itself religious in character, it must be remembered that we cannot have a whole which is not a whole of parts, nor parts which are not parts of a whole. Philosophy, as well as science, is concerned with detail; it does not exist in the rarefied atmosphere of a world aloof from facts. Nor does science take its facts in absolute isolation one from another and from a general scheme of the world; it is essential to science that the facts should be related to one another and should find each its place in the scientist's view of the whole. And any religion must take account of detail; for it is only in the details that the nature of the whole is manifested.

It is no doubt possible to forget the whole in laying stress on isolated parts, as it is possible to forget details in the general view of a whole. But each of these is a false abstraction; we cannot identify the former with science and the latter with religion or philosophy. The ideal, alike for philosophy and science, is to see the part in its place in the whole, and the whole perfectly exemplified in the part.

RELIGION AND MORALITY

We have arrived at the conclusion that all religion has an intellectual element, that this element is a creed or theology and at the same time a cosmology or philosophical theory of the world, and that therefore religion is so far identical with philosophy. But we have still to determine what other elements it contains, and how these elements are related to one another.

Religion, we are told again and again, is more than mere intellect, more than mere thought, more than philosophy. It may indeed find room within itself for an intellectual element, but that is not the whole of religion; there are other elements of equal value. Indeed, intellect is only one single aspect of life; and if philosophers sometimes treat it as if nothing else existed, that is only because philosophers are human enough to magnify their office. Granting freely that religion has its intellectual side, it has also a practical side which is no less important.

If this language is justified, religion is not merely a theory of the world; it is also a system of conduct. Just as any definite religion prescribes to its adherents certain definite convictions, so it inculcates certain definite modes of action. We have to ask whether this is true; and if we find that religion does really contain these two distinct elements, we shall be compelled to determine so far as possible the nature of their connection.

1. Parallel to the anti-intellectual theories examined in the preceding chapter are certain anti-moral theories of religion. These are directed to proving that religion does not dictate definite actions at all, or that if it does, this is not because these actions are moral but for some other reason.

(*a*) As a matter of common experience, it is often said, religion sometimes inculcates actions which are flagrantly at variance with the principles of a sound morality. Can we look back on

Reprinted from *Religion and Philosophy* (London: Macmillan & Co., 1916), pp. 21-36.

all the crimes done in the name of religion, the human sacrifices, the persecutions, the horrors of religious warfare, the corrupt connivance at wickedness, the torture inflicted on simple minds by the fear of hell—*tantum religio potuit suadere malorum*—and still maintain that religion stands for morality? Undoubtedly we can. The argument is a rhetorical jump from half-understood instances to an unfounded generalization. We might equally well quote the absurdities of ancient and the errors of modern scientists as proof that science does not aim at truth. If a great scientist makes a mistake, the importance of that mistake, its widespread effect, is due to the very fact that the man who makes it is a high intellectual authority; it is the exception which proves the rule that you can generally believe what he says. Religious persecution may be a crime, but it happens only because the persecutor believes it to be a duty. The crimes of the Church are a testimony to the fact that religion does dictate duties, and is believed to do so, for the most part, in a worthy manner.

Nor can we draw a distinction between the two cases on the ground that religious crimes are sometimes already condemned by their contemporaries and are therefore doubly unjustifiable, whereas the mistakes of a great scientist represent a point in the progress of thought as yet unattained by anyone, and are therefore pardonable. This would be to reduce the argument to a mutual recrimination between Church and State, each trying to fasten upon the other the odium of being the worse sinner. Into such a discussion we can hardly be expected to enter. Our distinction is between right and wrong, truth and falsehood; and if science teaches error or religion inculcates crime, extenuating circumstances are beside the mark.

If the argument were successful, it would prove not that religion was irrelevant to conduct (for the cases quoted prove the reverse; they are cases of religion definitely dictating conduct), but that it devoted its energies to the positive pursuit of immoral ends. And this would be to admit our main contention, that religion has a practical side, while maintaining that this practical side was the apotheosis not of good but of evil. But this fantastic notion would be advanced by no serious student of the facts, and we need not trouble to refute it. We are not concerned to prove that every particular mouthpiece of every particular religion is morally infallible, just as we do not assume it to be intellectually infallible. We tried to show in the last chapter that it was an essential note of religion to lay down certain statements and to say, "Believe these"; and that could only mean, "Believe these, for they are true." Truth is the governing conception, even if the dogmas propounded fail of reaching it. Similarly, religion always lays down certain courses of action and says, "Do these," that is to say, "Do these, because they are right." Not *merely* "because they are God's will," for God is a righteous God; nor *merely* "for fear he should punish you," for his punishments are just.

Historically, religions may have been guilty of infinite crimes; but this condemnation is a proof, not a disproof, that their fundamental aim is moral. They represent a continual attempt to conform to the good will of God, and the fact that they err in determining or in obeying that will does not alter the fact that the standard by which they test actions is a moral standard. But is the will of God always conceived as good? May it not be conceived as simply arbitrary? One phase of this question is considered in the next section.

(*b*) A second argument, of a type somewhat akin to the last, is drawn from anthropology. It appears that in primitive societies the morality of the tribe develops on lines independent of its religion. It is therefore supposed that morality and religion are two quite different things, which only in course of time come to be united in what is called the "moralization of religion." This argument takes it for granted—and indeed it can hardly be questioned—that the higher religions *are* moralized, that they conceive God's will as necessarily good.

As in the last chapter, we may dismiss this argument by showing that it is irrelevant. For us religion is already moralized, and we must accept it as it is and not pretend that religion as known to us is still the same thing that (on the theory) it is to the savage.

As in the case of the anti-intellectual argument from anthropology we were not content with dismissing it as irrelevant, but found it necessary to inquire more carefully into its own statements, so here it is desirable not simply to dismiss but to examine the argument. The word "moralization" is the real difficulty. If a thing has at the outset nothing to do with morality, no jugglery or alchemy will bring it into relation with the moral consciousness. You cannot arbitrarily impose a category on a thing which is unfitted to receive it. And, to suggest that "social evolution" can confer a moral value on a type of activity which has as yet no moral bearings whatever is calling in a *deus ex machina* to perform feats which involve a contradiction in terms.

The moralization of religion—the bringing of it into conformity with our moral standards—is certainly a real thing. But it is not a single event, once for all accomplished, in which religion leaves behind its old indifference to morality and learns to take cognizance of moral values. It is a continual process in which old standards are left behind and better ones adopted. If we look at the conduct of a class or nation or culture very different from our own, we are apt to imagine for a moment that it has no morality at all. But what we mistake for an absence of morality is really the presence of a different morality. Primitive religion does not inculcate civilized morality; why should it? It inculcates primitive morality, and as the one grows the other grows too.

(*c*) We now pass to a group of theories which arise not from the external, historical or psychological, investigation of the religious consciousness, but within that consciousness itself. These are determinist, antinomian, and quietist respectively.

Religious determinism results from a conviction of the omnipotence and universality of God, so interpreted that no power of initiation whatever is left to the human will. All that is done is done by God; God's plans are not conditional upon man's co-operation or overthrown by his rebellion, because God knew these things before, and indeed was himself the cause of them. This creed lays upon its adherent no commands in the ordinary sense of the word, for it does not hold him free to execute them. On the other hand, it does issue commands in the only sense in which it allows itself to do so; it teaches that one type of conduct is pleasing to God and another unpleasing, so that, if a man were free to choose, it would not hesitate to point out the kind of behavior that ought to be chosen. And indeed those who hold views of this kind often surpass all others in the rigorism and puritanism of their actual lives. This theory therefore does not really banish conduct from religion.

(*d*) Antinomianism springs from the same conception, as to the relation between God's will and man's, which underlies determinism. It causes, therefore, no fresh difficulty. But it is perhaps desirable to point out the element of truth which it contains. If morality is conceived as what St. Paul calls a "law of works," an external and apparently unreasonable code of imperatives, then such a morality is certainly, as the antinomian believes, superseded and done away with by religion. The external, compulsive law has been replaced by an inner spring of life. If a man is perfectly religious it is true that it does not matter what he does; not in the sense that he may commit crimes with impunity, but in the sense that he will not commit them, even if you forget to tell him not to. Thus religion appears as a release from the servitude of morality.

But this view depends on a false description of morality. The man to whose mind a moral law is a mere external command, grudgingly obeyed under compulsion, falls short not merely of religion but of morality. He is not really moral at all. He is in a state of heteronomy; it is not his own will, freely acting, that produces the result but the imposition upon his will of alien force. The very nature of the moral law is this, that it is not imposed upon us from without. We do not merely obey it; we make it. The member of the "kingdom of ends," the truly moral society, is not a mere subject; he is a sovereign. Thus the moral law has already that character of spontaneity, that absence of compulsion, which is typical of religion. The transition from heteronomy to autonomy which for St. Paul is marked by the passage from Judaism to Christianity—from the law of works to the law of faith—is not a transition from morality to religion, but a transition into morality from some infra-moral state.

What, then, is this infra-moral state? We might be tempted

to describe it as the stage of positive law, of civil law. But this would be equally unsatisfactory. Just as the really moral consciousness makes its own laws, and does not merely obey them blindly, so the really social will finds in the law of its society its own self-expression, and is sovereign as well as subject in the state in which it lives. This is an ideal, doubtless, to which few societies attain; but it is the ideal, none the less, of civil life as such. And, therefore, we cannot distinguish civil from moral law as characterized by heteronomy and autonomy respectively.

The difference is not between two types of law but between differences of attitude to one and the same law. The law may be divine, moral, or civil; in each case there are two ways of obeying it, either from within, when the law becomes the free self-expression of the acting will, or from without, the law appearing as a tyrannical force blindly and grudgingly obeyed. This is the distinction which the antinomian has in mind.

Antinomianism in the commonest sense, however, makes the mistake of supposing that the transition to autonomy cancels the duties which heteronomy enforced. Even this is in one sense true, for any "law of works" contains numbers of superfluous commands, presenting as duties actions which the autonomous will rightly sees to be valueless. But in so far as the external law enjoins real duties, the internal law comes not to destroy but to fulfil. Thus whatever in morality is really moral is taken up into religion; and the state of mind which marks it as religious, the free and joyful acceptance of it, is not peculiar to religion as distinct from morality. It is essential to morality as such.

(*e*) It remains to examine the view known as quietism. This view may be analyzed as a development from certain types of expression very common in all religion; for instance, that religion is not self-assertion but self-surrender, that in the religious life we wait upon God and accept his good will instead of imposing ours upon him, that the individual is lost in union with God and is no longer an independent will. Such language is often called mysticism, and the word may be usefully employed in this sense. It is, however, well to remember that the experience to which this language refers is an experience not peculiar to certain people called mystics, but common to every religious mind. Subject to this caution, we may use the word mystical as a description of that aspect of the religious life which consists in the fusion of the individual with God.

This question is one which we shall treat at length in a later chapter; and we shall there see reason to believe that this mystical language, so far from being a fanciful or confused description of the facts, gives a perfectly accurate account of that relation of God which is the essence of personal religion. At present we are concerned not with mysticism but with its offshoot, or rather perversion, quietism. Mysticism asserts the union of my will with the will of God, the total and complete fusion of the two into one. Quietism asserts that my will is negated, that it has simply disappeared and the will of God has taken its place. I am utterly lost in the infinity of God. The two things are really quite distinct: the former asserts a union of two wills in one person, the latter asserts that the person has only one will, and that not his own but God's. Theologians will recall the relation of the Monothelite heresy [1] to the orthodox Christology of the Church; and indeed we may suggest that quietism was only a revival in another context of the essential doctrine of Monothelitism, whereas mysticism exactly expresses the orthodox view as to the relation of the divine and human wills.

Quietism thus denies that conduct is a part of religion, because it believes that in religion the individual will disappears; religion is a state of complete passivity. This doctrine is due to the assumption (which we shall criticize later) that two wills cannot be fused into one, and therefore, feeling bound to preserve the unity of the individual, the quietist denies the human and keeps the divine. Pending our inquiry into the underlying principle, it is enough to point out certain objections. (1) The act of self-abnegation is definitely an act of will, and is represented as a duty, and a reli-

1. Consisting in the assertion that Christ had not (as laid down at Chalcedon) two wills, one human and one divine, but one only, the divine, and no human will at all. This was heretical as destroying the humanity of Christ.

gious duty; therefore the practical content of religion is not in point of fact denied. (2) This act is not done once for all; it is a continual attitude of the self to God, an attitude capable of being discontinued by an act of will, and therefore itself maintained by an act of will. (3) The union with God thus attained does not deprive the individual of all activity. Rather it directs and makes more fruitful and potent this activity. It affords a solution of all his practical difficulties and gives him the strength to carry out the solution; but it does not remove them from his consciousness and place him in a simply inactive sphere of life. In a word, the self-dedication of the will to God is not the end of the individual life, but the beginning of a new and indeed of a more active life. The union with God is a real union, not the annihilation of the self.

2. We have perhaps sufficiently shown that religion never exists apart from conduct. Just as all religion involves thought, as every religion teaches doctrine and a true religion teaches true doctrine, so all religion involves conduct; and whereas a good religion teaches good conduct, a bad religion teaches bad. And further, just as we found that all knowledge was already in essence religious, so we must now say that all morality is already religious; for, as we have seen, morality properly understood already shows in itself the freedom, the autonomy and devotion, of religion. It seems, therefore, that religion is not a simple but a complex thing, containing two (or, for all we yet know, more) different elements. It is necessary that we should do something toward determining the relation of these elements to one another. If they are really separate ingredients of a compound, then religion is merely the name for a life which contains both thought and action side by side; it is no third thing over and above these, but simply the one *plus* the other. Such a conclusion really negates the conception of religion altogether; for the different independent elements of which it is composed are capable of complete analysis and description each by itself, and there is no whole (religion) but only parts (thought, action).

As a means of approach to this difficulty, it would be well to ask whether it is necessary that the two elements should always coexist; or whether they are alternative modes of operation which can only exist one at a time, so that to speak of a kind of consciousness which unites the two, as we maintain that religion does, is meaningless.

(*a*) In any case of action, it is easy to see that some thought must be present. When we discussed the ritualistic theory of religion we found that unless ritual was simply meaningless and unmotived play it must be based on some definite creed. We may extend this principle further. Unless action is based on some knowledge it cannot take place at all. The most that can happen is some automatism of which the person, whose action we call it, is unconscious. An action is necessarily based on a large number of judgments, of which some must be true or the action could not be carried out, while others may be true or false but must at least be believed. If, for instance, a man wants to drown himself, he must know "here lies the water: good; here stands the man: good": otherwise he is not able to do it; and also he must believe rightly or wrongly that he will improve his circumstances and get rid of his present miseries by putting an end to his life; otherwise he will not desire to do it. Thus every act depends for its conception and execution upon thought. It is not merely that first we think and then we act; the thinking goes on all through the act. And therefore, in general, the conception of any activity as practical alone, and containing no elements of knowing or thinking, is indefensible. Our actions depend on our knowledge.

(*b*) The converse is equally true. If we can only do what we know how to do, we only know what we wish to know. Knowing is an activity just as walking is and, like walking, requires to be set in motion by the operation of the will. To think requires effort; it can be described as harder or easier; it is the outcome of a choice which deliberately determines to think and selects a subject of thought. There can be no activity of thought apart from activity of the will.

If this is so, it is no longer possible to uphold the familiar distinction between a life of thought and a life of action. The man of action, the statesman or the soldier, would never be able to act at all but for his intellectual grip on the problems of his profession. The best man of action is not simply the man of iron will, dear to the popular imagination, but the man who has the clearest insight into the necessities and peculiarities of the given situation. Indeed the notion of a strong will in itself, apart from strength of intellect, and still more the worship of an abstract "will to power" or "blind will" are mere absurdities. A will to power must know what kinds of power there are to have and which kind it wants, and a blind will that did not know what it was doing or what there was to be done would never do anything at all. The student or man of contemplation, on the other hand, does not simply know without willing. He wills to know; and his knowledge is the result of positive hard labor. No moment of thought is conceivable which is not also a volition, and no moment of will is possible which is not also an act of knowledge.

Thus if there is such a thing as the religious life, it must be one which, like any other, involves both thinking and acting; and the religious life, so conceived, is not, any more than a philosopher's life or a statesman's, the mere sum of two different lives. For of the two ingredients neither can ever exist by itself. It must exist in union with the other or not at all. Any real life must contain both elements, each playing as important a part as the other.

3. But although the duality, of which religion now seems to consist, cannot be broken up, in the concrete, into two separable elements, it is still a duality. Thought and action remain simply side by side and absolutely distinct, though each is necessary to the other. Religion, it appears, is simply a compound of philosophy and morality, though philosophy always involves morality and morality can never exist without philosophy; and therefore all life, as such, shows the composite character which is the mark of religion. It is not simply religion, but all the life of the mind, that is now subject to the dualism; and therefore there is the greater need of understanding it. What is this dualism between thought and action? We have seen that the two things mutually depend upon one another, but we have not inquired very minutely into the nature of this dependence.

(*a*) In the theory of the religious life offered by religion itself, there is no dualism at all between knowing and acting. The two things are united, for instance by the author of the fourth Gospel, in such a way that they are absolutely indistinguishable. The term used to express their unity is "love," an activity which in its perfect manifestation is represented as the perfection of the religious life. The whole of the great final discourse in John is an exposition of this conception; nothing can be clearer than the way in which the spirit of love is identified on the one hand with that of truth, and on the other with that of morality or obedience. And the two elements are not connected merely externally; knowledge is the way of obedience and obedience the approach to truth. The connection between the two is the most intimate conceivable; just as the perfect life involves the denial of all distinction between man and man, so it involves the denial of all distinction between man's two faculties of thought and will.

(*b*) Such denials of our ordinary distinction, even if they cannot in themselves be taken as conclusive, serve at least to arouse doubts as to its sufficiency. And if we ask how thought and action are actually distinguished, the answer is not very satisfying. They are not the operations of two different parts of the mind; that is admitted on all hands. The whole self wills, and the whole self thinks. Then are they alternative activities, like sleeping and waking? No; we have already seen that they are necessarily and always simultaneous. The only thing we can say seems to be that thinking is not willing and willing is not thinking. And this is simply to assert the existence of a distinction without explaining wherein the distinction consists. We cannot say that in willing we do not think, or that in thinking we do not will, for both these, as we have seen, we certainly do.

If I will to think, there are not two elements in this act but one. When I will to walk, I do not separately experience an internal resolve on the one hand, and a movement of my legs on the other; the act of will *is* the voluntary moving of the legs. To say "I will to walk" is the same thing as saying "I walk of my own initiative," that is, "I walk." And so "I will to think" means not two things but one thing: "I think." We never simply will in the abstract; we always will to do something; what we turn into a separate organ and call "the will" is only the fact of free activity, the voluntary doing of this thing or that. Walking is thus not something distinguishable from willing, a result, so to speak, of the operation of "the will"; it is nothing more nor less than the willing itself, the particular form which, on this occasion, free activity takes. Thus walking is a kind of willing, not something else; and equally, thought is a kind of willing.

But is there any other kind of willing? Walking is only one kind; is thinking only one kind? No; for if it were, there would be kinds of willing in which thought was not present. This, we have already admitted, there cannot be; and therefore, just as all thinking is willing, so all willing is thinking. Or, to put it in other words, there is neither consciousness nor activity considered as a separate reality, but always the activity of consciousness and the consciousness of activity. Nor can we say that in this second case there is a dualism between the activity of a mind and its own consciousness of that activity; for an activity is already by its very nature conscious of itself, and if it were not, it would be not an activity but a mechanism.

We conclude, therefore, not that one and the same thing, mind, has two manifestations, consciousness and volition, and that these two always exist side by side, but that all consciousness is volitional, and that all volition is conscious. The distinction between the two statements is not merely verbal. The former way of putting it suggests that there is such a thing as a mind, regarded as a thing in itself, and that this thing has two ways of behaving, which go on at once, as a machine might have both a circular and a reciprocating motion. This idea of the mind as a thing distinguishable from its own activities does not seem to be really tenable; the mind *is* what it *does;* it is not a thing that thinks, but a consciousness; not a thing that wills, but an activity.

(*c*) This somewhat tedious discussion was necessary in order to vindicate the real unity of the religious life against the view that it is a falsely conceived juxtaposition of heterogeneous functions with no unity and no interconnection. There is, we have argued, only one kind of activity, namely, that which is at the same time thought and will, knowledge and action; and if religion is the name of this activity, then all true life is religion. We cannot distinguish three kinds of life, the thinking life, the active life, and the religious life that unites the two. So far as anybody thinks, he wills to think, and is so far already in possession of the complete or religious life; and the same is true of anyone who wills.

It may be desirable to remark at this point that to say there is only one possible complete life, and that the religious, does not in the least abolish the differences between different people's abilities and ideals, or set up one out of a number of lives as the one to which all ought to conform. In a sense, it is to do the very opposite of this; for we have pointed out that whatever life is really livable, whatever is a life at all, is already for that very reason religious in its degree, and that no one type of life has any right to claim for itself the title of religious at the expense of any other.

In one sense we do certainly make a restriction in the variety of ideals; not in the number of possible lives, but in the ways in which such lives may be classified. While fully agreeing that there is a difference between the work of a statesman and that of a philosopher, for instance, we should not admit that this difference is of such a kind that the former can be correctly described as a man of action and the latter as a man of thought. And in the same way, we should not wish to deny the difference between a priest and a layman; but we should deny that the life of the one was religious and the life of the other secular. As every life includes, and indeed is, both thought and action, so every life is essentially religious; and the secular life, if that means a life negatively defined by the mere absence of religion, does not exist at all. If, however, the "secular" life is defined positively as consisting of interests from which priests are excluded, or of interests lying altogether outside the sphere of religion, we shall reply that no legitimate interest is foreign to all religious life, and that the question what is and what is not lawful for a priest, though a perfectly legitimate question, cannot be decided by an appeal to the conception of religion.

Every man has his own duties, and every class of men has duties proper to itself as a class; but just as the "man of action" is not freed from the obligation to truth, nor the "man of contemplation" from the obligation to morality, so the layman is as much bound as the priest by the ideals of the religion which in some form or other he cannot help professing.

RELIGION AND HISTORY

WE have till now, in our treatment of the intellectual side of religion, confined our attention to the philosophic or theological content; but if we are right in supposing the religious life to be all-inclusive, it must also include the activity of historical thought. Religion, as Coleridge said, must contain "facts" as well as "ideas."

The historical aspect of religion is not likely to suffer neglect at the present time. The application to religious problems of historical research has been the most conspicuous and brilliant feature in the theology of the last half-century. Even thirty years ago, so little was generally known of the origins and antecedents of Christianity that when the *Apocalypse of Enoch* was first produced in English in 1883, its editor could gloat with an almost comic delight over the publication of "the Semitic romance from which Jesus of Nazareth borrowed his conceptions of the triumphant return of the Son of Man." Today no writer, however ignorant of recent research, could compose such a sentence. Everyone knows that Christianity was deeply rooted in Judaism, and the relations of the two can be discussed without shocking the orthodox or causing malicious glee to the critics.

This great historical movement in theology has taken two chief forms. They cannot indeed be sharply separated, but they may be broadly distinguished for the sake of convenience. One is comparative religion, with its anthropological and psychological branches; the other is historical theology, concentrating upon the antecedents, origin, history, and development of Christian doctrine. Each of these has made enormous and most valuable contributions to theology; indeed whatever progress has been made in the last fifty years has been due almost entirely to their help.

1. The danger at the present time is not so much that the religious importance of history may be forgotten as that it may be

Reprinted from *Religion and Philosophy* (London: Macmillan & Co., 1916), pp. 37-55.

overrated. The great successes of historical theology and of comparative religion sometimes lead theologians to expect more from these methods than they ever really supply. There is a tendency to regard historical methods as the only respectable approach to religious truth; to suppose that the vexed questions of theology are soluble by historical means or not at all; in fact to imagine that theology has tried the method of speculation and found it wanting, and that it has now at length found the right method, a method which properly used will yield all the truth that can ever be known.

This theory I shall describe as historical positivism, by analogy with Comte's view that human thought was in his time emerging from a "metaphysical" stage and entering on a "positive," casting aside barren *a priori* speculation and waking up at last to the reality and all-sufficiency of *a posteriori* science, passing out of the region of ideas into the region of facts. Comte's forecast, it may be observed in passing, was just. Thought did from his time assume for a while a notably less metaphysical and more positive character. It had been well frightened by its own philosophical daring in the previous period. It had jumped in and found itself out of its depth; and Comte was the mouthpiece by which it recorded its vow never to try to swim again. Who has not made a similar vow? And who, after making it, has ever kept it?

As in the case of Comtian positivism, so this historical positivism in theology seems to imply a definitely anti-philosophical skepticism; it is a merely negative attitude. It is characteristic of two religious types which at first sight seem to have little in common. On the one hand, it is expressed by that extreme anti-speculative orthodoxy which takes its stand on the bald historical fact "so the Church believes and has believed"; on the other, it is found in the extreme anti-dogmatic view of many liberal Protestants, to whom "metaphysic" is anathema. These positions we shall not criticize in detail. We have already laid down in a former chapter the necessity to religion of a speculative creed, and there is no need to repeat the arguments there used. Instead of proving the impossibility of a totally unphilosophical theology, we shall consider two instances of unphilosophical representations of religion and try to show where and why they break down. These instances are abstract or one-sided forms of the two sciences mentioned above, namely, (*a*) comparative religion, and (*b*) historical theology.

(*a*) Comparative religion is the classification and comparison of different religions or of different forms of the same religion. Its aim is to determine the precise beliefs of such a people or sect. It is therefore on the one hand anthropological, as involving the comparison of different human types, and on the other psychological, as determining the religious beliefs of this or that individual considered as a member of a certain class, sect, or nation. Comparative religion or religious anthropology is therefore not really to be distinguished from the psychology of religion.

If we ask what constitutes psychology and distinguishes it from other sciences, we cannot answer merely that psychology is the study of the mind or soul. The philosophical sciences—logic, ethics, and so forth—attempt to study the mind, and they are not psychological. Nor can we say (as some psychologists say) that this is the reason for their unsatisfactory character; for these sciences exist on their own basis, and it is no criticism of one science to point out that it is not a different one. Again, we cannot define psychology as the study of conduct, because that title is already claimed by ethics. From these philosophical sciences psychology is distinguished not by its subject but by its method.

The method peculiar to psychology may perhaps be described as follows. The psychology of knowing differs from logic or the philosophical theory of knowledge in that it treats a judgment—the act of knowing something—as an event in the mind, a historical fact. It does not go on to determine the relation of this mental event to the "something" known, the reality beyond the act [1] which the mind, in that act, apprehends. Such a further investigation would be metaphysical in character and is therefore avoided by psychology. Now this formula can be universalized, and thus gives us the definition of psychological method. Take the mental activity

1. The description of judgment as a mental event or act which refers to a reality beyond the act is borrowed from Mr. F. H. Bradley's *Logic*. I use Mr. Bradley's language not because I entirely accept such a description of the judgment, but because I believe it to express the view on which psychology is based; and therefore psychology cannot be defined without reference to it.

as a self-contained fact; refuse, so far as that is possible, to treat of its metaphysical aspect, its relations with real things other than itself; and you have psychology. Thus in scientific thought as studied by logic we have a judgment in which the mind knows reality; psychology, treating the judgment as a mere event, omits its reference to reality, that is to say, does not raise the question whether it is true.[2] In religion, we have people holding definite beliefs as to the nature of God. Psychology studies and classifies those beliefs without asking how far they correspond with the real nature of God. In conduct generally we have certain actions, individual or social, designed to attain the ends of morality, utility, or the like; psychology will study these actions without asking whether they are right or wrong, but taking them merely as things done. In general, the characteristic of psychology is the refusal to raise ultimate questions. And since that is so, it is plainly not in a position to offer answers to them; or rather, in so far as it does offer answers these rest on an uncritical and quite accidental attitude toward the problems. For instance, the psychology of religion, consisting as it does in the collection of beliefs about God without determining their truth, evidently does not aim at discovering what God is and which opinions give the best account of his nature. The psychology of religion, therefore, unlike the philosophy of religion, is not itself a religion; that is, it has no answer of its own to the question "What is God?" It has, in fact, deliberately renounced the investigation of that question and substituted the other question, "What do different people say about him?"

Of course a religious psychologist may be willing to offer an answer of his own to the first question. But in so far as he does that he is abandoning the psychology of religion and falling back on religion itself, changing his attitude toward religion from an external to an internal one. When I describe the attitude of psychology as "external" my meaning is this. There is an air of great concreteness and reality about psychology which makes it very attractive. But this concreteness is really a delusion and on closer inspection vanishes. When a man makes a statement about

2. The same omission or abstraction is made by formal logic, which I take to be a psychological rather than a philosophical science.

the nature of God (or anything else), he is interested, not in the fact that he is making that statement, but in the belief, or hope, or fancy that it is true. If then the psychologist merely makes a note of the statement and declines to join in the question whether it is true, he is cutting himself off from any kind of real sympathy or participation in the very thing he is studying—this man's mental life and experiences. To take an example, a certain mystic says, "God is a circle whose center is everywhere and whose circumference is nowhere." The psychologist, instead of answering, "Of course," or, "Really?" or, "I don't quite see what you mean," replies, "That is an example of what I call the religious paradox." [3]

The mind, regarded in this external way, really ceases to be a mind at all. To study a man's consciousness without studying the thing of which he is conscious is not knowledge of anything, but barren and trifling abstraction. It cannot answer ultimate questions, because it has renounced the attempt; it cannot enter into the life it studies, because it refuses to look with it eye to eye; and it is left with the cold unreality of thought which is the thought of nothing, action with no purpose, and fact with no meaning.

These objections against the ideal of religious psychology or of the science of comparative religion only hold good so long as, from such collections of opinions, the philosophical impulse toward the determination of their truth is completely excluded. And the fact that this impulse is never really absent is what gives religious value to such studies. Indeed, this impulse alone gives them scientific value; for some degree of critical or sympathetic understanding is necessary before the bare facts can be correctly reported. It is notorious that the unintelligent observer cannot even observe. It is only owing to surreptitious or unconscious aberrations from its ideal of "objectivity" that psychology ever accomplishes anything at all.

(*b*) The ideal of a history of the Church as a substitute for philosophical theology is plainly open to the same general objections. It profits nothing to catalogue the heresies of early Christianity and get them off by heart, unless one enters with some degree of sympathy into the problems which men wished to solve, and tries to comprehend the motives which led them to offer their various an-

3. This instance is not imaginary.

swers. But this sympathy and understanding are purely religious, theological, philosophical; to understand a heresy one must appreciate the difficulty which led to it; and that difficulty, however expressed, is always a philosophical difficulty. The merely external history of dogma killeth; it is the internal history—the entering into the development of thought—that maketh alive.

The same applies, again, to the origins of Christianity. The "historical Jesus" can never solve the problem of Christianity, because there never was a "historical" Jesus pure and simple; the real Jesus held definite beliefs about God and himself and the world; his interest was not historical but theological. By considering him as a mere fact in history, instead of also an idea in theology, we may be simplifying our task, but we are cutting ourselves off from any true understanding and sharing of his consciousness. Historical theology is always tempted to lose itself in the merely external task of showing what formula he took over from current religion, and what he added to them, and what additions and alterations were superadded by the early Church; whereas all this is but the outward aspect of the reality, and the true task of historical theology is to find out not only what was said, but what was meant; what current Judaism, to begin with, meant by its formula, and how far its meaning was a satisfactory theology. Then we should be in a position to understand from within the new doctrines of Jesus, and really to place ourselves at the fountainhead of the faith. To speak of studying the mind of Jesus from within may seem presumptuous, but no other method is of the slightest value.

2. Historical positivism thus fails to give any answer to theological questions. It can tell us that the Church has anathematized certain doctrines. But what those doctrines mean, or why anyone ever held them, or what the Church meant to assert by condemning them, or even why it follows that we ought to condemn them too, pure history can never tell us. For the solution of these problems we are thrown back on speculative thought.

Hence, through condemnation of the overemphasis laid on historical truth, emerges a contrary theory, namely, that history is useless as a basis for theology. This anti-historical view may take two forms: (*a*) that history is itself too uncertain to bear such an important superstructure as theology; (*b*) that the two things are truths of different orders, so that one cannot have any bearing on the other.

(*a*) However well attested a historical fact may be, it is never more than merely attested. It is always possible that it may be wrong; we have no means of checking it; it is always conceivable that evidence might turn up sufficient to discredit the best established historical belief. And—still worse—the evidence might never turn up, and we should simply go on believing what was totally untrue. Seeing, then, how desperately uncertain history must always be, can we, dare we, use it as the foundation for all our creeds?

This argument introduces a new form of skepticism, which we may describe as anti-historical skepticism. It is in essence a statement of the unknowability of past fact simply as such, on the abstract ground that failure of memory, breach of the tradition, is always possible. This is entirely parallel to the anti-philosophical skepticism which declares that no inference is sound because of the unavoidable abstract possibility of a logical fallacy. Each is a fantastic and hypercritical position, and neither is really tenable. If inference as such is to be distrusted, the evidence that leads us to distrust it is discredited with the rest. If attested fact as such is liable to be misreported, the facts on which we base this generalization are as doubtful as any others. Indeed the theory puts a stop to every kind of activity; for if the human memory as such is the seat of the supposed fallacy, we cannot count upon any continuity whatever in our mental life; it may always be the case that my memory of five minutes ago is completely misleading. If I may not base a theory on facts reported in books of history, am I more entitled to trust those recollected by myself? Plainly there is no difference of kind here. But if the skeptic falls back on a question of degree and says that some facts are better attested than others, then of course one agrees with him and admits that one is always bound to ask whether these facts are well enough attested to serve as basis for this theory; whether the facts are two thousand years or two minutes distant in time makes no real difference.

(*b*) The other argument against the use of history in theology asserts that there are two categories of fact, historical and philosophical, and that since they are totally distinct, theological propositions, which are essentially philosophical in character, cannot be proved or disproved or in the least affected by historical arguments, just as discussions about the authorship of a poem do not in the least affect its beauty.

This argument is plainly right if it merely means that you cannot as if by magic extract a philosophical conclusion from non-philosophical premises. If you understand history as something entirely excluding philosophical elements, then any philosophical conclusion which you "prove" by its means will be dishonestly gained. But in this sense the statement is no more than the tautology that you cannot extract from an argument more than its premises contain; it does not help us to recognize a purely historical or philosophical argument when we meet one, or even convince us that such things exist.

It may, secondly, be interpreted to mean that when we cite instances in support of philosophical views the philosophical conclusion depends not on the historical fact but on the "construction," as it is called, which we put upon the fact. We look at the fact in the light of an idea; and the philosophical theory which we describe as proved by the fact is due not to the fact but to the idea we have read into it. Here again there is a certain truth. When A finds his pet theory of human selfishness borne out by C's action, and B uses the same action as an illustration of his own theory of human altruism, it seems natural to say that each starts from the same fact but with different preconceived ideas, and that the fact is really equally irrelevant to both the theories which it is used to prove. But this account of the matter is quite inaccurate. A's "idea" is that C's act was a selfish act; B's "idea" was that it was altruistic. But of these ideas neither was a mere "idea"; one was a historical fact and the other a historical error. Thus the distinction between the fact and the construction put upon it is false; what we call the construction is only our attempt to determine further details about the fact. And since the question whether C was acting selfishly or not is a question of historical fact, the doctrine that people act in general selfishly or altruistically is based entirely on historical fact, or on something erroneously imagined to be historical fact. The attempt to dissociate philosophy and history breaks down because, in point of fact, we never do so dissociate them. One simply cannot make general statements without any thought of their instances.

3. Positivism and skepticism both break down under examination. We cannot, it appears, do without either philosophical or historical thought. We seem therefore to have here a distinction within the region of the intellect parallel to that of intellect and will in the mind as a whole; and consequently we must investigate the relation between philosophy and history with a view to determining as accurately as possible the nature of the distinction.

(*a*) In the first place, it appears that history cannot exist without philosophy. There is no such thing as an entirely non-philosophical history. History cannot proceed without philosophical presuppositions of a highly complex character. It deals with evidence, and therefore makes epistemological assumptions as to the value of evidence; it describes the actions of historical characters in terms whose meaning is fixed by ethical thought; it has continually to determine what events are possible and what are not possible, and this can only be done in virtue of some general metaphysical conclusions.

It is not, of course, implied that no historian is qualified for his work without a systematic education in academic philosophy. Still less is it to be supposed that a philosopher dabbling in history is better able than the historians to lay down the law as to the value of such and such a historical argument. It must be remembered that by philosophy we mean, here as elsewhere, thought concerned with metaphysical problems, not acquaintance with technical literature and the vocabulary of the specialist.

(*b*) It is equally certain that philosophy is impossible without history; for any theory must be a theory of facts, and if there were no facts there would be no occasion for theory. But in asserting the necessity of history to philosophy we must guard against certain misunderstandings.

In the first place, the above statements may be interpreted to mean that philosophy develops or evolves along fixed lines, has a definite history of its own in the sense of a movement in which each phase emerges necessarily from the preceding phase, and therefore philosophy (*i.e.* the state of philosophical thought now) depends absolutely upon history (*i.e.* its own previous history).

As against such a view it must be pointed out that philosophy is a human activity, not a mechanical process, and is therefore free and not in any sense necessitated either by its own past or anything else. Doubtless every philosopher owes much to his predecessors; thought is a corporate activity, like every other. But the dependence of Hegel upon Kant, say, is of quite a different kind from the dependence indicated by the above theory. Hegel's work is based upon Kant, in the sense that many of Kant's truths are Hegel's truths too; but Kant also makes errors which Hegel corrects. The error is not the basis of the truth but the opposite of it. It may, and indeed in a sense must, lead to it, because an error cannot be refuted till it has been stated. But the statement of the error is not the *cause* of its refutation. The word "cause" is simply inapplicable; for we are dealing with the free activity of the mind, not with a mechanical process. And therefore this theory uses the word dependence in a misleading sense.

Secondly, philosophy may be said to depend on history in the sense that history, the gradual and cumulative experience of facts, is necessary before we can frame philosophical theories on a broad enough basis. The wider a man's experience, the more likely his generalizations are to be true. The same applies to the human race in general; we have been accumulating facts little by little for centuries now, and consequently we are a great deal better equipped for philosophizing than were, for instance, the Greeks.

This theory expresses a point of view which is always widely held; it is an attitude toward the world whose technical name is empiricism, and of which the dominant note is the abstract insistence on mere number or size. It reckons wisdom by the quantity of different things a man knows, and certainty by the number of different times a statement comes true; it holds that a man broadens his views by traveling, and stunts them by living at home; it measures everything in two dimensions, and forgets the existence of a third. As a matter of fact—one is almost ashamed of having to utter such truisms—he who accumulates information alone is very likely to accumulate not merely sorrow but indigestion of the mind; if he cannot understand himself, he is not necessarily the wiser for trying to understand others; if he cannot learn truth at home, he will certainly not learn it abroad. It is true that more facts of some kinds are known to the learned world now than in the time of Socrates; but it does not follow that we are all wiser than Socrates. The notion of establishing theories on a broad basis is, in short, an error, itself based upon a broad, but extremely superficial, theory of logic. What matters in the foundations of a theory is not their breadth but their depth, the thorough understanding of a single fact, not the feverish accumulation of a thousand.

History must be regarded not as a mechanical process, nor yet as a gradual accumulation of truths, but simply as *objectivity,* as the real fact of which we are conscious. History is that which actually exists; fact, as something independent of my own or your knowledge of it. In this sense there would be no philosophy without it; for no form of consciousness can exist without an object. We are not expelling from history the notion of movement; for if we are asked, what is the nature of this reality of which we are conscious? we shall reply that it is itself activity, growth, development, but not development in any automatic or mechanical sense.

4. We are now able to suggest more fully the relation of history to philosophy. Neither can exist without the other; each presupposes the other. That is to say, they are interdependent and simultaneous activities, like thought and will. The question is whether, like thought and will, they are fully identical.

Each is knowledge; and if they are different, they must be the knowledge of different objects. How can we distinguish these objects? History, it is sometimes said, is knowledge of the particular, philosophy knowledge of the universal. But the particular is no mere particular; it is a particular of this or that universal; and the universal never can exist at all except in the form of this or that particular. "The universal" and "the particular" considered as separate concrete things are fictions; and to equate the distinction of philosophy and history with such a fictitious distinction is to admit at once that it is untenable.

Nor can we distinguish them as the knowledge of the necessary and of the contingent respectively. This distinction is due to the fact that a theory explains some things but leaves others unexplained; and this remnant, relatively to the theory, appears as "the contingent." Contingent, therefore, is only a synonym for unexplained; it cannot mean inexplicable, for if there is a sense in which anything is explicable, we cannot assume that anything is in this sense not explicable. In the last resort necessary probably means no more than real: when we say that a thing is necessarily so, we mean that we understand it to be really so. And therefore whatever is real is necessarily real. In point of fact, it is possible that the distinction between necessity and contingence is only a restatement of that between the universal and the particular.

It would, again, be a repetition of the same idea if we tried to distinguish things that happen in time (history) from things that are true independently of time (philosophy). For there is one sense in which every truth is temporal, as for instance the nature of God is historically revealed, and the fact that twice two is four is grasped by adding, on a definite occasion, two and two; and there is another sense in which every fact is independent of time, as it is still true and always will be true that the battle of Hastings was fought in 1066. The difference between a temporal event and a timeless truth is a difference not between two different classes of things, but between two aspects of the same thing. This attempt to distinguish philosophy and history suggests a dualism between two complete worlds, the one unchanging, self-identical, and known by philosophy, the other subject to change and development, and known by history. But a world of mere self-identity would be as inconceivable as a world of mere change; each quality is the reverse side of the other. To separate the two is to destroy each alike.

History, like philosophy, is the knowledge of the one real world; it is historical, that is, subject to the limitation of time, because only that is known and done which has been known and done; the future, not being mechanically determined, does not yet exist, and therefore is no part of the knowable universe. It is philosophical, that is, all-embracing, universal, for the same reason: because historical fact is the only thing that exists and includes the whole universe. History *a parte objecti*—the reality which historical research seeks to know—is nothing else than the totality of existence; and this is also the object of philosophy. History *a parte subjecti*—the activity of the historian—is investigation of all that has happened and is happening; and this is philosophy too. For it is incorrect to say that philosophy is theory *based upon* fact; theory is not something else derived, distilled, from facts but simply the observation that the facts are what they are. And similarly the philosophical presuppositions of history are not something different from the history itself: they are philosophical truths which the historian finds historically exemplified.

History and philosophy are therefore the same thing. It is true, no doubt, that each in turn may be interpreted abstractly, abstract history being the mere verbal description of events without any attempt at understanding them, philosophy the dry criticism of formal rules of thinking without any attempt at grasping their application. Abstract history in this sense is a failure not because it is unphilosophical, but because it is unhistorical; it is not really history at all. And similarly abstract philosophy becomes meaningless, because in eliminating the historical element it has unawares eliminated the philosophical element too. Each alike must also be the other or it cannot be itself; each in being itself is also the other.

5. The value of historical theology, then, consists in the fact that it is already philosophical. It does not merely supply philosophical theology with materials; it is itself already grappling with the philosophical problems. Religion cannot afford to ignore its historical content, nor can it treat this content as something inessential to the establishment of its speculative doctrines. History must bear the weight of speculative superstructure to the best of its ability; but in return it may derive help from philosophical light thrown thereby on its own difficulties. In this way the distinction between philosophical and historical theology disappears; there is seen to be only one theology, which is both these at once. It may be presented with comparative emphasis on constructive doctrine, as in the later chapters of this book; but if so, it does not omit or ignore history. It is woven of strands each of which is historical in character, and the whole presents itself as a historical fact. Similarly, theology may be written from a historical point of view, with the

emphasis on temporal development; but it is only theology so long as it is clear that the thing that is developing is really doctrine all the time.

An illustration may serve to indicate the necessity to theology of its historical aspect. In view of the criticisms often brought against the records of the life of Jesus, many are inclined to take up a skeptical attitude and to declare that our tradition is hopelessly incorrect. But, they go on to ask, what then? We learn many valuable lessons from the Good Samaritan, though we do not believe him to have existed. We learn, too, from Homer, even if Homer never wrote what we ascribe to him. We have the tradition in black and white; it bears its credentials on its face; all else is a side-issue. Is there anything we learn from the Christ-history that we could not equally learn from the Christ-myth?

The simple religious mind would, I believe, emphatically reject such a suggestion. And this would be perfectly right. It is easy to say that the Christ-myth embodies facts about God's nature which, once known, are known whether they are learnt from one source or from another. That is by no means the whole truth. The life of Christ gives us, conspicuously, two other things. It gives us an example of how a human life may satisfy the highest possible standards; and it puts us in contact with the personality of the man who lived that life.

The whole value of an example is lost unless it is historical. If an athlete tries to equal the feats of Herakles, or an engineer spends his life trying to recover the secret of the man who invented a perpetual-motion machine, they are merely deluding themselves with false hopes if Herakles and the supposed inventor never lived. The Good Samaritan's action is the kind of thing that any good man might do; it is typical of a kind of conduct which we see around us and know to be both admirable and possible. But if the life of Jesus is a myth, it is more preposterous to ask a man to imitate it than to ask him to imitate Herakles. Any valid command must guarantee the possibility of carrying it out; and the historical life of Jesus is the guarantee that man can be perfect if he will.

Further, in that perfection, or the struggle toward it, the religious man somehow feels that he is in personal touch with a risen

Christ. We do not at present demand an explanation of this feeling, or ask whether there is a real intercourse; it is enough that the feeling exists and is an integral part of the Christian consciousness. The presence of Christ is as real to the believer as the love of God. But it can hardly be real if Christ is a myth.

It must be observed that we are not arguing for the reality of Christ's presence now, or his historicity in the past, on the strength of this feeling. Such an argument would be extremely hazardous. We are merely concerned to show that Christianity would not be absolutely unchanged by the demonstration that these things were mythical. The belief that Christ really lived, whether it is true or false, colors the whole consciousness of the believer.

The same holds good even of purely "intellectual" doctrine. If a doctrine is simple and easy, containing nothing very new or paradoxical, a fiction is enough to drive it home. But if it is difficult to grasp and conflicts with our preconceived notions, our first impulse is to challenge the reality of the fact which serves as an instance. A scientist propounds some new and revolutionary doctrine; at once we ask whether the experiments on which it is based were fairly carried out as he describes them. If not, we dismiss the doctrine. No doubt to an absolutely perfect mind a fiction would be as illuminating as a fact, because *ex hypothesi* such a mind would have no special difficulty in grasping any truth, however subtle, and would stand in no need of, so to speak, forcible conviction. A person who was the equal or superior of Jesus Christ in spiritual insight could give up his historicity and not lose by it. But such a description only applies to God. And in God, we can no longer distinguish between the historical and the imaginary. If, speaking in a Platonic myth, we describe the course of history as a story told to himself by God, it makes no difference whether we say the story is imaginary or true.

But for us objective fact, history, is necessary. We all have something of the spirit of Thomas, and must know a thing has happened before we can believe its teaching. Is this, perhaps, one reason for the difference between the parables that Jesus spoke and the parable he acted? He knew the limitations of his audience; he saw what they could understand and what they could not. Some things about God he could tell them in words, and they would believe his words; but one last thing—how could he tell that? And if he could find words to tell it, who would not mock him for a visionary or shrink from him as a blasphemer? There was only one way—to act the parable he could not speak. We are accustomed to think of the death of Jesus as the sacrifice for our sins. Was it not also, perhaps, a sacrifice for our stupidity?

RELIGION, SCIENCE, AND PHILOSOPHY

AN ancient Greek argued that, the structure of matter being what it was, motion was impossible. Another sage, when asked to criticize the argument, refuted it by walking across the street. It may not have been a satisfactory refutation, from a strictly academic point of view, but it served its purpose; for it emphasized the great principle that facts are the ultimate test of theories.

There is a theory current today that religion has been discredited by the advance of science. People who put forward that theory invariably shrink from the test of fact; and rightly. For the facts are fatal to their theory. Of the admittedly great scientists in the world's history, there is, so far as I can discover, not one who has regarded his scientific thought as subversive of religion; it is notorious that, for the most part, the greatest scientists have been genuinely religious men. And what was true in the seventeenth, eighteenth, and nineteenth centuries is still true in the twentieth. Many have, no doubt, found their scientific interests absorb so much of their attention as to leave little room for religion; precisely as many have found that absorption in science turned them away from interest in poetry or music. But that only proves the smallness of their minds, not the incompatibility of science and religion.

Yet there is a quarrel between religion and science, and it is no use trying to deny it. And the source of the quarrel is this: religion has in the past tried to usurp, in certain respects, the place of science, and science has retaliated, in more recent times, by trying to usurp the place of religion. In the last century, to go no farther back, advances in geological science were met by certain schools of religious thought with a horrified incredulity because they contradicted the geological views enshrined in the book of Genesis. (In the same way, one may recollect, the new astronomy of the six-

Reprinted from *Truth and Freedom,* II (1926).

teenth century had been persecuted in the name of religion because it disagreed with "Biblical astronomy.") It soon became apparent to every unbiased person that the new geology was in the right and the geology of Genesis, in the light of modern knowledge, indefensible. But the champions of religion had made it appear that the whole credit of Christianity was bound up with the geology of Genesis; so that, by their own admission, you could not give up the geology and keep the religion. Consequently it seemed as if religion, at any rate in the shape of orthodox Christianity, was bankrupt; and those who drew this inference either rejoiced over the termination of what they considered a disgraceful episode in human history—the religious episode—or else, if they understood anything of human nature, they began to ask themselves where they were going to find a new object for the innate and ineradicable religious impulses of mankind. The result of this was an extraordinary series of artificial and mechanical religions, chief of which was the "religion of humanity" advocated by the positivists. And the modern rationalist, whether consciously or unconsciously, is always trying to divert the religious impulses—which he instinctively feels to be ineradicable—into some new channel: to represent the vast material universe, or the inexorable laws of nature, or the mysterious working of the life-force, as the fit object of an awe and veneration which, when properly analyzed, are seen to be strictly religious in character. Many of them, indeed, are quite frank about it, and openly advocate something which they call "the religion of science." There is a rationalist journal of high repute which professes on its title page to be the organ of such a religion. Probably none of its promoters realizes that in preaching a religion derived from science he is glorying in having made the same blunder which the early Victorians made when they preached the geology of Genesis as a scientific doctrine consecrated by religion. For the business of good science is to be scientific, and the business of good religion is to be religious; and to recommend a religion because it is in accordance with, or verified by, or derived from science is just as silly as to recommend a scientific theory because it is consecrated by religion. In both cases the proposed criterion is wildly irrelevant, as irrelevant as the criterion of mathematics applied to the beauty of a sonnet, or the criterion of pleasant taste applied to ink.

The quarrel between religion and science, then, is based on sheer confusion of thought, first perhaps arising in the heads of the champions of religion, and now chiefly observable among the champions of science. But people never make mistakes without a reason; and in this case the reason is that they have not clearly thought out the relation of religion on the one hand, and of science on the other, to that central and most obscure activity of the human mind which is called philosophy. Philosophy is the knowledge of ultimate reality; and both religion and science are just enough concerned with ultimate reality to facilitate a hasty identification of both with philosophy and therefore with each other. And if they are both identical with philosophy and therefore with each other, it follows that there must be war to the knife between them, because they are trying to do the same work and trying to do it with different tools, in different ways, with inevitably different results. Certainly the God of religion is ultimate reality; but in religion we seek not to grasp this reality in an act of knowledge, but to achieve a living unity with it, consciously adoring it and enjoying it in the act of adoration. And certainly, the Nature of science is ultimate reality; but in science we are analyzing it, dissecting it into features each of which is by itself an abstraction, a fiction of scientific understanding. The living unity of the object of religion is in science dismembered and scattered broadcast into an infinity of particles. Now both these methods of approaching the ultimate reality are possible and, so far as they go, valid; more, they are both necessary; and without practicing them both, no human mind can approach reality at all. But there is something else we can do to reality, something that is neither religion nor science but philosophy: we can know it, not in its fragments, as the scientist knows, but in its wholeness; yet not living in its wholeness only as we do in religion, but knowing ourselves as living in it and it as living in ourselves. And in this knowledge, which is philosophy, we see for the first time that religion is not philosophy and that science is not philosophy, but that each is a necessary part of that life which, when it comes to reflect upon itself, recognizes itself as the life of philosophy.

No one wholly lacking in a certain sphere of experience can realize his own lack. It is only when we begin to know that we discover our own ignorance; till then, we think we know everything.

So, in the profound communion with God, with in the life of religion we enjoy, we are apt to think that we not only worship but know, that what we now possess is not only religion, but philosophy. And similarly, in the scientist's triumphant analysis of nature, he is apt to think that he is not merely analyzing but knowing, that his science is not only science but philosophy. And between these two points of view there must always be enmity.

What is the remedy? One remedy, and always one, and only one: the struggle to cast off false philosophies and progress toward the truth. And the truth, when we find it, if we ever do, will most certainly show us *how* religion and science are, what *somehow* they certainly are, complementary and mutually helpful; not enemies at all, but harmonious and equally necessary elements in human nature.

Part Two. Religion as a Scale of Forms: The Dialectical Theory of Rapprochement

INTRODUCTION

I. TRANSITION FROM RELIGION AS ABSTRACT REASON TO RELIGION AS A FORM ON A DIALECTICAL SCALE

The conclusion of *Religion and Philosophy* concerning the relation between history, philosophy, and the other sciences, is that they are "the same thing." This identity is achieved by what appears to be a single criterion, the criterion of their being concerned with the same object, variously described as the one real world, the totality of existence, and the historical fact. By means of this same criterion Collingwood arrived at a theoretical basis for establishing the unity of the sciences. But this required his treating the sciences as "univocal" expressions of the single act of knowing.

In *Speculum Mentis* and *An Essay on Philosophical Method,* as we have already noted, the identity of the sciences is reaffirmed, but the criterion according to which it is established is reinterpreted so as to take more adequate account of specific differences. The result is that the "univocal" system of relations gives way to a dialectical system according to which the various sciences form a logical hierarchy or scale of overlapping forms which reflects, in ways which have yet to be explained, the dialectical growth of consciousness itself:

> the conception of different philosophical sciences as treating distinct aspects of the same subject matter, or expressing distinct attributes of one substance, will be modified by conceiving them as terms in a scale, each penetrating more deeply than the last into the essence of its subject matter and expressing the nature of the one substance more adequately (EPM, 189).

According to this new theory, the sciences are still concerned with the same object, but this time differences are not reduced merely to differing views of one aspect of the same object. Collingwood repudiates this notion at the very outset of *Speculum Mentis:*

> There is an obstacle which we must here remove from our path. This is the theory of art, religion and the rest as co-ordinate species of knowledge, species of a genus, each valid and autonomous in its own sphere but each limited to a single aspect of reality, each constituting a single aspect of mind. (SM, 46; cf. also EPM, 35 and 40).

At first sight this appears to be a repudiation of the very views which Collingwood had earlier defended in *Religion and Philosophy*. It must be pointed out, however, that there is in *Religion and Philosophy* an implicit contradiction between what is intended and what is actually accomplished. It is clear, for example, that while Collingwood's intention in *Religion and Philosophy* was to establish a "concrete identity" among the various sciences, his actual achievements fell far short of this. The explicit achievements of *Religion and Philosophy* amounted, in fact, to a philosophical error, the error of falsely conceiving the forms of knowledge as species of a genus. But every error contains an implicit truth, and *Speculum Mentis* may be regarded as the attempt to explicate this truth, which in the case of *Religion and Philosophy* is that the very act through which each form identifies itself with every other form is at the same time its source of differentiation. Or, to put it another way, the implicit truth of *Speculum Mentis* is that the generic essence, rather than simply transcending the specific differences which are univocally related to it, is, on the contrary, identical with these differences which coexist in a perpetual state of tension, so that the universal itself is also in a state of perpetual tension. Thus *Speculum Mentis* is not simply a repudiation of *Religion and Philosophy* but an attempt to supply the conceptual framework from which the explicit aims of *Religion and Philosophy* may be finally realized—an interpretation which may be supported by Collingwood's own remarks in *Speculum Mentis* concerning *Religion and Philosophy.* In *Religion and Philosophy,* he writes, the identity of the forms of experience is too "abstract" and does not account for the important "concrete" distinctions which exist between them. This error may be overcome, however, through the application of what Collingwood calls the principle of "the distinction between explicit and implicit" (SM, 108):

> I contended throughout that religion, theology, and philosophy were identical, and this I should not so much withdraw as qualify by pointing out that the "empirical" (i.e., real but unexplained) difference between them is that theology makes explicit what in religion as such is always implicit, and so with philosophy and theology (SM, 108).

Suppose we now apply the distinction between what is implicit and what is explicit to the interpretation of Collingwood's own writings. In this case we find, as I have already argued, that *Speculum Mentis* renders explicit what is implicit in *Religion and Philosophy* in the same sense that philosophy, for example, renders explicit what is implicit in each of the other forms. The dialectical relation between *Religion and Philosophy* and *Speculum Mentis* may be further explicated by seeing how the very definition of reality which is explicit in *Religion and Philosophy* would, if developed in terms of certain implicit assumptions concerning the nature of mind which Collingwood appears to accept, lead straight to the position of *Speculum Mentis*. In the former work, reality is defined as the object of all the sciences—in effect, as the whole forming a univocally related system of appearances. But what kind of reality can possibly satisfy this criterion of completeness, and how can such an object be characterized? I would suggest that it was in the attempt to answer this question that Collingwood advanced from the position of *Religion and Philosophy* to the position of *Speculum Mentis*.

Under the influence of Bradley and Hegel, Collingwood's thought would most likely have taken the following direction. Reality is not something other than appearance but is appearance itself. Appearances, however, can constitute themselves only within the experience of conscious mind. Thus the answer to "What is reality?" presupposes an answer to "What is mind?" Given a variety of assumptions about the nature of mind, which even in *Religion and Philosophy* Collingwood appears to accept—that it is identical with its acts, that it makes itself through these acts; in effect, that it undergoes dialectical development—it follows that reality itself, and truth, must be subject to the same dialectic of self-making. Thus the appearances of mind (and consequently the sciences which are founded upon these appearances), rather than being univocally related, are, on the contrary, related according to a dialectical system, so that one form of knowledge grows out of another as a result of internal stresses and strains.

This is precisely the position of *Speculum Mentis* which is explicitly described as an analysis of experience, conceived as a system of appearances, a series of successive attempts on the part of mind to mediate itself through the construction of external worlds, so that each stage is the dialectical product of a previous one and the presupposition of a further one. This process requires, however, that each particular standpoint present itself as absolute and therefore as standing in opposition to every other standpoint. Collingwood writes, "Every person who is actually absorbed in any given form of experience is by this very absorption committed to the opinion that no other form is valid, that his form is the only one adequate to the comprehension of reality" (SM, 307; 284). What is more, it is only the philosophical error of thinking that there are such distinctions that gives rise to the sciences in the first place and makes them what they are (SM, 309; 285).

From the absolute standpoint, of course, philosophy recognizes that there are "no autonomous and mutually exclusive forms of experience" (SM, 306; 283). But this transcendental insight is available only to philosophy and must be achieved by each generation for itself. This necessity to work toward transcendental insights through error—i.e., by first attempting to vindicate the autonomy of the separate standpoints—is the ground of the finiteness and historicity of philosophy. Yet, insofar as this insight has been arrived at at all, it is transhistorical and infinite. "A mind which knows its own change," writes Collingwood, "is by that very knowledge lifted above change" (SM, 301; 301). The self-development of man as finite (the achievement of the historical sciences) is at the same time the assertion of himself as infinite (the achievement of absolute or transcendental philosophy). Once the standpoint of transcendental philosophy has been reached, rapprochement between the various disciplines becomes explicitly possible. Philosophy can now apply to the other standpoints insights which it has achieved into its own nature. The result, in the case of religion, is what I have previously called third-level religious consciousness, the philosophical expression of which is represented by the readings collected together in this section.

2. THE DIALECTICAL RAPPROCHEMENT BETWEEN FAITH AND REASON

The first explicit discussion of third-level religious consciousness appeared in 1927 in an article entitled "Reason Is Faith Cultivating Itself." In this article Collingwood cites Descartes' *Cogito* as an example of a rational certainty (i.e., a universal and necessary truth) which is at the same time a matter of faith in that it rests not on argument but on direct conviction (RFCI, 8; 114). Collingwood credits Descartes with the discovery that the foundation and source of all knowledge whatever is intuitive certainty or faith:

> This conception of Descartes solves the problem of the relation between faith and reason. Reason itself is henceforth seen to depend for its cogency on that immediate and indemonstrable certainty which is faith; faith is henceforth no longer severed from reason or given a field of its own to operate by itself, but becomes as it were the soul of which reason is the body (RFCI, 9; 114).

In our awareness of our own responsibility and spontaneity, of our timeless and eternal reality, and of the existence of an infinite mind upon which our finite nature somehow depends, we are, Collingwood argues, in possession of certainties of the same kind as Descartes' *Cogito.* They cannot be proved because they lie too close to us. They are the presuppositions of all proof whatever: not like the Aristotelian axioms which enter into particular arguments as their premises, but rather as the conditions of their being any arguments at all (RFCI, 9-10; 115).

Not only is faith the ground and source of reason, but reason itself, according to Collingwood, is no more than the development of faith into an articulated system (RFCI, 12; 118). Reason, in other words, is implicit in faith in the sense that (a) only through reason can faith reveal its own nature to itself and (b) all scientific and philosophical ideas, before they have been worked out in explicit intellectual terms, are present to men's minds in the form of religious beliefs (RFCI, 13; 119):

> The faith that sets out in search of understanding is a faith already endowed with sufficient understanding to recognize its need for more. And in searching for more understanding it is searching not for an extraneous addition to itself, but for a development and confirmation of its own nature . . . reason is nothing but faith cultivating itself (RFCI, 14; 120-121).

If *Speculum Mentis* may be cited as an example of faith cultivating itself—in the sense that reason is there shown to render explicit what is already implicit in faith—then the identity that exists between faith and reason and between religion and the other sciences must be an identity in difference. Thus, in rendering explicit in reason what is implicit in faith, concrete differences are introduced which may then become the basis for distinguishing the standpoint of faith from other standpoints.

These differences are given some attention in the pamphlet published in 1928 entitled "Faith and Reason," which relates and analyzes the two forms according to the rules of the logic of the overlap of classes. Faith is defined as our attitude toward reality as a whole; reason as our attitude toward its details as distinct from each other (FR, 24-26; 220-222; 140-142).[1]

Within the realm of faith itself further dialectical distinctions emerge. Conceived as an attitude toward the universe as a whole, faith may be either (a) theoretical, (b) practical, or (c) emotional. Theoretical faith is knowledge that the universe as a whole is rational. This is a basic and universal presupposition of science. Indeed, Collingwood later describes it as an absolute presupposition.

1. References to *Faith and Reason* are given first to 1928 edition, second to the 1929 edition, and finally to this edition.

Practical faith consists in the certainty that life is worth living, in the belief that the world is open to possibilities and in the knowledge that we are free. These are the absolute presuppositions of moral existence. Finally, the emotional aspects of faith are present in art, conceived as a feeling toward the universe as a whole (FR, 25-26; 221-222; 141-142).

Corresponding to the dialectic of faith is the dialectic of reason. Reason, the scientific habit of mind, is the attitude which we take toward things as parts of a whole, as finite things distinct from one another and connected with one another by a network of relations which it is the business of thought to trace out in detail. Theoretical reason treats things as objects to be studied. Practical reason selects particular ends to pursue. Finally, there is an emotional aspect in which everything excites in us a feeling proper and peculiar to itself (FR, 26-27; 222; 142).

Thus the proper sphere of faith is everything in the collective sense, i.e., everything conceived as a whole. The proper sphere of reason is everything in the distributive sense, every separate thing, all finite things. Reason, says Collingwood, cannot come into open conflict with faith because reason can operate only in a system whose general nature has first been determined by faith:

> So far from a conflict between faith and reason being inevitable from the nature of things, they are in point of fact necessary to each other.
>
> Faith cannot exist without reason. The infinite is not another thing which is best grasped by sweeping the finite out of the way; the infinite is nothing but the unity, or as we sometimes say, the "meaning," of finite things in their diversity and their mutual connections. (FR, 27; 223; 143).

Thus the interdependence of faith and reason is affirmed as the paradigm structure of the interdependence of all the other forms of knowledge as well, of art, religion, science, history, and philosophy. Faith cannot exist without reason, for faith must be accompanied by an attempt to embody itself in reason by developing its own assertions (which as undeveloped would be mere abstractions) into a system of thought and conduct (FR, 28; 224; 143). Likewise, reason cannot exist without faith. Reason rests on presuppositions concerning the nature of the universe as a whole which are not scientifically discovered or ascertained but embraced by an act of faith (FR, 28-29; 224-225; 144-145).

> A person who sees that the whole of life, regarded as a whole, is the sphere of religion, and that the same whole, regarded as made up of details, is the sphere of science, must see that it is possible to be religious without ceasing to be genuinely scientific and scientific without ceasing to be genuinely religious. And a person who sees that the whole lives in the details, and the details in the whole, must see that it is only possible to be genuinely scientific by being genuinely religious, and *vice-versa* (FR, 30; 226; 145).

Collingwood elaborates further on the rapprochement between faith and reason through a series of reflections on the ontological argument. The implicit meaning of the ontological argument, according to Collingwood, is the doctrine that there is at least one unique object *id quo maius cogitari nequit* (beyond which nothing greater can be thought) and of whom we can say *est id quod est* (it is a unity of existence and essence). But this object is precisely the object of reason whenever it becomes philosophical. Unlike the objects of mathematics and natural science, the objects of philosophy cannot be conceived independently of their existence (EPM, 124-127). The life of philosophy is therefore founded on a rapprochement between thought and action. For just as in the case of Being, essence cannot be conceived apart from existence, so in the case of philosophy (when applied to the analysis of life), truth cannot be divorced from experience, nor thought from action. A man does not first know the truth and then act according to it; rather he acts in order to know. But what is thus discovered through acting is only what is already implicit. Knowledge presupposes knowledge. This according to Collingwood is the fundamental principle of philosophy:

> The principle that in a philosophical inquiry what we are trying to do is not to discover something of which until now

> we have been ignorant, but to know better something which in some sense we knew already; not to know it better in the sense of coming to know more about it, but to know it better in the sense of coming to know it in a different and better way—actually instead of potentially, or explicitly instead of implicitly, or in whatever terms the theory of knowledge chooses to express the difference (EPM, 11; cf. also NL, 5-6).

It is this very principle that the ontological argument (as Collingwood understands it) is intended to vindicate.

That this principle is part of the meaning of the ontological argument is affirmed for Collingwood in the correspondence between Anselm and Gaunilo in which Anselm admits that the ontological proof of the existence of God proves the existence of God only to a person who already believes it. Concerning this aspect of the argument, Collingwood writes in his article of 1928 on "Faith and Reason":

> Thus Anselm, searching for a proof of God's existence, hit upon the famous ontological proof; and the odd thing is that when a kindly critic pointed out that his proof was logically conclusive only to a person who already believed in God, Anselm was not in the least disconcerted. "I believe" to quote his own words, "in order that I may understand; for this I know that unless I first believe I shall never understand" (FR, 18; 213; 135).

This aspect of the argument points up the rapprochement between faith and reason: unless we already believed on faith in the existence of God, we could never receive a rational account of it. This is really a variation of the principle, *Nihil est in intellectu quod non fuerit in sensu.* If, following Collingwood's instructions in the earlier *Hibbert Journal* article of 1927, we read for intellect, "scientific thought," and for sense, "religious intuition," "we may say with substantial truth that the intellect discovers nothing that faith has not already known" (FRCI, 14; 120). Indeed, Collingwood declares, we may view the whole life of man as *fides quaerens intellectum.* But this principle is paradigmatic of all other rapprochements, including the rapprochement between "essence" and "existence." Let us therefore read for *sensus* "experience" or "existence," and for *intellectus* "essence," or whatever is the object of philosophical thought (not any thought, just philosophic thought). *Then nothing can be an object of philosophy which does not exist in experience.* But this is simply a further variation of the principle that philosophy renders explicit what is already implicit in experience—reveals, if you like, the presuppositions of experience. And in so far as our behavior is determined by implicit presuppositions which are perhaps "unconscious," we may therefore be said to act on "faith" or according to "belief."

A final example of the application of the logic of the overlap of classes to the solution of a religious problem is "The Problem of Evil" (1926). The problem arises, according to Collingwood, because evil is usually posited along with goodness and omnipotence as though these three concepts were mutually exclusive—i.e., as though they were three classes of externally related entities. But the employment of an abstract logic of classification and division gives rise to the following "dilemmatic" argument: If God wills the evil which exists, he is not good; if he does not will it, he is not omnipotent. But since it certainly exists, he either wills it or does not will it. Therefore he is either not God or not omnipotent. The "problem" consists in the attempt to refute this dilemma without denying the reality of any of the three terms, since none can be denied without the destruction of our religious belief (PE, 67; 148). To the solution of this problem Collingwood employs what he later came to call the logic of the overlap of classes, which involves manipulating the terms of the dilemma by a criticism and reexposition of the conceptions involved until they are no longer incompatible and irreconcilable (*ibid.*).

In keeping with the spirit of *Speculum Mentis* and the *Essay on Philosophical Method,* Collingwood declares that the problem of evil, like all speculative problems, is in one sense insoluble (i.e., in the sense that it can never be solved definitively such that it need never be reconsidered in the light of new thought); but in quite another sense it *is* soluble (i.e., in the sense that every attempted solution sums up the problem thus far). Part of the difficulty in reconciling evil with the other concepts lies in the identification of pain with evil. So long as pain is regarded as evil, the existence of pain will serve as a refutation of the goodness of God. This identification, however, rests on a philosophical error or fallacy (i.e., the fallacy of false identity) the responsibility for which rests with utilitarianism which bestows goodness upon consequences, events, things, or conditions, rather than, as Kant had emphasized, on will. For utilitarianism, the goodness of the will is secondary; it is merely the goodness of a means to an end. Collingwood contrasts utilitarianism with what he calls the "ethical outlook." The ethical (or Kantian) outlook recognizes that the problem of evil can never be solved so long as we continue to judge goodness and evil according to their consequences. A solution to this problem can be forthcoming only by treating the problem of goodness as the problem of the good will and the problem of evil as the problem of the evil will (PE, 70; 152). For the ethical habit of mind, the division of evil into both pain and sin is fallacious. In fact, only the problem of sin is relevant to the discussion (PE, 71; 153).

The question with which we began was, "How can a world created by God's will contain evils?" According to the ethical standpoint, it makes a difference whether we are using the terms good and evil in their strictly moral sense or in the utilitarian sense. According to the former, which is the proper one, God's will is good in itself, as are the evils we speak of. Evils are acts of *sin,* i.e., acts of the evil will (PE, 71; 153). To call a thing evil is, therefore, to call it *an act of somebody's will.* Nothing that merely exists or merely happens can be called evil. Evil applies only to things done, to actions. Mere events, by themselves, have no moral predicates. Thus the question, "Is pain an evil?" presupposes, when raised from the ethical standpoint, that pain is the product of somebody's will (PE, 72; 154-155). In saying that pain is evil, then, we are saying that God (or the Devil) creates pain by an act of will, which is a wicked action. In other words, the goodness or badness of a thing is a reflection of the character of the volition. Taken by itself, pain is neither good nor evil. When it results from an evil will, it is evil. But when it is willed by a good will, it is good. There is, therefore, no contradiction in supposing that pain is caused by a good will, or in believing that it may be good for us to have pain. It is only when things are judged solely by their consequences that a contradiction between pain and goodness obtains.

Not only does Collingwood propose a solution to the problem of evil by showing that in fact the concepts of goodness and pain overlap, but he argues as well that the antithesis between the utilitarian and the ethical points of view can itself be resolved by placing each on a scale of forms, instead of viewing them as competing answers to the same question. These standpoints are not, he declares, coordinate species of a common genus. They are, on the contrary:

> alternative presentations of the entire problem from opposing points of view. From the ethical point of view the problem is solely the problem of sin; the problem of pain is seen to be a quite different problem presenting a quite different character. From the utilitarian point of view the real problem is the problem of pain; the problem of sin is either simply solved by the conception of human freedom, or else remains as a particular case of the problem of pain. If we regard the will as means (utilitarian view) the problem of the bad will disappears into the problem of bad events or states of things, typified by pain. If we regard the will as end (ethical view) the problem of undesirable things or events, such as pain, is swallowed up in the problem of the evil will. But if instead of adopting either of these two views, we merely halt between two opinions, then our treatment of the problem of evil will fall into the two heads which we have enumerated (PE, 73; 156).

In effect, then, Collingwood has ruled out what I have here called the first and second levels of dogmatism: the totalitarian claim that the whole of the problem of evil must be viewed from one or other of a set of mutually exclusive standpoints, and the more democratic claim that it can be looked at from many standpoints together. He proposed instead what he calls a synthesis—involving what he later called a logic of the overlap of classes (as opposed to a logic of classification and division into genus and coordinate species). He declares: "Pain and sin . . . are not two kinds or divisions of what evil is. To treat them as co-ordinate heads of one and the same problem is to stand in self-confessed contradiction as to the fundamental nature of the problem at issue" (PE, 74; 157). In other words, according to Collingwood, each is a different problem requiring a different solution, and as such gives rise to different questions demanding different answers.

REASON IS FAITH CULTIVATING ITSELF

THE conception of faith belongs to that large and important group of ideas whose place in European thought is due to Christianity. We find the conception, it is true, in Plato; but in him it is simply one of those hints which Plato is always throwing out and not following up—a kind of experiment in ideas, how serious we cannot tell. Plato uses the term "faith" for our belief in the reality of the world we see around us—chairs and tables, animals and men. If anyone denies that these exist, we cannot prove him wrong; but, all the same, we are perfectly certain he *is* wrong. It is this indemonstrable certainty, this conviction indefensible by argument, that Plato calls faith; and, however strange his terminology may appear to us, accustomed as we are to the antithesis between faith and sight, we must not forget that, negatively, Plato's use of the word is the same as Paul's: in each case the word implies the absence of any possibility of proof or verification.

But the Greek mind, for good and ill, was radically intellectualistic; that is to say, its instinct was to demand an argued demonstration of everything. Faith, therefore, was to the Greek a rather scandalous thing, a thing clean contrary to his scientific cast of mind. And no doubt that is why Plato's experimental use of the conception was not taken up and developed by subsequent Greek thought. Aristotle put forward a theory of knowledge according to which everything required syllogistic proof except the ultimate first principles from which this proof was in the last resort derived. And these ultimate truths were not matters of faith; they were themselves provable in a special sense, by showing that any attempt to deny them contradicted itself when developed. And all the best Greco-

Reprinted from the *Hibbert Journal,* XXVI (1927).

Roman thought devoted its powers to elaborating and manipulating this beautiful instrument of precision, the Aristotelian syllogism.

Into a world so occupied, Christianity, however truly foreshadowed and prepared by many tendencies of the Greco-Roman mind, came as a destructive and revolutionary force. Instead of syllogistic logic, it preached faith as the organ of knowledge; instead of a natural world, it set up, as the sole object of that knowledge, God. Human thought, hitherto dissipated in a syllogistic network over the infinite field of natural fact, was now to be focused upon a single point, and in that concentration to substitute immediate conviction for reasoned argument. Thus the Platonic position was reversed. Plato had considered faith an inferior kind of knowledge, because it could not, when challenged, argue in its own defense. Christianity saw in the same fact a ground of its superiority. It is important to understand why this fact was regarded as a superiority. It was because the object of faith is God; and God, being infinite, has no relation to anything outside himself by which he can be indirectly known. A finite object—a chair or a geometrical figure—has its causes outside itself. Hence, in order to know it completely, you must start outside it, you must know it by its causes, for the cause, in Aristotle's own words, is the middle term of the syllogism. Thus Aristotle's own doctrine proves that, *if* there is an infinite uncaused being, this being cannot be known syllogistically, its existence cannot be proved by argument; it must be grasped by some kind of direct intuitive act. But this intuitive act cannot be the intellectual intuition by which, according to both Plato and Aristotle, we grasp the ultimate truths of science; for those truths are still finite truths, finite in that each of them is not the others, and finite in that each is, in abstraction, distinct from the particular facts that exemplify it. There is no resemblance between God and a Euclidean axiom; and the intellectual intuition that grasps the axiom cannot grasp God. Yet the whole of Christianity depends for its value on the assurance that God is revealed to us; and that implies on our part some faculty capable of accepting the revelation. That is the primitive Christian conception of faith.

To the Greek mind it necessarily appeared a reactionary and

confused conception. It seemed to imply giving up all the ground that Greek thought had conquered, and sinking back into the primeval and pre-scientific attitude of the barbarous and superstitious East. "The triumph of barbarism and religion," as Gibbon called it, seemed involved in the triumph of the Christian mind.

But the truth was the opposite of this. The Greek view of life involved cutting human thought into two parts, the one scientific, syllogistic, argumentative, and intellectually respectable; the other intuitive, immediate, irrational, and in the last resort merely superstitious. Under the first head fell philosophy and the sciences; under the second, religion and everyday perception. Now Christianity did nothing so simple or so silly as to invert the Greek view and exalt religion and everyday perception at the expense of science and philosophy. It abolished the old classification altogether and substituted a new one. Instead of grouping religion and everyday perception together, it separated them. Greek thought had grouped them together for the merely negative reason that they were both non-argumentative forms of thought. Christianity, more Aristotelian than Aristotle, recognized that two faculties whose objects were so widely different must themselves widely differ: the faith by which we apprehend the infinite and wholly spiritual nature of God must be utterly unlike the perception by which we apprehend the particular finite things in the world of sense. Hence the distinction between faith and sight. In exalting faith above reason, therefore, Christianity was not in any sense undoing the work of Greek thought, but rather building upon it. The Greek conception of reason as the syllogistically-articulated knowledge of the natural world, the world of finite objects, was left standing; the superiority of reason, still in the same sense, to the perception by which we immediately recognize the appearances of these objects, was left unchallenged. What Christianity added to Greek thought was the idea of a yet higher kind of knowledge, a knowledge in which we apprehend not the finite but the infinite, not nature but spirit, not the world but God.

When I say that this idea was the gift of Christianity I am not forgetting its presence in Neoplatonism. I am rather intending to suggest that Neoplatonism was not exactly a Christian heresy, but a product of the same spiritual movement which found expression in Christianity. The Neoplatonists certainly grasped the conception of a knowledge of the infinite, and expressed their conception in eloquent language; but where Neoplatonism differed from Christianity it differed for the worse. It never appreciated the oldness of the bottles into which it was pouring its new wine. It did not realize that its own sense of the divine brought it far nearer to the Christianity which it opposed than to the Plato whom it admired, and that its allegiance to the traditional schemes of Greek thought was profoundly inconsistent with its mystical theology. The knowledge of the finite or of nature is an aristocratic thing, and expresses itself outwardly in the figure of the philosopher, scientist, or sage, aloof from the world and absorbed in his own thought; but faith, the knowledge of God or of the infinite, is a democratic thing, and takes outward form in the body of a church composed of believers and entered, not by competitive examination, but by a simple pledge of loyalty. Here Christianity was consistent. Its new thought clothed itself in a new form truly appropriate to its spirit. Neoplatonism, less logical than Christianity, clung to the conception of the philosopher and rejected that of the Church.

But the rise of Neoplatonism is an eloquent witness to the fact that Christianity, with its profoundly un-Greek view of man and the world, satisfied a need of which even contemporary paganism was conscious. The Greeks had already pushed the conception of knowledge as knowledge of a natural world of finite objects as far as it would go; scientific and philosophical thought had reached a *cul-de-sac,* and its own self-imposed limitations prevented it from progressing further. The Orientalizing of Greek thought in Neoplatonism was as necessary as the Orientalizing of the Roman Empire by Diocletian. In both cases the original impulse was exhausted, the original strain had become sterile, and it was necessary to import new blood into the stock, to effect a compromise with principles that had hitherto been strictly kept at arm's length. You cannot go on forever concentrating your thought upon the finite natural object. Thought so concentrated becomes in time a barren and tedious intellectualism, a mere game of logic-chopping. Nor, for that matter, can you concentrate your thought permanently upon the infinite; if you do, it evaporates into a sickly mysticism which out of its own corruption generates a host of saprophytic and verminous finite objects, the creatures of a superstitious fancy. And if a mind too rigidly concentrated on the infinite thus creates for itself an arbitrary world of finite objects, so, in the same way, a mind too closely bound to the finite revenges itself by kicking over the traces and plunging into pseudo-metaphysics and a fantastic theology.

Greek thought stood for the ideal of knowledge as knowledge of the finite object; the infinite object it simply denied as an object, relegating it to the sphere of superstition and mental pathology. Christianity, without denying the Greek ideal, added to it, as a higher ideal, knowledge of the infinite object. Faith and reason thus stood side by side, faith the higher of the two; and that is the situation accepted and theoretically developed in the Middle Ages. Each faculty has its own sphere and its own powers; each is competent in its own sphere; neither can overstep the boundary that separates them; but, nevertheless, it is clear that faith is the higher faculty by as much as the infinite is higher than the finite.

This medieval theory begins to show its weakness when worked out in detail. Had it been a wholly true theory, its application would have been easy, for there would have been no question as to where the field of reason began and that of faith ended. There would have been no more temptation to mutual encroachment than there is between the eyes and the ears. But in practice it was soon found that in a science like theology difficulties arose as to the precise share of the work allotted to reason and to faith respectively. A compromise was no doubt effected; it was generally agreed that certain theological doctrines were matters of reason, and others matters of faith; but the terms of the compromise were highly disputable and both sides must constantly have wondered whether, on principle, a compromise was possible at all. For surely, if God exists and if some of his attributes are matters of demonstration, there can be no valid reason to deny that all can be demonstrated; and if some cannot, why should any? Doubts of this kind visibly underlie the voluminous medieval discussions about the proof of the existence of God. Anselm, searching for a proof of God's existence that should be absolutely convincing, discovered one which convinced only a person who already believed in God; and the strange thing is that when this was pointed out to him he does not appear to have been in the least disconcerted. He could move across from the position of reason to the position of faith without feeling that he had moved. His successors attempted to guard against such transitions by laying down a precise boundary; but their boundaries were always arbitrary.

The weakness of the medieval compromise between faith and reason was really due to the fact that faith and reason are not two faculties, but two theories of knowledge as a whole, and are therefore mutually contradictory. To separate faith and reason means separating God from nature, the finite from the infinite; the infinite, set outside the finite, becomes merely another finite, being now limited by the finite as something other than itself, and therefore the infinite as such disappears. So long as there is a legitimate sphere of reason there cannot be, outside it, a legitimate sphere of faith; what was given to faith must be claimed as the *irredenta* of reason. And conversely, if the infinite is the proper object of faith, and if the infinite is truly infinite, the finite falls not outside it, but within it, and reason must be swallowed up in faith. This dilemma may seem a mere freak of abstract logic, but unless one takes it seriously one cannot understand what the men of the Renaissance were worrying about, any more than Gibbon could understand what the Arians and their orthodox opponents were worrying about.

The solution of the dilemma appears first in the early seventeenth century, and belongs characteristically to Descartes. Was it by reason or by faith that Descartes assured himself of his own existence? Not by reason, because, as he pointed out, the thing was an ultimate intuition. And not exactly by faith, because faith had always hitherto contained a suggestion of arbitrary adhesion to a belief which, if one had so wished, one might have denied. Now the conviction of one's own existence is a conviction which one cannot help having. It is not in one's power to have it or to reject it. Its possession does not depend on one's having undergone certain special kinds of experience. Some experience one must have; but any experience will do.

What Descartes has done here is to indicate a point at which faith and reason absolutely coincide. In the certainty of my own existence I have a conviction which is rational in the sense that it is universal and necessary, but a matter of faith in that it rests not on argument, but on direct conviction. Descartes' methodic doubt is not *fides quaerens intellectum,* nor yet *intellectus quaerens fidem;* it is a search for something absolutely certain, which anybody, however situated, must recognize as absolutely certain. Its certainty does not depend on proof, not even, like that of the Aristotelian first principles, on indirect proof, but on the fact that it cannot be denied. Now a man full of the consciousness of God cannot deny God; but not everyone is always full of that consciousness. Descartes has shown that our knowledge of our own existence is of exactly the same kind as this direct knowledge of God by faith, with this difference, that it can never desert us when we acquire its presence.

But Descartes has done more than that. He has shown that this intuitive certainty is the foundation and source of all knowledge whatever. If I make a syllogism, my conclusion no doubt in a sense rests on reasoning; but how do I know that I *am* reasoning? Only in virtue of my self-consciousness, which enables me to say, "I know that, this time, I am not talking nonsense, but really seeing the necessity that binds my premises to my conclusion." Every single step in my reasoning depends for its convincingness upon my being able to say this, to assure myself that I really am reasoning and not associating ideas together in a random way.

This conception of Descartes solves the problem of the relation between faith and reason. Reason itself is henceforth seen to depend for its cogency on that immediate and indemonstrable certainty which is faith; faith is henceforth no longer severed from reason or given a field of its own in which to operate by itself, but becomes as it were the soul of which reason is the body. Hence, when Kant, working out Descartes' ideas a stage further, says, "I must abolish knowledge in order to make room for faith," he does certainly mean that God, freedom, and immortality cannot be proved; but this is not because they are not real, for in his view they *are* real, nor because he thinks we cannot or need not be absolutely certain that they are real, for nothing is further from his mind than the suggestion that they are mere postulates or hypotheses, the suggestion that we ought to act *as if* God existed, whether he does exist or not. Kant was a hard-headed person with a sense of humor, and he would have treated as a joke the suggestion that if God doesn't really exist there could be any point in acting as if he did. God, freedom, and immortality are truths, according to Kant, of which life itself assures us: all life, not merely this or that special form of experience, like undergoing conversion or seeing ghosts. These special experiences do not prove anything in particular, for the conversion may be a nerve-storm, and the ghost a fraud or a hallucination. But in our universal and necessary experience of every day we are actually aware, if only we can detect and isolate this awareness, of our own responsibility and spontaneity, of our timeless and eternal reality, and of the existence of an infinite mind upon which our own finite nature somehow depends. These are certainties of precisely the same kind as Descartes' *cogito ergo sum.* They cannot be proved, because they lie too close to us; you cannot demonstrate them any more than you can button up your own skin; they are the presupposition of all proof whatever, not like the Aristotelian axioms, which enter into particular arguments as their premises, but rather as the conditions of there being any arguments at all.

They reckon ill who leave me out;
When on they fly, I am the wings;
I am the doubter and the doubt,
And I the hymn the Brahmin sings.

That is not quite Kant's position. He was no pantheist. The infinite is not completely and indifferently present for him in any and every finite thing. Rather, it is not present in them at all; they are in it, dependent upon it, maintained by it, and therefore witnesses to it rather than instances of it. God is not the doubter, nor yet the doubt; He is the truth which the doubter thinks he is doubting, but of which he is really quite certain—if he were not, he could not doubt.

But if this is the meaning of faith, how is it possible for anyone not to have it? If Kant is right, everyone must know that God is real, and be as much convinced of it as he is of his own existence; and if Descartes is right, no one can ever doubt his own existence for an instant. Yet surely we are not all of us born with a clear and distinct idea of ourselves, and neither are we born with a clear and distinct idea of God.

The answer is that there is a distinction between being certain of a thing and recognizing that one is certain of it. It is impossible for anyone not to be certain of his own existence; but it requires an effort of detached and reflective thought to recognize this certainty for what it is. Until a person has made this effort and made it successfully, he cannot correctly use words like "I" and "you"; if he does use them, he attaches wrong meanings to them, as anyone knows who has talked to very small children. But the child comes to recognize that it has, or is, a self; and this recognition comes not through any special type of experience, but simply through learning to reflect on experience in general. And we become conscious of God in an analogous way; we come to recognize a certainty which we possessed in some obscure form long before we came to recognize it. If anybody says he does not believe in God, that may be simply because he has not successfully reflected on his own experience and detached from it the certainty which he cannot but have; but it is more likely to be because someone has confused his mind by putting before him a definition of the term "God" which does not connect itself with anything in his personal experience. Early missionaries frequently report the discovery of savages innocent of the idea of God; but modern anthropologists cannot find such savages, and do not believe them to exist; and the explanation certainly is that the early missionaries found an idea of God so different from their own that they failed to recognize it.

This, I think, is the meaning of the term "faith" in Kant. I can perhaps best illustrate his view by contrasting it with Herbert Spencer's. Spencer, as everyone knows, thought that some things were knowable and others unknowable. The knowable was the sphere of reason, of science, and the unknowable was the sphere of religion, of faith. Now the unknowable means that which cannot possibly enter into human experience; and thus Spencer's view was that the object of religious belief could not possibly become a factor in the actual life of man. That is another way of saying that no human being could in any circumstances have any kind of religious experience. Why, that being so, he should wish to believe in God, Spencer does not explain. Now, for Kant, human thought in all its forms is concerned with phenomena only; that is, with things just so far as they enter into human experience. The God in whom Kant is interested, therefore, is not a metaphysical abstraction, not the First Cause of philosophical theology, but the God of religion, the God of actual human experience. This God is for him in a sense unknowable; that is, he cannot be made the object of scientific inquiry; that is just because he is not a particular finite thing, but an infinite spirit. But though we cannot devise scientific experiments or logical arguments to demonstrate God's existence and attributes, that is not because we are not certain of them; it is just *because* we are certain of them that we know these methods of proof to be inapplicable.

I have stated Kant's position at some length, because it lies at the root of all that is best in modern thought on this subject. The crucial point is the fact that reason and faith no longer for us, as for the Middle Ages they did perforce, appear as separate and independent cognitive faculties. We cannot nowadays maintain that certain problems or propositions belong to the sphere of faith, and others to the sphere of reason. Both faith and reason have been reinterpreted in the light of a long experience of both science and religion, and we ought now to be able to recognize that all real knowledge partakes of the character of each. Religion, when it tries to preserve its purity uncontaminated by science, tends to regard itself as wholly a matter of faith. By so doing it degrades itself into an irrational thing, and its object into a contingent finite fact. Science, when it emasculates itself into a mere chain of reasoning from hypotheses arbitrarily laid down, does so only by forgetting that the cogency of each link in its demonstration must itself remain undemonstrated. Faith, properly understood, is not irrational, for it is not so much dependent on reason as the ground and source of reason; reason is not the negation of faith, but its development into an articulated system. Every act is fundamentally an act of faith; but it is not a completed act of faith unless it develops into a rational and self-explanatory system of thought. Hence faith that remains mere faith and keeps reason at arm's length is in error, not because it is only faith, but because it is *not* faith; it has not sufficient faith in itself to state itself clearly and abide by the result. This is not faith, but lack of faith, just as it is lack of faith to say, "I believe this bridge will bear me, but in order to preserve my faith uncontaminated by reason I won't try to walk across it." People who claim to have a lively belief in God and shrink from expressing this belief in the reasoned terms of theology and philosophy are obviously victims of this lack of faith.

Yet faith cannot be the product of reason. You cannot add finite quantities together and make the infinite; you must first assume the infinite from which to make your selection, and only so can you get your finite quantities. So you cannot produce faith by arguing. Faith is presupposed in the argument itself. People do not, and never can, come to believe in God, or in anything else, as a result of ratiocination. The function of ratiocination is not this, but the development or reasoned statement of what faith finds within itself. To say that is not to deny all value to apologetics and to debates; that would be hardly necessary, for everyone knows that the value of these things is extraordinarily slender if they are to be judged by their net result in the shape of conversions. They have a very real value in leading people to answer the question, "What do I believe?" and that is a question always worth answering. Indeed, if the view I have been maintaining is right, anything that led people to answer this question would be in the interest of religion; for on this view everyone believes in God, if only he could be brought to see it. Reason cannot generate faith, but reason alone can reveal faith to itself, can display to it its own nature.

Hence, too, it is only reason that can display to faith the nature of its own object. It is by faith that we grasp reality, whether we call that reality by the name of God or by any other name, as immediately and certainly present to us; but what it is that is thus present to us faith alone could never say. It could at most only assure us that something was present to us, something real but wholly undefined, a mere empty presence. The work of reason is to ask what this is that is present to us, to determine its name and its nature by discovering how it works upon us and how it affects our experience.

All this is true of religious experience, and equally true of experience at large. All knowledge begins with an immediate, unreasoned, and indemonstrable conviction that there is something here to be known, and goes on to ask what it is. All action begins with the immediate, indemonstrable, and irresistible feeling that we are filled and sustained by some power as yet unexpressed, which is to reveal itself through our action; and thus action, no less than knowledge, begins in faith and rests on faith; indeed, faith is as much an active as a cognitive thing, as much a practical force as a theoretical enlightenment. But though all knowledge, all conduct, rests on faith, there is in two ways a special connection between faith and the specifically religious side of our nature. First, faith is, as I said at the beginning, a distinctively Christian idea, a conception which Christianity first introduced to the European mind, and one which we can never entirely dissociate from its Christian origin. Secondly, the interplay of faith and reason as I have just described it goes on not only within every single act and thought, but also, in a larger rhythm, within the history of human knowledge as an interplay between religion and science. It is a fair generalization that all scientific and philosophical ideas, before they have been worked out in explicit intellectual terms, are present to men's minds in the form of religious beliefs. The doctrine of the Trinity, taught as a revelation by early Christianity and expressly excluded by medieval thought from the sphere of reason, becomes in Kant and his successors a demonstrable and almost alarmingly fertile logical principle. The conception of personality is another which we owe first, in religious terms, to Christianity, and secondly, in scientific terms, to modern philosophy and psychology. Karl Marx may have been unduly fanciful when he seemed to find his own conception of economic law in the theological determinism of Calvin, and Mr. Cornford may be simplifying the facts when he finds in Greek philosophy a mere restatement or refinement of Greek religion; but the principle is sound. *Nihil est in intellectu quod non fuerit in sensu,* said the schoolmen; if for intellect we read scientific thought, and for sense religious intuition, we may say with substantial truth that the intellect discovers nothing that faith has not already known. But this conversion of a given thought from terms of faith to terms of intellect does not deprive faith of anything. *Fides quaerit intellectum*; and when it finds it, it is only finding itself.

So we come back to Anselm, and define not only the philosophy of religion but the whole life of man as *fides quaerens intellectum.* But we must be allowed to interpret the phrase in our own way. Anselm thought that, to a faith already complete and full grown, understanding could be added without in the least altering its nature; but we have now seen that to add understanding to faith means revealing faith to itself, teaching it what it is and what it believes. And therefore, as faith could never seek understanding unless it had already to some degree found it, a complete, full-grown faith wholly devoid of understanding nowhere exists. The faith that sets out in search of understanding is a faith already endowed with sufficient understanding to recognize its need of more. And in searching for more understanding it is searching not for an extraneous addition to itself, but for a development and confirmation of its own nature. If we wholly believed, if we did not feel the need of help for our unbelief, we should not need to think. We could rest wholly satisfied with our faith. And anybody who thinks he is perfect in his faith may logically and morally refuse to torment himself by following the stony path of reason.

But anyone who finds his faith less clear and strong than he would wish it must take steps to amend it; and these can only be of one kind. Faith, in and by itself, cannot be cultivated; that is the essence of its intuitive immediacy. But reason can; and if I have made myself clear, I shall be understood when I conclude by saying that reason is nothing but faith cultivating itself.

FAITH AND REASON

INTRODUCTION

Faith is a habit of mind which accepts without criticizing, pronounces without proving, and acts without arguing. It knows nothing of analysis and classification, hypothesis and induction and syllogism; for the machinery of thought it has no use. Nor does it inquire into causes and effects, forces and their combinations, bodies and their interactions; in a mechanical world it is not at home. Yet somewhere it has a home, and thought of a kind it certainly is; and however it came into human nature, whether by the disposition of an all-wise providence or by the survival of the fittest, it is a habit of mind that exists in men and finds its proper expression in their religions.

Reason is a habit of mind which aims at criticizing before it accepts, proving before it pronounces, and arguing before it acts. Instead of relying on its own unanalyzed and instinctive intuitions, it thinks out a method, a logic, for itself; it invents a logical machine to think with, and it thinks of the world as, at bottom, itself a machine. Cause and effect, action and reaction, part and whole, are the categories of its thought, whereas faith seems to break down these categories by thinking of an uncaused cause, an action that has no reaction, and a whole not divisible into parts. Reason, like faith, is plainly a real element in human nature; and its proper expression is in what we call science.

The affirmation to be made in the following pages is that both these habits of mind are natural and necessary to man, and that, in spite of their opposite characteristics, they are not really at bottom opposed. But they certainly seem to be opposed; and therefore we must begin by looking carefully at this appearance of opposition.

A pamphlet in the "Affirmation Series" (London: Ernest Benn, 1928). Reprinted in A. A. David, ed., *God in the Modern World* (New York: Putnam, 1929).

THE CONFLICT BETWEEN RELIGION AND SCIENCE

Not many years ago an eminent scientist resolved to settle once for all, by strictly scientific methods, whether prayer was of any use. He decided, no doubt correctly, that, on the whole, members of the royal family and children of the clergy were more prayed for than any other classes in the community; and he inferred that, if prayer had any value, these persons, being specially protected as a result of their well-wishers' prayers, would on the average have longer lives than persons not so protected. Statistics showed him that this was not the case; therefore, he concluded, the efficacy of prayer was *nil.*

Here you have, in a nutshell, the whole quarrel between religion and science, in the form in which it exists today. In the middle of the nineteenth century it took a somewhat different form. Then, orthodox religion stood committed to certain views on biological and geological subjects which the advance of scientific inquiry was undermining. Just as the Copernican astronomy had aroused the antagonism of ecclesiastical authority centuries earlier, so the new geology and the newer biology of the eighteenth and nineteenth centuries encountered an opposition of very much the same kind, based on very much the same motives.

Galileo was right, and the Inquisition wrong; Darwin was right, and his opponents wrong. No one whose opinion is worth taking today has the slightest desire to rehabilitate either the pre-Copernican astronomy or the pre-Darwinian biology. No doubt Copernicus and Darwin left problems unsolved and gave us theories open, in many important ways, to modification. But not even the most malignant adversary of science could pretend to believe that on this account they were wrong, and their opponents right, on the main point at issue.

The moral, no doubt, is that on subjects falling within the sphere of science, science is the sole arbiter. When scientific thought is still in its infancy, and has not delimited its own sphere and elaborated its own methods, the priest discharges the scientist's duties as well as his own, and teaches not only religion but also biology and astronomy, meteorology and medicine. But on these topics he is powerless to speak with the authority that belongs to genuine knowledge. His authority on scientific matters rests on the false assumption that if he knows about the gods he probably knows about the stars as well; and the only sanction of this authority is superstition. Hence, when scientific thought, firmly possessed of its proper methods of research, and confidently claiming a certain field for the employment of those methods, produces results at variance with the authority of the priest, that authority must give way and accept these results with a good grace. No other course is barely decent, let alone worthy of a director of consciences.

But what subjects *do* fall within the sphere of science?

In the nineteenth century the scientists were still fighting a defensive battle, fighting for permission to accept certain results which scientific thought had actually achieved, though they admittedly contradicted the Biblical story of creation. The question of principle remained in the background. And for this reason people who wished both combatants to survive the battle could suggest the terms of a possible treaty, according to which certain gains should be secured to science and a certain authority left to religion, each being mistress in her own house.

Suppose, however, it is maintained that *all possible subjects fall within the sphere of science.* In that case the house of science is the whole house of life; and religion seems to be left homeless.

This is what has happened in the case of the scientist whom I quoted at the beginning. He is assuming that the inductive methods of science are applicable, not simply to questions generally recognized as scientific, but to all questions whatever, including those generally recognized as peculiarly reserved for religion.

For observe: most people, if asked whether prayer was of any value, would reply that, if it is, its value is a value of a peculiar kind; a value not capable of being measured or weighed by the scientist; a value only to be apprehended by a religious mind and in terms of religious experience. Most people would smile at Huckleberry Finn's argument, that prayer was valueless because he didn't get what he prayed for ("once I got a fish-line, but no hooks; it war'n't any good without hooks"), and would agree with Miss Watson that the things one ought to pray for are "spiritual blessings." That being so, the question whether prayer is answered is a question on which vital statistics throw no light whatever. But our eminent scientist was not so grossly ignorant as not to know that. His scientific disproof of the value of prayer was no doubt intended as a deliberate, though tacit, rejection of the ordinary belief, in the interests of a theory that *all* values are to be apprehended by scientific observation and *all* beliefs tested by scientific induction. At any rate, that is the implication which leads another distinguished scientist to quote the argument with approval in a recent book.

The present position of the conflict between religion and science, then, is that the scientists, having won an important victory in the last phase of the war, are now attacking the position which then they never dreamed of attacking—the position that religion has a sphere of its own within which it has the same kind of competence that science has in such spheres as that of biology.

The main force of this attack depends on the results achieved and hoped for by psychology. Just as religion once falsely arrogated to itself the power to make assertions about astronomy and biology, so now (it is said) it claims the same power with respect to psychological questions, and no less falsely. But psychology has already entered into some part of its inheritance at the expense of religion, and will in time make good its claim to the rest. And then religion will have been driven from its last stronghold—the stronghold of man's inner consciousness.

The full force of the attack will never be recognized until we see that within their own limits the scientists are right. It seems quite reasonable to think that we ought not to pray for "material" things but for "spiritual" things; but if we try to escape disease by sanitation rather than by petition, to secure our harvests by scientific agriculture and our voyages by scientific navigation, it is idle to suppose that the utility of science must forever stop short at the threshold of the mind. Ever since the seventeenth century we have been much influenced by an exaggerated and therefore false separation between mind and matter; and we have found it easy (and on the whole useful) to assume that matter is the proper sphere of scientific inquiry, while mind cannot be grasped by scientific thought and must be reserved either for religion, or for philosophy, or for a partnership of the two. But we are coming to realize that this separation of mind and matter, which seemed so obvious, was only a working hypothesis, and one whose term of usefulness is drawing to a close. The tide of scientific inquiry is still rising, and imminently threatens to obliterate the whole distinction. And nobody will arrest that tide by taking a chair down to the seashore and sitting down in it, with however dignified a gesture.

Indeed, nobody wants to. I spoke of the adversaries of science, but I do not really imagine that such people exist. We all want science to go on thriving and to achieve greater and greater triumphs in the future. At least, we all want this when we think clearly of what it involves. When we fail to think clearly, we can belittle the progress of science by identifying science with useful inventions, and then taking the high line of depreciating a "mere increase in material prosperity." Certainly, if the advance of science meant nothing but an increase of comfort, it would be a thing that might well be opposed to the highest interests of mankind. But though the advance of science does incidentally involve an increasing complexity and delicacy in the mechanical devices which men use, this is only an incident in a process whose essence lies elsewhere. Essentially, the advance of science means the advance of the scientific spirit, the critical and inquiring spirit which takes facts as they stand and analyzes them in order to discover their laws. And this spirit is one of the highest and finest things in human life. The world could get along very well without wireless telephony; but it would be a very poor place without the kind of man whose thought has made wireless telephony possible. It is not so much that it would be an uncomfortable place; one soon gets used to discomfort, and finds that it does not much matter; but it would be a stupid, slothful, dull-minded place, ruled by blind prejudice and terrorized by crude superstition.

If, then, we want the scientific spirit to flourish, and believe in it as a thing of genuine value in itself, we must take the consequences. We must ask what are the conditions in which it can thrive, and see that these are fulfilled. "Conditions" here does not mean *external* conditions. I am not suggesting that there may be certain climatic or racial or political or economic conditions which may be specially favorable or unfavorable to the scientific spirit. I mean *internal* conditions: that is to say, states of mind. I am raising the question, what must a scientist's mental attitude toward the world be, if the scientific spirit in him is to thrive?

Obviously, his attitude must be the scientific attitude: the attitude of critical analysis, the attitude which treats facts as things to be taken to pieces to see how they work. But *what* facts? That is the question which puzzled us before.

We can now answer it: *all* facts. Why? Because it is a question of principle. The scientific spirit is a spirit, not a dodge; it lives by living up to an ideal, not by inventing marketable gadgets. The reason why it treats certain facts analytically and inductively is not because these particular facts happen to lend themselves to that treatment, but just because they are facts and, being facts, grist to the scientific mill. It is therefore hopeless to draw a magic circle round any particular group of facts and say to the scientist, "Keep to your own sphere, and hands off mine." If the scientist is a real scientist, if the scientific spirit is hot within him, he will be powerless to obey you. In any case, he cannot obey you without disobeying his own conscience and denying the spirit of science.

Modern scientists are aware of this; and that is why, from their point of view, the old distinction between mind and matter has ceased to have the force of an international frontier. They no longer regard their own work as coextensive with the sphere of matter, and stopping short, for some mysterious reason, of mind. Whatever is recognizable as a fact, capable of being observed and recorded and tabulated, they now recognize as a proper object of their own inquiries. And therefore they would, I imagine, on the particular point at issue, sympathize with Huckleberry Finn and accuse Miss Watson of evading the issue. "You have given up," they would say to Miss Watson, "the simple and natural religious idea of praying for whatever you want—a fine day or a fishing-line or a new pair of boots—because you have come to realize that, so far as these things can be acquired at will, they are acquired by purely natural means. But you still think you can acquire *spiritual* blessings by prayer; that is, that you can become peaceful and happy and good by supernatural means. But psychological science is in a fair way to prove that these blessings are just as natural—just as much subject to ascertainable laws—as the others; and therefore just as little within the sphere of prayer."

It does not matter whether psychological science has yet reached this point or not. The question is now one of principle: it is a question, not of what science has done, but of what (if anything) it can undertake never to do in the future. And if religious experience is to live on the margin of life left over from scientific analysis, if religion is to be a residual phenomenon inhabiting a region as yet unpenetrated by the pioneers of science, then the right of religion is only squatter's right and it can never have any home that it can call its own.

That is the true significance of the conflict between religion and science, in the form which it has now taken. Formerly, science was asking for a bare foothold in selected portions of a world the whole of which was in principle claimed by religion. Nowadays, religion is trying to retain a bare foothold in selected portions of a world the whole of which is in principle claimed by science. And the attempt is bound to fail. If the gods have been driven from our hearths and gardens, our fields and roadsides, to lurk in the forests and wild places, we have only to extend the area of cultivation until all the gods are dead.

Does this mean that religion is doomed to perish?

Certainly not. It only means that the future of religion would be desperate, *if it depended on protecting a certain region of human life from scientific inquiry.* In most current discussions, it is assumed that this is the case: that religion and science must agree to draw a boundary between their respective territories, and that the only real question at issue is where this boundary is to be drawn.

To assume that, is to commit oneself to the conclusion *either* that religion must perish as a pre-scientific, antiquated, superstitious form of experience, *or* that science is not a matter of principle but a trick for inventing gadgets. If you believe in religion as a serious thing, you can settle the boundary problem by assuming that science is a mere haphazard collection of useful dodges. On that view, there is only one sacred principle at stake—the principle of religion; and then you can afford to make concessions to science on the ground that, after all, religion *need* not assert the astronomical centrality of the earth or the special creation of each kind of animal. Conversely, if you believe in science as a serious thing, you can settle the boundary problem by assuming that religion is a mere weakness of the mind, and allowing it to squat anywhere on the margins of life until such time as science is ready to oust it from that particular point. But if you realize (as every religious man does) that *religion* is a serious thing and a matter of principle, and also realize (as every scientific man does) that *science* is a serious thing and a matter of principle, then you only need a little clear thinking in order to see that no boundary can be drawn, and that, in the truceless war that must spread from point to point over the whole of human life, every engagement will be a fresh defeat for religion.

The only reason why this inference is so seldom drawn is that comparatively few people realize the seriousness both of religion and science. People who are keenly religious very often fail entirely to appreciate the high spiritual and ideal quality of the scientific mind; and conversely, scientific people whose whole life is a living sacrifice to truth are apt to see in religion a phenomenon of mainly archeological interest. These pages are being written for readers who believe that neither religion nor science is a trivial thing, who believe that each represents a value, an ideal, whose enrichment of human life is not to be measured in terms of comfort, whether of body or of mind. If the reader joins with me in this belief, and agrees with me in thinking that some solution must be sought for a conflict between two things that are both so necessary, he will perhaps bear with me while I go on to explain where, I think, the solution is to be found.

In order to do this it is desirable to make clear a few outstanding points in the history of the ideas of faith and reason. The quarrel between religion and science is as much an event in human history as was the medieval quarrel between the Empire and the Papacy; and in both cases a proper understanding of the grounds of the quarrel, the necessary preliminary to its composition, must depend upon some understanding of its origin.

ORIGINS AND HISTORY OF THE CONFLICT

The idea of logical scientific thought, which we are calling reason, can be traced in a direct line back to the ancient Greeks. It is true that Greek logicians emphasized the deductive side of science, whereas modern logicians tend to emphasize the inductive; and this shows that the modern idea of reason is no longer precisely the Greek idea. But it is still true today, even after all the innovations in logic which have been made since the time of Bacon, that modern logic is substantially the logic of Aristotle, which means that our idea of reason is in its main lines the Greek idea.

Faith, on the other hand, is not a Greek idea at all. Its prominence in modern European thought is due to Christianity. Only by close scrutiny can we discover that the Greeks knew such a thing existed. Plato in one passage used the word "faith" for our belief in the reality of the world we see around us—the world of chairs and tables, animals and men. If someone took it into his head to say that the table on which I am writing is not really there, I could not prove him wrong; but I should be perfectly certain that he *was* wrong. This indemonstrable certainty, this conviction indefensible by argument, is what Plato calls faith. To us, his use of the term seems strange. That is because we are accustomed to distinguish between faith and sight, and this distinction, as we shall see, is what Christianity added to the idea and thus made it what it has been ever since. But in one sense, a merely negative sense, Plato's use of the term is the same as our own: in both cases, faith implies the absence of proof or rational argument.

This Platonic use of the term "faith" remains undeveloped, a mere passing suggestion, thrown out and dropped. Plato never discussed the matter again in his dialogues, and later Greek writers did not take it up. They did not realize what an important and fertile idea had, for a brief moment, seen the light. This was because the whole energies of Greek philosophical thought were being devoted to the development of the opposite idea, that of reason. The Greek mind, for good or ill, was radically intellectualistic; its instinct was to demand an argued demonstration of anything. And the culmination of Greek philosophy was the Aristotelian theory of the syllogism, a theory according to which the ideal of thought is to demonstrate everything except the ultimate first principles from which all demonstrations were in the last resort derived. Nor were these ultimate first principles matters of faith. They were demonstrable; but demonstrable in a special sense, namely, by proving that any attempt to deny them contradicted itself. All the best Greco-Roman thought devoted itself to elaborating and manipulating that beautiful instrument of precision, the Aristotelian syllogism.

Into a world so occupied, Christianity, however truly foreshadowed and prepared by many tendencies of the Greco-Roman mind, came as a destructive and revolutionary force. Instead of syllogistic reason, it preached faith as the organ of knowledge; instead of a world of finite entities and natural facts, it set up, as sole true object of that knowledge, God. Human thought, hitherto dissipated in a syllogistic network over the infinite field of natural fact, was now to be focused upon a single point. The result of this was to substitute immediate conviction for reasoned argument; because syllogistic argument consisted in pointing out the relations between fact and fact, and therefore presupposed the dispersion of thought over a plurality of facts.

Thus the Platonic relation between faith and reason was reversed. Plato had considered faith an inferior kind of knowledge because it could not, when challenged, argue in its own defense. Christianity saw in the same fact a ground of superiority. This change of attitude was perfectly logical. It was not a mere question of taste. The Greek philosophers had laid down that the value of any kind of knowledge was proportionate to the value of the object known by it. Now, according to Aristotle, the only things that really exist are individual substances—this chair, this man, and so forth. Each of these is a finite object, whose causes are to be sought outside itself. And to know a thing is to know its causes. Hence to know anything you must, first, know it as a particular finite thing, and, secondly, know it in its relations to other particular finite things. But the object of faith, as understood by Christianity, is God; and God is an infinite being, who is not limited or caused by anything other than himself. Hence, by a corollary of the strict Greek view, God cannot be known syllogistically; you cannot, that is, demonstrate his existence or attributes, because to demonstrate a thing is to think of it as standing in the relation of effect to something else that is its cause. In order to know God, therefore, we must grasp his existence by some kind of direct intuitive act. This intuitive act cannot be the intellectual intuition by which, according to the Greek view, we grasp the ultimate truths of science; for these truths are still finite objects in the sense that each of them is a particular truth different from the others and from the particular facts that exemplify it. God is not a Euclidean axiom; and the intellectual intuition that grasps the axiom cannot grasp God. Yet the whole of Christianity depends for its value on the assurance that God is revealed to us; and this implies on our part some faculty capable of apprehending the revelation. This is the primitive Christian idea of faith.

To the Greeks, the idea was foolishness. It seemed a reactionary idea, a retrograde movement in philosophy. It seemed to imply giving up all the ground that Greek thought had conquered, and relapsing into the primitive and pre-scientific attitude of the superstitious East. The triumph of the Christian mind with its cardinal idea of thought as faith seemed to involve (in Gibbon's words) "the triumph of barbarism and religion."

But this was a false diagnosis. The new idea was really a step forward, not backward; instead of failing to maintain what the Greeks had won, it solved a problem that had defeated the Greek mind.

The Greeks had cut human life into two parts: the one

scientific, argumentative, and intellectually respectable; the other intuitive, irrational, and in the last resort superstitious. Under the first head fell philosophy and the sciences; under the second, religion and everyday perception. Now, Christianity would have taken a retrograde step if it had merely inverted the Greek view; but it did not; it modified it by distinguishing between religion and everyday perception, and putting them in separate classes. Greek thought had grouped them together for the merely negative reason that they were not syllogistic, not argumentative. Christianity, while agreeing that this was true, pointed out a distinction which Greek thought had overlooked: namely, that perception was concerned with finite sensible objects, whereas religion was concerned with an infinite object not apprehensible by sense. Thus the faith with which we apprehend the infinite and wholly spiritual nature of God must (on the principles of Greek philosophy itself) be utterly unlike the perception with which we apprehend the finite things of sense.

This was the distinction between faith and sight. The consequence was that faith, as the apprehension of the supreme reality, God, became the supreme organ of knowledge; and reason, as the syllogistically-articulated knowledge of the natural world, was not in any way attacked or disparaged, but simply subordinated to it. The superiority of reason over sense was left exactly as the Greeks had established it; but Christian thought added a third term to the series, and asserted the superiority of faith over reason.

To convince oneself that this Christian idea of faith, as knowledge of the infinite, was an idea which satisfied a need already felt by ancient thought and solved a problem which it had felt but had not as yet solved, it is only necessary to consider the case of Neoplatonism. The great Neoplatonists were ostensibly opponents of Christianity; but the motives which underlay their thought were the same as those which underlay the Christian doctrines. If you compare the Neoplatonic philosophy with that of Plato and Aristotle—the classical Greek systems—you find one great fundamental difference amid all the resemblances of detail. For the classical Greeks, knowledge proper is knowledge of finite objects in their mutual relations. For the Neoplatonists, knowledge proper is knowledge of the one infinite object. Hence the classical syllogistic *reason* gives place, in Neoplatonism, to an intuitive type of thought really identical with what the Christians were calling *faith*.

This sense of the infinite, this emphasis upon faith, brought the Neoplatonists far nearer to the Christians whom they opposed than to the classical Greeks whom they admired; and their allegiance to the letter of classical philosophy was at bottom profoundly inconsistent with their mystical theological temperament. This inconsistency rendered Neoplatonism sterile in just those points where Christianity was fertile. The knowledge of natural or finite objects expresses itself outwardly in the life of the intellectual specialist, the sage or wise man, ancient philosopher or modern scientist, aloof from the world and absorbed in his own special line of inquiry. The knowledge of God or the infinite, faith, expresses itself outwardly in the life of a church composed of believers and entered not by competitive examination but by a simple pledge of loyalty. Here Christianity, organizing its outward life into the form of a church, was consistent with the inner significance of the idea of faith; Neoplatonism, clinging to the classical conception of the philosopher and the philosophical school, failed to clothe its new thought in an appropriate social form, and thus injured that thought itself.

The victory of Christianity is the beginning of the Middle Ages. Faith and reason are now recognized as two modes of knowledge: faith is that by which we apprehend God as the infinite, reason that by which we apprehend natural facts as finite. Faith therefore is superior to reason as the infinite to the finite, but, subject to that superiority, each has its own proper sphere and competence.

This is the theory accepted and developed by the Middle Ages. But it was never a wholly satisfactory theory. Had the distinction between the spheres of faith and reason been as clear as the theory implied, it would have been easy to see where the one began and the other ended, and there would have been little danger of friction. But there was always friction from the first. In a science like theology it was impossible really to settle what exact share of the work should be done by reason and faith respectively. No doubt a compromise was effected; it was generally recognized that certain theological doctrines were matters of reason and others matters of faith; but the terms of the compromise were always open to objection, and it was always possible to raise the question whether, theoretically, a compromise was justifiable at all.

This appears very plainly from the medieval discussions concerning the proofs of God's existence. If the principle of the distinction between faith and reason had been grasped, it would have been asserted that God's existence cannot be proved. Yet on the whole, and with very important reservations, medieval opinion inclined to the view that it could. Thus Anselm, searching for a proof of God's existence, hit upon the famous ontological proof; and the odd thing is that when a kindly critic pointed out that his proof was logically conclusive only to a person who already believed in God, Anselm was not in the least disconcerted. "I believe," to quote his own words, "in order that I may understand; for this I know, that unless I first believe I shall never understand." Here faith is given an absolute priority over reason; but the very demand for a proof of God's existence contradicts this by implying the priority of reason over faith. To the question "Is it faith or reason that assures us of God's existence?" Anselm has no answer; or rather, he has two incompatible answers. The same is true of medieval thought in general. This difficulty is an inevitable result of the medieval compromise, and it must recur wherever a similar compromise is attempted. Faith and reason were given two distinct spheres, each lying outside the other. Now, faith is the knowledge of the infinite, reason the knowledge of the finite. To separate the sphere of faith from that of reason means separating the infinite from the finite and setting them side by side with a dividing line between them. But anything which is divided off from something else lying outside it is thereby shown to be a finite thing, for to be finite simply is to be limited by something else. The so-called infinite is therefore infinite only in name; really it is another finite.

And therefore what has been called faith is not really faith but only reason over again, reason not recognized for what it is.

Thus, so long as reason has a legitimate sphere, there cannot be outside it a legitimate sphere for faith. What is given to faith under such a compromise must always be an *irredenta* of reason. But conversely, if there is a legitimate sphere for faith, that sphere is the infinite; and if it is really infinite, the finite falls not outside it but inside it; and therefore reason is swallowed up in faith, and nothing is left for reason as such.

This dilemma may look like a mere freak of abstract logic; but it is a very real difficulty, and without understanding it one cannot understand the Reformation, or the Inquisition, or why Spinoza used *Deus* and *natura* as synonymous terms. And these facts are the true antecedents of the modern conflict between religion and science.

The germ of a new attitude toward the dilemma is to be found in Descartes; but it is no more than a germ, though a fertile one. Descartes wanted to construct a system of science which should be really secure and well founded; and he thought that the chief thing needed for this was an absolutely firm starting-point. He therefore went in search of some truth which should be undeniable: undeniable not metaphorically but literally, not relatively but absolutely. By the practice of methodic doubt he discovered that innumerable things were deniable which were not usually denied; but he found one thing that no one could possibly deny—the doubter's own existence.

Now, was it by reason or by faith that Descartes assured himself of his own existence? Not by reason in the ordinary sense, because, as he rightly pointed out, his conviction of it was intuitive, and it could not be expressed, without falsification, as a syllogism. *Cogito ergo sum* was his way of putting it; but the *ergo* was, he said, not the *ergo* of inference. Nor was it a matter of faith in the ordinary sense, because faith contained a suggestion of voluntary adhesion to something which one might, had one wished, have denied; whereas the conviction of one's own existence is a conviction which one cannot help having. It is not in anyone's power to reject it, nor does it depend on one's undergoing any special kind of experience.

The peculiarity of the *cogito ergo sum* is that Descartes here found a point at which reason and faith coincide. The certainty of my own existence is a matter of faith in the sense that it does not rest on argument but on direct intuition; but it is a matter of reason in the sense that it is universal and necessary and cannot be denied by any thinking being. It resembles the religious man's knowledge of God in its immediate certainty; but not every man is always religious, and faith in God may desert us. It resembles the knowledge of the Aristotelian first principles in being universal and necessary; but the Aristotelian first principles are deniable and thus lack the absolute and immediate conviction that is inseparable from the *cogito.*

It was something—in fact it was a great achievement—to have discovered a common point in the spheres of faith and reason. But it was a great achievement only because it indicated a line of possible progress. This line Descartes himself did not follow; it was explored by his successors, and notably by Kant, who saw more clearly than most people the true nature of the problem involved in the distinction between faith and reason. Turning his back on all the philosophers who had exhausted their ingenuity in devising proofs of the existence of God, Kant laid down that there could be no such proof: God, freedom, and immortality, the three traditional objects of metaphysical speculation, were objects of faith, not of scientific demonstration. Not that Kant thought their reality doubtful. He did not; he regarded them as truths of which all our experience assures us. We do not demonstrate them, not because they are too uncertain, but because they are too certain: they lie too close to our minds to be proved, they are too inextricably interwoven with our experience to be argued about. To prove them is like buttoning up your own skin.

Kant was trying to treat God, freedom, and immortality as certainties of the same kind as Descartes' *cogito ergo sum:* that is, as universal, necessary, and so far rational, but indemonstrable and so far matters of faith. Descartes had shown that, whatever may be said about this or that *detail* of my conscious life—however much it may be open to discussion whether this is a toothache and that a love affair—there is always something that holds good of this conscious life *as a whole,* namely, that it is all mine: that it hangs together in the peculiar way in which a system of experiences must hang together in order to be one person's experiences. This subjective unity of experiences, their unity regarded as the unity of the mind that enjoys them, was what Descartes discovered to be a certainty transcending the distinction of faith and reason. Now, this subjective unity corresponds to an objective unity: that is, the unity of my experiences regarded as the unity of the world present to me in experience. It is this objective unity that Kant is emphasizing. Whatever may be said about the *details* of the world, there is always something that may be said about the world *as a whole,* namely, that it *is* a whole: a whole within which all distinctions fall, outside which there is nothing, and which, taken as a whole, is the cause of itself and of everything in it. The details of the world are the proper theme of scientific thought; but its characteristics as a whole, its unity and the implications of that unity, are not matters for scientific inquiry. They are, rather, a foundation on which all scientific inquiry rests. If it was possible to deny them—which it is not—scientific inquiry would instantly cease.

We can see the kind of thing Kant had in mind if we ask ourselves such questions as this: "Why do we believe that there are laws of nature?" "Why do we believe that if conclusions follow logically from true premises they are themselves true?" To these questions people sometimes thoughtlessly reply, "They are mere assumptions." It is a thoughtless answer because it is made without reflecting on the meaning of the word "assumption." And assumption is an optional thing; if I assume $x = 12$, that implies that I might have assumed $x = 13$. But if we try, we shall find that we cannot assume that there are not laws of nature or that untrue conclusions can follow logically from true premises.

Another thoughtless answer is that "our minds are so made that we must believe these things." This is a contradiction in terms;

because if anyone really thought that the only reason why he believed a thing (call it T) was that his mind was so made as to compel him to believe it, this very thought would be equivalent to a disbelief in T; because it would be equivalent to thinking that his only reason for believing T was a bad reason.

A third wrong answer is: "We learn them by experience"; for unless we were already certain of them, we could not, at any given moment, begin accumulating that mass of detailed information which in bulk is called experience.

The only right answer to questions of this kind is: "Because we know that it is so." And if we are asked "How do you know?" we must reply: "That is an illegitimate question, because it implies that we ought to have reasons for these pieces of knowledge, which we haven't, and, in the nature of the case, do not need." If then we are told that this reduces them to mere matters of faith, we shall reply, "Not at all: faith they are, but not mere faith, because the faith which they express is a rational faith in the sense that it is universal in everyone—even in you, who pretend to doubt it—and necessary to all thought, even the thought by which you pretend to criticize it."

We thus possess certain pieces of knowledge about the world which we did not acquire, and cannot criticize, by scientific methods. The knowledge in question is our knowledge of the world, not in its details, but as a whole. And not only is it not acquired by scientific thought, but it is the very foundation of such thought; for only in so far as we know, for instance, that there are laws of nature, can we reasonably devise methods for discovering them.

Kant thought that our certainty of God, freedom, and immortality belonged to this kind of knowledge: God, because God stands to us for the rationality, the trustworthiness, of the objective world; freedom, because freedom means our own power of determining our own actions, which certainly cannot be tested by a scientific inquiry into this or that type of action, but must be found, if anywhere, in our actions taken as a whole; immortality, because immortality means the ultimate harmony between human purposes and the destiny of the universe, and that, again, is a question not of detail—it has nothing whatever, for instance, to do with ghosts and "spirit messages" and "phenomena" which, just because they are admittedly "phenomena," cannot be "spiritual"—but of the relation of mind as a whole to its world as a whole.

I have dealt with Kant's view at some length, instead of pursuing the history of the ideas in question into its more recent phases, partly because these later phases are well known, and partly because Kant's view, though on the whole neglected in these later phases, involves certain principles which, if carefully developed, seem to supply exactly what is needed for the solution of our original problem. The main principle is this: the finite falls within the infinite, not outside it; therefore the sphere of faith and the sphere of reason are not two mutually exclusive spheres, but the sphere of reason falls within the sphere of faith. Faith is our attitude toward reality as a whole, reason our attitude toward its details as distinct and separate from each other. Consequently any attempt to revive the medieval compromise, by which certain problems or prepositions are assigned to faith and others to reason, is foredoomed to failure; and this is no doubt the reason why, as we saw at the outset, the conflict between religion and science, conceived as an attempt to delimit their respective spheres, has led to no permanent settlement. Let us now try, in the light of this historical review, to reconsider the terms of our original problem.

TOWARD A SETTLEMENT

Faith is the religious habit of mind. That is to say, it is the attitude which we take up toward things as a whole. There is a certain analogy to it in the attitude which we take up toward a relative or limited whole like our country. We come to know what our country is, what it means to us, by living in it, and acting and thinking as parts of it; we love it in knowing it, and certainly could not know it without loving it. Our devotion to it, our willingness to sacrifice our personal welfare and even our lives to its honor, are elements in our attitude toward it as a whole, and therefore religious elements; but in so far as it is not *the* whole but only *a* whole, that is, at bottom only a finite thing, it is at best only an earthly god and our worship of it is not pure worship but in part idolatrous.

We have an attitude of the same kind toward the universe. This is not always recognized; but it is always there. It takes various forms: theoretical, practical, emotional.

Faith as a kind of knowledge, or theoretical faith, is the knowledge that the universe as a whole is rational. It is only because we know that this is so, that we can be certain of finding in this or that detail of it a fit and possible object of scientific study. The scientist may be unconscious that the experiment which he is making rests upon his certainty that the universe as a whole is rational; but his unconsciousness of the fact does not alter the fact. Without an absolute confidence in the "uniformity of nature," or whatever name he gives to the rationality of the universe, he would never try any experiments at all.

But faith is just as much a practical thing as a theoretical. In this aspect, it is a practical attitude toward the universe as a whole. Our acts, like our knowledge, are concerned in part with matters of detail within the universe, in part with the universe in its entirety. The question "What is the good of this or that?" is not the only question that can be asked about our actions; there is also the question "What is the good of anything?" and the person who answered "Why, nothing," was exhibiting a (no doubt transient) failure of practical faith. Practical faith consists in the certainty that life is worth living, that the world into which we have been unwillingly thrust is a world that contains scope for action and will give us a fair chance of showing what we are made of; a world in which, if we turn out complete failures, we shall have only ourselves to blame. Practical faith means "accepting the universe," or, what is the same thing, knowing that we are free.

Faith is also present to us in the form of feeling. We have feelings toward this or that finite object, but we also have feelings toward the universe as a whole. Nor can these two kinds of feeling be completely separated; our feeling toward a particular thing is very often, perhaps always, more or less conditioned by a sense that the thing is somehow typical or symptomatic of things in general. Few people, except through mere failure to observe their own experiences, will deny that they sometimes have feelings about the world at large: we feel the world sometimes as a familiar place, as our home, sometimes as alien and strange, and formidable or menacing in its aloofness, sometimes as cold and rigid, sometimes as palpitating with life, sometimes as a single concentrated focus of meaning, a thing that could be completely expressed in a single word if we knew the word, sometimes as a riot of differences inexhaustible to the most patient enumeration. Poetry (that is to say, the work of people who make it their business to express feelings accurately) is full of the record of such cosmic emotions, which are the emotional aspect of faith.

Reason, the scientific habit of mind, is the attitude which we take up toward things as parts of a whole, as finite things distinct from one another and connected with one another by a network of relations which it is the business of thought to trace out in detail. Here, again, we have a theoretical aspect, in which reason treats things as objects to be studied and thought about; a practical aspect, in which we select particular ends to pursue, and distinguish between what we are doing and what we are not doing; and an emotional aspect, in which everything excites in us a feeling proper and peculiar to itself.

The proper sphere of faith is everything in the collective sense—everything as a whole. The proper sphere of reason is everything in the distributive sense—every separate thing, no matter what. All finite things are proper objects of this scientific habit of mind. There is no fact or class of facts which can be withdrawn from its analysis or spared its criticism. Superstition means the denial of this. To be superstitious is to select certain finite things from among the rest and withdraw them from the sphere of reason; but it is precisely the duty of reason to fight superstition wherever it finds it, even if (as it always does) it shelters itself behind the name of religion.

But reason cannot possibly come into conflict with religion itself though it is always more or less in conflict with superstition, and superstition is always more or less confused with religion. Reason builds on a foundation of faith, and moves within a system whose general nature must be determined by faith before reason can deal with it in detail.

So far from a conflict between faith and reason being inevitable from the nature of things, they are in point of fact necessary each to the other.

Faith cannot exist without reason. The infinite is not another thing which is best grasped by sweeping the finite out of the way; the infinite is nothing but the unity, or as we sometimes say, the "meaning," of finite things in their diversity and their mutual connections. To look for the infinite by throwing away the finite would be very much like making the players stop playing in order to hear the symphony. What they are collectively playing *is* the symphony; and if you cannot hear it for the noise they are making, you cannot hear it at all. The notes are, so to speak, the body of which the symphony is the soul; and in that sense we might say that the finite is the body of which the infinite is the soul; though, if we say that, we must beware of the materialism which would delude us into talking of disembodied spirits, and remember that it is of the essence of spirit to embody itself. A faith unaccompanied by reason, therefore, is no true faith. The spirit of faith is shown to be a real spirit by embodying itself in reason, that is, by developing its own assertions, which as undeveloped would be mere abstractions, into a rational system of thought and conduct. If you really believe in God you will behave in detail like a man who believes in God. If you believe in the rationality of the world and the trustworthiness of human thinking (these two beliefs are the same belief stated in different terms) you will embody your belief in detailed scientific inquiries. A person who says he believes in God, but shrinks from developing his belief into a science of theology, or a person who professes his faith in the rationality of the world but will not say how exactly this rationality manifests itself in detail, is like a man who says, "I believe this bridge will bear me, but I would rather not walk across it." To speak like that is to show not the purity of your faith, but its absence.

Reason, conversely, cannot exist without faith. The finite is nothing except as part of a whole. We cannot evade this by calling it a part of a part of a part of a part . . . and so on without ever speaking the word "whole"; for the longer we go on refusing to speak it, the more insistently it rings in our ears and forces its repressed meaning upon our minds. Unless there is a whole, a universe, an infinite, there is no science; for there is no certainty beyond the certainty of mere observation and of bare particular fact; whereas science is universal or nothing, and is bankrupt unless it can discover general laws. But this discovery, as every student of logic knows, rests on presuppositions concerning the nature of the universe as a whole—laws of thought that are at the same time laws of the real world, not scientifically discovered but embraced by an act of faith, of necessary and rational faith.

From these general considerations, what inferences can we draw as to the relations which we would wish to see established between organized religion and organized science in the world of today?

In the first place, it is no use thinking that, because science has defeated religion (or rather, superstition) over Copernicanism and Darwinism and so forth, religion itself is worse off than it was. It is better off. The defeat of superstition is a victory not only for reason but for faith too. Nothing could more thoroughly consolidate the position of religion than that science should systematically drive it from every position of detail that it holds, because nothing could more thoroughly enforce the lesson that if religion is to exist at all it must base its claims not on a reading of this fact or that but on its reading of human experience in its entirety.

Therefore we must expect the scientific spirit to lay violent hands on a good many particular facts which religion (or rather superstition masquerading as religion) has claimed as exceptions to scientific law and on which, as so exceptional, it has staked its existence. We must expect the belief in miracles, whether past or present, to go the way of a good many other beliefs whose antiquity alone made them respectable; and we may be perfectly sure that, as a consequence, religion will be not a penny the poorer.

In the second place, we must get rid of the belief in a separation between religious people and scientific people. We must realize that if faith rejects reason and if reason rejects faith, each is cutting off its own nose to spite its face. We must expect and demand a scientific spirit in our professional men of religion and a religious spirit in our professional men of science.

This will be both possible and inevitable as people come to realize that there can be no division of territory between reason and faith. A person who sees that the whole of life, regarded as a whole, is the sphere of religion, and that the same whole, regarded as made up of details, is the sphere of science, must see that it is possible to be religious without ceasing to be genuinely scientific and scientific without ceasing to be genuinely religious. And a person who sees that the whole lives in the details, and the details in the whole, must see that it is only possible to be genuinely scientific by being genuinely religious, and *vice versa.*

On the other hand, we must not expect to find that the religion of scientific men will be exactly what religious people would wish it to be. It will, very likely, be contemptuously disposed toward many things to which religious people are traditionally attached. And conversely, the science of religious people will not be very like the "science" of nineteenth-century positivism, that compendium of empiricist logic and materialist metaphysics which to the best modern scientists appears so quaintly archaic a thing, and is thought by many other people to be what the best modern scientists believe in.

And in the third place, we must hope and believe that a rapprochement between religion and science will *not* mean the rise of a bastard kind of thought which is neither religious enough to be good religion nor scientific enough to be good science. Science must not try to ingratiate itself with religion by diluting itself with pseudo-religious ideas like that of a life-force or a purpose in nature. Science is good science only so far as it is rigidly and scrupulously scientific; so long as it measures and weighs its objects and treats them as mechanisms acting according to inviolable laws. And religion must not try to ingratiate itself with science by substituting for the divine spirit of its worship a scientific abstraction like humanity or nature or the reign of law. Each must win the respect of the other by fearlessly being itself and making the claims which it knows are demanded by its conscience. This is essential to a right understanding between the two; for the quarrel between them is really due to a failure, on both sides, to be content with their own proper work. The religion of a scientist is the very best kind of religion; the "religion of science" is bad religion misbegotten of bad science. Conversely, the science of a religious man may be very good science, if we may judge from the fact that Mendelism was invented by an abbot; but religion posing as science is at best "Christian Science," which is about as scientific as it is Christian.

Three things, therefore, must happen simultaneously. Religion must set its house in order by scrupulously searching for superstitious elements within itself and seeking to eradicate them. Science must set its house in order by abandoning mythologies and occult forces and being really scientific. And as these processes go forward—they are not things that can be done once for all—the quarrel between religion and science will die away, and each will gradually learn to find in the other not a rival and enemy, but a friend and ally.

This triple process is undoubtedly going forward today. On both sides, the leaders of opinion are tired of the traditional enmity, and are beginning to realize that a science that is content to be scientific and a religion that is content to be religious need not fear one another. It is even beginning to be recognized that they are necessary to one another. This movement of mutual tolerance and good will is intimately connected with a new and stricter conception of the true scope and limits of science on the one hand and of religion on the other; and that is what makes it a genuine advance and enables us to see in it the hope of a genuine reconciliation.

The war between faith and reason is drawing to a close. The

stage was set for it in the Middle Ages; it has been raging with varying intensity, but without intermission, since the Renaissance; and we are now taking part in its concluding phase. Reason has won every battle; but faith has won the war, because by its defeat it has learnt to be itself and to claim for its own not this detail or that within human life, but human life as a whole.

NOTE: The movement to which I refer at the end may be studied in many recent books: e.g., Canon B. H. Streeter's *Reality;* Joseph Needham's *Science, Religion and Reality,* by various authors; and the same writer's *Man a Machine;* J. B. S. Haldane's *Possible Worlds* (to which I owe my reference to Galton's proof of the futility of prayer), etc. The parallel between our relation to the universe and our relation to our country I have borrowed from Sir Francis Younghusband's paper on "Religious Experience" in the *Proceedings of the Aristotelian Society* (1927-1928). The substance of my second chapter has been repeated, with kind permission, from an articie of mine called "Reason Is Faith Cultivating Itself," in the *Hibbert Journal* for January 1927.

WHAT IS THE PROBLEM OF EVIL?

THE object of this paper is to point out what seems to be a confusion of thought as to the exact nature of this problem and the ground it covers. In any form the problem involves three terms: the goodness of God, His omnipotence, and the existence of evil. These three terms give together a dilemmatic argument in the following shape. If God wills the evil which exists, He is not good; if He does not will it, He is not omnipotent. But, since it certainly exists, He either wills it or does not will it; therefore He is either not good or not omnipotent. The "problem of evil" consists in the attempt to refute this dilemma without denying the reality of any of the three terms, since none can be denied without the destruction of our religious beliefs.

As stated, this is an impossible task. The dilemma does not admit of direct refutation. Only three courses are open: to give up the problem—that is, to abandon the whole of theology and the whole of philosophy (for the problem of evil, *mutatis terminis,* reappears with exactly the same force in every moral philosophy); to give in to it—that is, to accept the dilemma as cogent and to deny the reality of one of the three terms, it does not much matter which; or thirdly, to manipulate the terms of the dilemma, by a criticism and re-exposition of the conceptions involved in the hope of so reinterpreting them that they are no longer irreconcilable. The first method is the suicide of religion; the second its violent self-mutilation, likely to result in its bleeding to death; the third is arduous and responsible, but alone possible.

The backbone of any discussion of the "problem of evil" will therefore be a critical exposition of the three conceptions of omnipotence, goodness, and evil. In so far as any discussion has at all

Reprinted from *Theology,* I (1920).

cleared up one of these conceptions, it has justified itself; in so far as it has defined them all in a way which both satisfies their function in the religious consciousness and at the same time dissolves the original dilemma, the problem will have received at any rate some kind of a solution.

It is not the object of this paper to contribute anything positive toward this end—an end, however, which must not be regarded as in any special sense unattainable. There is a sense in which every speculative problem is insoluble—for no problem can ever be solved in such a way that it need never be reconsidered in the light of new thought; in another sense all are soluble, the problem of evil no less than the others. My object here is only to clear the path for such an advance by removing a certain confusion as to the scope of the conception—and therefore the problem—of evil.

It is usual to begin any discussion of the problem by distinguishing two or more aspects of it—that is to say, two or more main ramifications of the concept of evil. The two most commonly enumerated are sin and pain; evil in the sense of undesirable actions and evil in the sense of undesirable passive states. Sin is evil in the sense that a person who sins is wicked, and therefore one who causes (or when he could prevent it allows) another to sin is wicked; therefore the existence of sin disproves the goodness, or, if not the goodness, the omnipotence, of God. Pain is evil in the sense that it ought not to exist, and therefore one who creates it by inflicting it upon another (or permits another to suffer it when he could prevent it) is wicked; therefore the existence of pain leads independently to the same conclusion.

On the whole, more weight is commonly laid on the "problem of pain" than on the "problem of sin." This is because it is often felt that the latter difficulty is alleviated, if not entirely removed, by the recognition of the necessity for human freedom. It is taken as self-evident that man is free, and free by the will of God; and if free, free to sin. But there is no such mitigation of the "problem of pain"; and therefore when people speak of the "problem of evil" as a serious difficulty in religion or apologetics they often refer primarily, if not exclusively, to this problem.

I shall try to show in this paper that the identification of the problem of pain with a part or the whole of the problem of evil is a fallacy, due to a philosophical error which was vigorously preached in the last century and is still by no means extinct, especially in this country, where it is on its native soil. Until this error has disappeared from the popular mind it is vain to hope for a better understanding of the problem of evil, or, indeed, of any ethical question whatever.

The philosophical error to which I refer is the doctrine that when we call an act good we do so with reference to certain good consequences which it produces or is intended to produce. That which is "good" *par excellence* is a thing, an event, a condition; the will is called good only in a secondary sense, in so far as it creates or tries to create things and conditions which are good. A good act is thus defined as such by reference to its consequences, whether actual, probable, or intended; but a thing or event is good (or bad) simply in itself. The good will is good because it is a means to good ends.

This idea, which I shall call utilitarianism, because it is as a matter of fact the fundamental principle of the ethics known as utilitarian, is thrown into sharp relief if we compare it with the famous opening of Kant's great essay on the good will. "There is nothing in the world, or even out of it, which can be called good without qualification, except a good will." Physical and mental endowments, the virtues and the affections, the gifts of fortune—all these things are doubtless good in a sense; each of them is good in certain respects, and relative to certain ends or conceptions of the end; but none of them can be called good without qualification, because each can be turned to the service of evil. Thus, whatever goodness we ascribe to these things is, as it were, a mere reflection of the goodness of the will. The only sense in which we can ascribe to them a goodness of their own is that they possess a kind of secondary goodness—the goodness of means to an end.

But this is exactly the kind of goodness which utilitarianism ascribes to the will. Thus, the two views are exactly antithetical. For Kant, whose view I shall designate by the name ethical, the good will alone is in the strict sense good—good as an end in itself; all other things are only good in a secondary or derivative sense, good as means. For utilitarianism, the good will is good in just this secondary or derivative sense; all that is fully and strictly good —good as an end—is the things which the will sets out to create.

We may perhaps conveniently distinguish the two views by making a distinction in the meaning of the word good. Good may mean, first, good in itself, as an end; or, secondly, good in a derivative sense, as a means. The utilitarian view of morality consists in maintaining that the good will is good in the latter sense, which we shall accordingly refer to as the utilitarian sense of the word. The ethical view maintains that the good will is good in the former sense; this sense, therefore, we shall name the ethical sense of the word. The utilitarian view implies that the phrases "duty," "morally good," and so on, as applied to actions or to the will, mean "good in the sense of means to an ulterior end"; the ethical or Kantian view interprets these same expressions as meaning "good in the absolute, unqualified sense—good, that is, as an end in itself."

This distinction between the utilitarian and the ethical or Kantian view of the good will is of course familiar to every student of philosophy, but it seems desirable to state it here with the utmost possible clearness because it underlies every discussion of the problem of evil. The utilitarian conception has had great influence in this country over a long period of time, and the criticisms of it, however damaging and final, have hardly touched the popular mind. The Kantian doctrine would imply that an event, a state of things, something that simply is or simply happens, can never claim the title good in its own right. It is only good if the will which created it was a good will; otherwise it may be useful for this or that end, but it cannot be properly described as good; and when it can be so described, this is only because it takes a moral coloring from the morality of the will to which it was due. In England the utilitarian morality has sunk so deeply into our minds as to make this seem a paradox. We have been schooled to believe that the word "good" attaches primarily to events and states of things, independently of the question who created them and why; and that when we call a will good, we only call it so because the events it produces are in themselves good, are events which ought to happen. This point of view makes the will a means, and never anything but a means; the will so conceived does not by being good confer goodness on the things it does, but it derives goodness —a reflected glory—from these things, when they are good.

This paper is not an essay on pure moral philosophy, and therefore I do not intend to discuss the merits and defects of utilitarianism. I only wish to point out its fundamental feature—namely, its conception of the good will as a means, not as an end, as opposed to the Kantian conception of the good will as an end in itself—and to express the conviction that in this matter the utilitarian point of view is hopelessly wrong, and the Kantian conception at least sound on fundamentals. Out of the utilitarian view no sound or healthy philosophical results have proceeded or are likely to proceed; in order to make any progress in moral speculation one must begin by agreeing with Kant that the problem of goodness is the problem of the good will; and if this is so, the problem of evil is the problem of the evil will.

It is true that Kant did not succeed in his attempt to develop his conception into a system of ethics. The attempt broke down with great completeness. But it is possible to admit this and yet to maintain that his starting-point was right—was, in fact, the only possible one. Kant's system broke down because he never discovered how to make use of his starting-point; he never found the road away from it, the link by which he could connect it with the concrete facts of the moral life. It is the germ of a system, but in his hands it remained a germ. Here, again, I am summarily expressing philosophical conclusions which this is not the place to defend or even to expound in detail.

The problem of evil, then, is the problem of the evil will. For that alone is evil which ought to have been and might have been good; and if the term good in its moral sense is applicable to the will alone, so is, in the same moral sense, the term evil. And this is the sense which the word bears when we speak of the problem of evil. No doubt the utilitarian sense of the word good (good for some end beyond itself) is paralleled by a utilitarian sense of the word evil. We speak, and quite legitimately, of bad boots, just as we speak of good boots. But when we speak of a pair of boots as good, we mean good for some special purpose—good for country wear, or the like. So, when we speak of bad boots, we mean bad for the purpose which we had in mind, though possibly quite good for other purposes—for fuel, or for starting sweet-peas in. But this sense of the word bad can hardly be said to give rise to a problem of evil. At most, it raises the question why we should want to use things for purposes to which they are not adapted; and this may lead us, by way of the conception of stupidity, to the problem of error and so back to the problem of evil; but the connection is a remote one.

Let us now return to the division which we found observed by the common discussions of the problem of evil. As we saw at the beginning, we are in the habit of subdividing it into some such heads as (*a*) the problem of pain, in man and in the lower animals, and (*b*) the problem of sin. Other heads are sometimes added, but on criticism they soon resolve themselves into by-forms of one or the other. The thesis of this paper is that the latter head alone has a right to be discussed—is, in fact, a problem of evil at all; that the former, the problem of pain conceived as a division of the problem of evil, is a confusion due to the persistence of a utilitarian habit of mind.

This contention follows immediately from our main principle as to the nature of the good will. When we raise the question, How can a world created by God's good will contain evils? we are using the terms good and evil in a definitely moral sense, not in the utilitarian sense. God's will is conceived as having not the kind of goodness which we predicate of tools or implements, the goodness of a means to an ulterior end, but the absolute and self-contained goodness of an end in itself. Therefore the same sense must here attach to the term evil. The evils of which we are speaking must be things not merely evil in relation to some further end or purpose, but evil absolutely and in themselves. That is to say, they can only be sins, acts of the evil will.

It may be useful to develop this conclusion in a little more detail by some observations on the subject of the so-called "problem of pain" regarded as one side of the problem of evil.

The "problem of pain" consists in the question, how can God, being omnipotent and benevolent, cause or permit pain? The crucial point in this question is the introduction of the word benevolent as a substitute for the word good. The two terms are not equivalent. To be benevolent is to shrink from the pain of another; it is the opposite of being cruel or vindictive. An amiable trait, certainly; but not an adequate description of the whole content of the good will. A will that was benevolent and nothing more would be very far from ideally good; and, in fact, we do not use the epithet as in any sense fully descriptive except in the case of a certain type of slightly imbecile old gentleman whom we meet in the pages of *Punch*. The God of Judaism is a just and a terrible God; and if the God of Christianity is a God loving and loved, no longer terrible, this is only because perfect love casts out fear, not because the God of Christianity has foregone any of the justice and holiness which made Him terrible to the Jews. Love is a fine and significant image for the relation of the good will to its own objects, an image nobler and truer even than justice; benevolence is a caricature, and expresses nothing of the nature of the good will except a mere negation, the absence of cruelty. As a predicate of God, therefore, it has value only so long as we are in danger of conceiving Him as actively and maliciously cruel. And today perhaps the opposite danger is more real—the danger of conceiving God as a doting father, pushing forgiveness to the verge of sentimentality.

The fact is that in surreptitiously introducing the word benevolent as an equivalent for the word good we are guilty of an anachronism. We are unconsciously harking back to the ethics of two centuries ago, an ethics long outworn and discredited, the philosophy of the sentiments; a philosophy which today survives only in theological tags of this kind.

If, then, we substitute for the word benevolent the right word, good, the difficulty either disappears or at least undergoes a profound alteration. To call a thing evil (or for that matter good) in the moral sense is to call it an act of somebody's will. Nothing that merely exists or merely happens can be called an evil, but only something that is done, an action. So far as anything merely happens to us, so far as it has the quality of an event, it can have no moral predicates. "Is pain an evil?" We can only reply, "To whose will are you attributing it?" "Pain ought not to exist." We must reply, "To say ought is to speak of a person, not a thing; an act, not an event."

In saying that pain is an evil, then, we are saying "God (or the devil) creates pain, which is a wicked action." Why do we call it wicked? Because pain is in itself an evil? No; that is to argue in a circle. The goodness or badness of a thing is a reflection of the character of the volition, not the other way round. If we know from what motives God or the devil creates pain, then we can say whether the pain so caused ought or ought not to exist. Otherwise the most we can say is that it is painful, and this must not be confused with saying that it is bad.

Much ink has been spilt over the question whether pain in itself is or is not an evil as if it were a question of opinion or of argument; but the fact seems clear that in the moral sense it is neither evil nor good, since nothing can have these predicates except the action of a will; while in the utilitarian sense it may or may not be an evil according to circumstances and to the end in view. In no case is there any contradiction in supposing that pain is caused by a good will. Indeed, it is not hard to think of cases in which the only thing a good will can do is to cause pain. Therefore the "problem of pain," whatever it may be, is not the dilemma with which we started—the flat contradiction between a good and omnipotent God on the one hand, and the existence of things which no good will could permit on the other. If we believe in God's goodness, we believe that He does not torture us out of wantonness. And if we believe in His omnipotence, we are confident that He does not let us be tortured out of helplessness. We can believe, and there is absolutely nothing in the nature of things to prevent our believing, that it is good for us to have pain; that pain is a thing to thank God for, a thing without which our life would be worse than it is, a thing which marks our communion with a crucified God.

There is nothing in the nature of things to prevent our believing this. It involves no internal contradiction. On the contrary, we may acclaim it as more than a blind act of faith, as in some degree a truth of experience. We do at least dimly recognize that pain justifies itself in relation to our life as moral beings; we have even invented a phrase—self-contradictory, because it perpetuates the utilitarian confusion of pain with evil—to express this justification; we speak of the "teleological value of evil." If anything still remains of the "problem of pain," it is simply the question whether the pain of the lower animals can be justified in the same way; and here, perhaps, the act of faith must remain an act of faith.

It is not contended that the "problem of pain" vanishes entirely on examination. Our analysis of it has left two distinct residues; first, the question how exactly pain is productive of the values which could not have existed without it; and secondly, the question whether this necessity or justification of pain rests in the last resort upon the existence of the evil will; whether it can be maintained that a sinless world would be a painless world. These are problems; but they are, so to speak, straightforward problems: they are quite distinct from the problem of evil, for they have not the character which that problem has of a hopeless and unavoidable dilemma.

The result of our analysis seems to be something like this. Traditionally, the problem of evil is presented in two parts: the problem of sin and the problem of pain. These two parts are really not co-ordinate parts, but alternative presentations of the entire problem from opposing points of view. From the ethical point of view the problem is solely the problem of sin; the problem of pain is seen to be a quite different problem, presenting a quite different character. From the utilitarian point of view the real problem is the problem of pain; the problem of sin is either simply solved by the conception of human freedom, or else remains as a particular case of the problem of pain. If we regard the will as means (utilitarian view) the problem of the bad will disappears into the problem of bad events or states of things, typified by pain. If we regard the will as end (ethical view) the problem of undesirable things or events, such as pain, is swallowed up in the problem of the evil will. But if, instead of adopting either of these views, we merely halt between two opinions, then our treatment of the problem of evil will fall into the two heads which we have enumerated.

There is certainly no royal road to the solution of the problem of evil. But there are ways of making it easier or harder to advance toward a solution. And one way of making it harder is to hesitate between two incompatible views of the nature of goodness. To those who feel that of the two opposing views each must contain some part of the truth, I would say, these parts of the truth, if they are such, can only be properly developed by careful segregation, by working out each side by itself, taking the utmost care not to confuse it with its opposite, and not attempting a synthesis before each side has become perfectly definite. To mix up the two points of view at the outset is to destroy all possibility of synthesis, because it destroys the conceptions themselves.

Pain and sin—this is our conclusion—are not two kinds or divisions of evil, but two conflicting definitions of what evil is. To treat them as co-ordinate heads of one and the same problem is to stand in self-confessed contradiction as to the fundamental nature of the problem at issue. If anyone prefers the utilitarian conception of evil, let him take it up and work it out. I have expressed my conviction that this utilitarian view is bankrupt, though I am well aware that it is maintained by perhaps a majority of modern authorities; but no one will deny that the two views are in sharp opposition, and that a treatment of a moral problem which is based on merely confusing the two is doomed in advance to failure.

Such a treatment, I suggest, we do actually find in the current approach to the problem of evil. Those who discuss the problem give one treatment of it under the heading of sin, as a concession to the ethical conception of good, and another under the heading of pain, as a concession to the utilitarians, having themselves not really made up their minds which conception they are going to adopt as their own. But this is a safe method of courting disaster. The problems are hard enough in any case; there is no need to make them harder by treating them from the standpoint of a quicksand of shifting and undetermined conceptions.

Here, in fact, as in many other cases, it is difficult to resist the conclusion that much of what now passes for "philosophy of religion" in this country—and elsewhere, for that matter—is vitiated at the start, and before the start, by a kind of philosophical eclecticism. It is seldom based on anything like a critical study of first principles; it collects its first principles from any and every source, regardless of their coherence or of their ability to stand a searching criticism. *Non tali auxilio nec defensoribus istis.* . . . Religious genius has no need of philosophical spade-work; and for the insight of religious genius the problem of sin and the problem of pain are alike solved on the Cross of Christ. But so long as religion seeks the aid of philosophical thought, she betrays her own trust if she accepts any but the best; and the best will never be so good but that it sorely needs bettering.

Part Three. Religion as Philosophical Anthropology: The Metaphysics of Human Self-Making

INTRODUCTION

NOT only does religion occupy a place on a general scale, which includes all of the various forms of knowing; but, like each of the other forms, religion contributes to the understanding of a number of particular phenomena, such as intersubjectivity, personal identity, self-making and self-knowledge. Implicit in religion, in other words, is a philosophical anthropology or philosophy of mind, and it is with a view toward establishing the contribution of Collingwood's philosophy of religion to the field of philosophical anthropology that the readings collected together in this section have been arranged.

1. INTERSUBJECTIVITY AND PERSONAL IDENTITY

Religion and Philosophy largely consists of a critical discussion of a number of false metaphysical views of religion. In particular Collingwood attacks what he calls the doctrine of pure immanent pantheism, which proclaims man and God to be absolutely identical (RP, 149 ff; 253 ff) and "positivism" or "absolutely transcendent theism" (RP, 109 and 149 ff; 180 and 253 ff). Against these views Collingwood contends that the relation between man and God is dialectical, and the criterion according to which the dialectical identity of man and God is established is made the basis for a rapprochement between intersubjectivity and personal identity (RP, 104 ff; 175 ff). In other words, just as a person derives his individual and human identity through union with God, so in an analogous fashion he comes to enhance his individuality through intersubjectivity at the personal level. Both union with God and intersubjectivity are expressions of the same concrete identity in difference.

In religion the individual constitutes himself by submitting his will to the will of God. But this act of submission is not to be confused with the mystical union of Quietism in which the individual will disappears completely through passive self-abnegation. On the contrary, because the religious union with God is an act of will, it is a choice which must be maintained by a continuous act of will and which can always be suspended by another act of will. Such a union does not, therefore, deprive the individual of autonomy, and it most certainly does not deprive him of the power of action. As Collingwood puts it, "the self-dedication of the will of God is not the end of the individual life, but the beginning of a new and indeed of a more active life. The union with God is a real union, not the annihilation of the self" (RP, 29; 66).

Personal identity is also achieved through intersubjectivity, which is established in *Religion and Philosophy* according to the criterion that if two minds are identical with the same object then they are identical with each other:

> . . . union consists of the fact that both are dealing with the same problems; for in so far as any two minds are conscious of the same reality, they are the same mind (RP, 161; 263).

In any act of knowing there must always be a concrete identity between my mind and its object in the sense that my thought about the object is not something "like" the object but "is" the object *as I know it.* Since the *esse* of mind is not *cogitare* simply, but *de hac re cogitare* (RP, 100; 172), mind is therefore identical with its thoughts, and to the extent to which these thoughts are therefore identical with their objects, the identity between mind *per se* and its object is also established. This is the basis from which Collingwood eventually developed his famous doctrine of history as the "re-enactment of past thought" (IH, 282 ff and A, 111), and it must therefore be taken into account if we are fully to understand such statements as, "the historian of a certain thought must think for himself that very same thought, not another like it" (A, 111). Collingwood writes in *Religion and Philosophy:*

> My thought of the table is certainly not something "like" the table; it is the table as I know it. Similarly, your thought of the table is what you know of the table as known to you; and if we both have real knowledge of the table, it seems to

> follow that our thoughts are the same, not merely similar; and further, if the mind is its thoughts, we seem to have, for the moment at least, actually one mind; we share between us that unity of consciousness which was [earlier (RP, 99; 171)] said to be the mark of the individual (RP, 101; 173).

This doctrine of intersubjectivity tends partly to explain why Collingwood believed that the historical study of the past was one way of overcoming the fragmentation of modern life and establishing a genuine community of spirit.

Intersubjectivity is achieved not only through knowledge of the same objects but also through the intentional act of willing the same ends (RP, 104; 175). In this case what constitutes intersubjectivity is not just that each wills the same thing, but that each does so as a matter of choice in a state of perfect freedom. But, as is the case in religion, this very freedom to will, which is the source of unity, is also the source of disunity; for just as the mind is free to maintain a state of intersubjectivity through an exercise of will, so the same mind is free to dissolve the relationship through its own self-betrayal (RP, 105; 177). The risk of disharmony, which perpetually threatens whatever unity has been achieved, and which creates, therefore, an immanent and inescapable tension, is the ground of difference on the side of the subject. Indeed, the fact that unity is accomplished not as a fixed and unchangeable state of affairs but only through the continuous exercise of free-will is what saves the intersubjectivity of minds as well as the union with God from being a mere abstract self-identity.

There is also, according to Collingwood, a source of differentiation on the side of the object—although this too turns out to have its origins in the conditions of subjectivity. What stands out about the object of mind *qua* mind is the fact that it is never merely abstract and undifferentiated, a pure uninterpreted datum. If there were such objects, then the relation between any two minds knowing them would be a blank unity without difference. But Collingwood declares:

> Any truth or ideal of conduct expresses itself under infinitely various aspects. A single truth never means quite the same thing to different minds; each person invests it with an emphasis, an application, peculiar to himself. This does not mean that it is not the same truth; the difference does not destroy the identity any more than identity destroys difference. It is only in the identity that the difference arises (RP, 106; 177).

In this statement Collingwood combines the epistemological doctrine that all knowledge is mediation with the metaphysical doctrine of the concrete universal. The latter is particularly evident in Collingwood's claim that the object of any particular mind is only one moment of a totality which includes the contributions of other minds. Indeed, the object's very existence as an object for me depends upon the existence of all the other moments. Collingwood writes:

> I desire the existence of a whole to which I can contribute one among many parts. The other parts must be contributed by other people; and therefore in willing my part I will theirs also (*ibid.*).

Thus, I am not only responsible for contributing to the possibility of there being a world of ideals for others to will, but my very presence as a knowing subject who desires the existence of a world is a condition of the other's responsibility to act in similar ways. This dual responsibility is the condition of intersubjectivity.

Finally in this discussion of intersubjectivity there is a clear anticipation of the doctrine advanced in *Speculum Mentis* that truth, the perfect state of freedom, the concrete identity, must be achieved by means of a progressive development through a scale of errors. Collingwood writes in *Religion and Philosophy* that unity or concrete identification is not the starting point but the goal of human endeavor. But in achieving this goal the mind advances "like a spiral tunnel of an Alpine railway: it ends, if not where it began, at least immediately above it. The end is not the antithesis of the beginning, but the same thing raised to a higher power" (RP, 107; 178) (Cf. OPA, 94-95; SM, 317; 291-292).

2. RELIGION AS SELF-KNOWLEDGE AND FINITE SELF-MAKING

There is no more urgent concern in Collingwood's thought than to understand the conditions of self-making through self-knowledge. Since the mind is what it does and since the most important thing a mind can do is know itself, it follows that the mind makes itself through self-knowledge. Art, religion, science, history, and philosophy are precisely such modes of self-knowledge.

The theory that mind makes itself by knowing itself underlies the whole of Collingwood's thought. In *Religion and Philosophy,* for example, mind is defined as the pure act of thinking:

> The mind seems to be not so much that which thinks as the thinking itself; it is not an active thing so much as an activity. Its *esse* is *cogitare* (RP, 100; 172).

But, Collingwood continues, the activity of the mind is an activity with a content:

> . . . there is no thought in general but only particular thoughts about particular things. The *esse* of mind is not *cogitare* simply, but *de hac re cogitare* (RP, 100; 172).

In *Religion and Philosophy* the theory of mind as *de hac re cogitare* is explained by an analogy to the concrete universal, as an activity of identity in difference. The ontological character of the self, its source of identity, derives from its relations, which are at the same time the source of differentiation (RP, 112; 182). The specific acts through which the mind relates itself, and hence constitutes itself, are at the same time the very acts through which the mind differentiates itself. In the case of the mind, these relations are simply acts of thought and imagination, such as art, religion, science, history, and philosophy. In the *Idea of History* Collingwood explains how the mind makes itself through the conscious appropriation of the past:

> Since mind is what it does, and human nature, if it is a name for anything real, is only a name for human activities, this acquisition or ability to perform determinate operations is the acquisition of a determinate human nature. Thus the historical process is a process in which man creates for himself this or that kind of human nature by re-creating in his own thought the past to which he is heir (IH, 226; cf. also, 169 and 171).

But whereas through history the mind makes itself as finite, through religion it makes itself as both finite and infinite, and this it does both by living in unity with God (through faith, devotion, and prayer) and by reflecting on the meaning of this experience through philosophy. God is therefore the ground of transcendence because he is an object through the knowledge of which each finite mind achieves unity with all other finite minds. To experience such a unity through knowledge of God is to experience transcendence.

God therefore plays the role in *Religion and Philosophy* that the absolute plays in *Speculum Mentis.* In fact, in *Religion and Philosophy* the terms absolute and God are used interchangeably. Neither the absolute nor God should be conceived as a mere abstract universal. The formless and empty absolute of abstract metaphysics, writes Collingwood, "perished long ago in the fires of Hegel's sarcasm" (RP, 116; 186; and SM, 299; 299-300). "A real philosophy," he continues, "builds its absolute . . . out of the differences of the world as it finds them, dealing individually with all contradictions and preserving every detail that can lend character to the whole" (RP, 115; 185).

In place of the abstract metaphysics of being, Collingwood advances a concrete metaphysic of being conceived as pure act, the "concrete identity of activity" (RP, 116; 186). The abstract identity of mind is changeless, permanent, and eternal. The concrete identity of mind, however, explicitly presupposes change. Not only is change an intrinsic property of this concrete self-identity, but understanding the conditions of change is an act of transcendence: "A mind which knows its own change is by that very knowledge lifted above change" (SM, 301; 301).

The absolute or God of *Religion and Philosophy,* like the

absolute mind of *Speculum Mentis,* is infinite truth, free of all contradictions (RP, 116; 185). It is therefore the object of transcendental philosophy or *speculum speculi.* In the course of its historical development, finite mind acquires of itself a *speculum mentis,* which is of course a constantly changing picture of itself. Yet at the center of the mind's constantly changing picture of itself there exists a more unified or transcendental knowledge (*speculum speculi*) which is what the mind achieves in its moment of self-transcendence, when, viewing the world *sub specie eternitatis,* it becomes (through philosophy) identified with the absolute, or through faith, devotion, and prayer, identified with God. But this identity is possible only because God or the absolute is with us from the start. God or the absolute, in other words, the *a priori* ground of the possibility of being and knowing, is immanent as well as transcendent. The activity of finite mind therefore consists, when through thought it raises itself to the level of philosophy or through faith it constitutes itself as religion, of the attempt to render explicit the implicit self-identity of absolute knowledge. Thus the very same process through which mind makes itself finite is the source of infinite or absolute self-making as well.

The concept of self-making as a process through which the immanent criterion of absolute knowledge is rendered explicit is further discussed in an essay called "the Devil" (1919), which was published shortly after *Religion and Philosophy.* This essay forms an interesting bridge between *Religion and Philosophy* and *Speculum Mentis.* In "The Devil" Collingwood argues that the primordial condition of the self is to be unformed and incomplete, and hence always in process of communicating itself to itself (D, 474; 232). It is for this reason, Collingwood argues, that the self is in need of a standard according to which it can complete itself. This standard is absolute truth which appears to thought as reality and to religious consciousness as God (D, 475; 232). But this standard becomes explicit only in the course of the actual practice of the forms of life which exemplify it, such as when the self engages in the activity of questioning the grounds of its being by humbly opening itself before the judgment of God. Self-questioning is therefore an act not only of self-knowledge but of self-creation: not the self-knowledge that derives from introspection, from the inspection of the self that *is* (for such knowledge can never become a source of creativity) but the self-knowledge that derives from an examination of the self that is *to be.* But what the self will be depends upon how it relates to its own immanent truth, the immanent presence of the absolute. In philosophy this is achieved through the gradual realization of truth as a scale of forms. In religion it is achieved whenever a person submits his will to the will of God and so creates the condition of trust in which he acts according to a truth which can be *known* only after the deed, but which must nevertheless be *believed* before that deed can even be performed.

PERSONAL IDENTITY AND INTERSUBJECTIVITY

. . . IF the universe is a whole of consciousness, of activity, of something that is at least better described as mind than as matter, in what relation does each part of it stand to the other parts and the whole? Is every part an independent and entirely individual mind (or piece of matter, if we prefer to call it so), or is there only one mind, of which every separate thing in the universe is a fragment and no more?

These two alternatives are generally known as pluralism and monism respectively. A thorough-going pluralism is intended to preserve at all costs the freedom and reality of the individual; but it does not tell us in what relation the individual stands to other individuals; indeed, it does not tell us what in the first place constitutes individuality. For if the human being is an individual, what of the atoms of which his body is composed, or the many acts which make up the history of his mind? Are they not individuals also? And if so, how can he be at once a single individual and a group of individuals?

It is equally easy for a thorough-going monism to assert the reality of the whole at the expense of the parts, to deprive the human being of all true freedom and self-existence, and to reduce him to the position of a mere incident in the life of the universe. Of these extreme theories neither is satisfactory; and in the present chapter we shall attempt to reach a less one-sided view of the nature of personality.

What constitutes the self-identity of a person? What is it that makes him one? And what, on the other hand, is the bond which makes a society one? Are these two bonds at bottom the same; that is, can a mind be at the same time one person and many persons,

Reprinted from *Religion and Philosophy* (London: Macmillan & Co., 1916), pp. 96-121.

or is the self-identity of a person one thing and that of a society something totally different?

1. In order to answer these questions we shall not inquire into the abstract meaning of the word personality. Many people maintain that personality, in its very meaning, implies limitation, finitude, imperfection, distinction from other persons, and the like; and to make or to reject such assumptions at the outset would be to beg the question which we wish to answer. We shall begin by examining the relations which subsist between different persons as we know them, in the hope of thereby throwing some light on the nature of personality itself; and these relations are the facts which we describe, on the side of thought, as communication, and on the side of will, as co-operation. For this purpose we can define a personality as this, if nothing more: the unity of a single consciousness; while a society might be defined as the unity of different and co-operating consciousnesses. These definitions are only provisional; but more than this we cannot say at the present stage of the inquiry.

(*a*) The fact of communication seems to be that two or more persons can actually share the same knowledge. The condition is not satisfied by supposing that the one has a piece of knowledge merely resembling, however closely, the knowledge possessed by the other; the two pieces of knowledge must be the same. There is a thory of knowledge which maintains that what I know is always peculiar to my mind, an "idea," as it is sometimes called, not an "object"; a state of my own consciousness, not an independently existing thing. If this were the case, no two people could have the *same* knowledge, any more than two objects can have the *same* weight; their weights might be equal, but the weight of each would be its own weight and not the other's. One thing cannot communicate its weight to another; but one mind can, as we believe, communicate its thoughts to another. If this belief is true, knowledge is not a state or attribute of my mind in the sense in which weight is an attribute of objects.

But is the belief really true? Is there such a thing as this communication at all? Is it not rather the case that no two people ever quite understand one another, or ever see eye to eye? Do not the facts rather favor the view that everyone is sealed up in a world of his own ideas from which there is no egress and no channel of communication into the mind of anyone else? There is much truth in these contentions; and we may grant—at least for the sake of argument—that no two people ever quite understand one another, that A never thinks in exactly the same way as B. But is the inference just, that communication is impossible? We may not succeed in conveying our deepest thoughts to each other, but we continue to try; and if the thing were an axiomatic and self-evident impossibility, how shall we account for the continuance of the attempt? After all, a theory of knowledge must accept the fact of knowledge as a starting-point; and it cannot be denied that partial, if not complete, communication is a fact. Nor can it be argued that this partial communication, which is all we can attain, is satisfied by the theory that my knowledge may resemble yours without being identical with it. For however incomplete our communication may be, we have before us the ideal of complete communication; and the very imperfection of our attainment, our consciousness of its imperfection, proves that this ideal is really our constant aim.

We are justified, then, in dismissing these skeptical objections with the remark that, if they were true, they would falsify not only all else but themselves; for the skeptic cannot seriously believe his own contentions so long as he tries to communicate his skepticism to us.

The unity of an individual was defined as the unity of a single consciousness. But if two people are conscious of the same object, have they not thereby the same consciousness? We may be answered: no, because there is more in any act of knowing than the mere object. The knowing mind (says the objector) does not, so to speak, lose itself in the thing it contemplates. If it did, then there would be no difference between my mind and yours so far as we were conscious of the same thing; but as it is, knowing is a relation between two things, the subject and the object, the knowing mind and the thing unknown. To forget the object makes communication impossible; but to forget the subject makes all knowledge impossible.

This objection brings up one of the most difficult problems in philosophy, and one which it may seem both indiscreet to raise and presumptuous even to attempt to answer in brief. But the attempt must be made, if we cannot hope to give a very satisfactory solution.

To say that the mind is one thing and the object another is doubtless true; but we cannot rest content with the statement. It is true also that the relation between them is unique, and that attempts to describe it by analogy with other relations must always be as misleading as they have been in the past. But it does not follow that, because it cannot be described by analogy, therefore it cannot be described at all; still less that because it is unique therefore it cannot be understood.

Even to say that the mind is one thing and the object another may mislead. The mind is specifically that which knows the object; and to call it a "thing" already suggests conceiving it as an object one of whose qualities is that it knows other objects—as this table is an object one of whose qualities is that it holds my paper—or, still worse, as a machine which turns out a kind of work called thinking, as a typewriter or a dynamo turns out its own peculiar product. The mind seems to be not so much that which thinks as the thinking itself; it is not an active thing so much as an activity. Its *esse* is *cogitare.*

Again, just as the mind is not a self-identical thing persisting whether or no it performs its functions, but rather is those functions, so the consciousness in which it consists is not an abstract power of thought which may be turned to this object or that, as the current from a dynamo may be put to various uses. All consciousness is the consciousness of something definite, the thought of this thing or of that thing; there is no thought in general but only particular thoughts about particular things. The *esse* of mind is not *cogitare* simply, but *de hac re cogitare.*

I hardly think that anyone will deny all this; but it may still be said that though A's mind is nothing but his consciousness of *x,* and B's mind nothing but his, yet A's mind and B's remain absolutely different and individual; since, though the object is the same and each admittedly knows the object, A's thought of it is distinct from the object itself and therefore from B's thought of the same object. It has already been admitted that each knows the same thing, but it is now argued that each knows it by having a "thought about it" which is peculiar to himself. I suspect this distinction between the object and the thought about it to be an instance of the confusion noted in the last chapter between thinking in the sense of knowing and thinking in the sense of imagining. My imagination of a table is certainly a different thing from the table itself, and to identify the two would be to mistake fancy for fact; but my knowledge of the table, my thought of it in that sense, is simply the table as known to me, as much of the table's nature as I have discovered. In this sense, my "thought about" the table—what I think the table to be—only differs from the table itself if and in so far as I am ignorant of the table's real nature. My thought of the table is certainly not something "like" the table; it is the table as I know it. Similarly, your thought of the table is what you know of the table, the table as known to you; and if we both have real knowledge of the table, it seems to follow that our thoughts are the same, not merely similar; and further, if the mind is its thoughts, we seem to have, for this moment at least, actually one mind; we share between us that unity of consciousness which was said to be the mark of the individual.[1]

If it is said that the mark of the individual is not so much consciousness of an object as self-consciousness, and that each person's self-consciousness is unique, this is in one way, I think, true. It is true in the sense that in all knowing I am conscious of myself as knowing, and also in the sense that I am aware of my own history as an active and conscious being. But I am not aware simply of my own awareness in general, but of this object as a thing I am thinking about; I may know that I am thinking, but not that I

1. I believe that the argument I have tried to express contains little if anything which contradicts the principles of either realism or idealism in their more satisfactory forms. There is an idealism with which I feel little sympathy, and there is a so-called realism which seems to me only distinguishable from that idealism by its attempt to evade its own necessary conclusions. But I do not wish to appear as a combatant in the battle between what I believe to be the better forms of the theories. Indeed, if they are to be judged by such works as Joachim's *Nature of Truth* on the one hand and Prichard's *Kant's Theory of Knowledge* and Carritt's *Theory of Beauty* on the other, I hope I have said nothing with which both sides would not to some extent agree; though I can hardly expect to avoid offending one or other—or both—by the way in which I put it.

The reader who has not studied the latter works should be warned that the "New Realism" criticized in, e.g., Professor Watson's *Philosophical Basis of Religion,* pp. 113-135, has no connection with the realism which they defend.

am thinking in the abstract, only that I am thinking about this thing. Self-consciousness is not in this sense, so far as I can see, distinguishable from consciousness of reality in general. In the other sense, self-consciousness being taken as knowledge of myself as a historical person, this knowledge is by no means confined to myself; others may in this sense know me better than I know myself.

Another possible objection depends on distinguishing two elements in knowledge, or two senses in the word knowing. There is, first, knowledge in the sense of what I know, the object; and secondly, there is the activity of knowing, the effort which is involved as much in knowing as in anything else. Knowledge as a possession —the things we know—may be common to different minds, but, it may be said, knowledge in the sense of the activity of knowing is peculiar to the individual mind. It may perhaps be replied that since knowledge is admittedly an activity, an effort of the will, there is no difference between thinking and willing to think. And if two minds are identical in thinking the same thing, they are equally and for the same reason identical in willing to think the same thing. All knowing is the act of knowing, and therefore whatever is true of thinking *sans phrase* is true of the act or volition of thinking.

But the objection leads on to the second part of our subject. To distinguish thought as the consciousness of an object from thought as an act of the will is to appeal, as basis for the absolute plurality between persons, from the conception of knowledge to that of action; and with this point we must proceed to deal.

(*b*) Every person, like every other fact in the world, is unique and has his own contribution to make to the whole; a contribution which cannot be made by any other. This need not be emphasized, and certainly cannot be questioned. It is as true of the intellect as of the will; and yet we found that the statement "my knowledge is my knowledge" must not be so interpreted as to exclude the complementary statement that my knowledge may also be yours. This fact, the fact of communication, led us to the conclusion that if and when knowledge became in this way common property, the minds concerned became the same mind. But if two people can by communication share their knowledge, it seems equally certain that they may by co-operation share their aims and volitions. My actions are my actions; but yet they are not exclusively mine.

Just as our intellectual life consists very largely of the acquisition of knowledge from one person and the passing it on, when we have added what we can, to others, so our active life consists very largely of working at ideals which are the common property, if not of all mankind, at least of our particular society. Man does not struggle with either his intellectual or his moral problems in solitude. He receives each alike from his environment, and in solving them he is doing other people's work as well as his own.

Now if there is in this sense co-operation of wills, if two or more wills are bent on the same object, what is the consequence?

A will is not, any more than an intellect, an engine which produces certain results. We are sometimes tempted to think of the will as a central power-installation somewhere in the depths of our personality, which can be connected up with a pump or a saw or any other machine we may desire to use. In this sense we distinguish the will from the faculties, the one as the motive power and the other as the machine which it operates. But the will is not simply crude energy, indifferently applicable to this end or to that. Will is not only the power of doing work but the power of choosing what work to do. It is not in need of another faculty to direct and apply its energy. Will is, in short, always the will to do this or that: it is always particular, never merely general. The distinction between the will and the things which it does is a quite abstract distinction, like that between human nature and men. Human nature simply means the various kinds of men; and my will is nothing more nor less than the things I do.

We seem therefore to be led to the same conclusion here as in the case of thought. If two people will the same thing, the personal distinction between them has given way to an identity, in virtue of which the two can be described as one mind.

2. It may be asked, if this identity were ever really established would it not be in fact self-destructive? If the distinction between the two persons was absolutely cancelled, of what elements would the unity be composed? For a unity that is composed of no elements

at all cannot be anything. Not only does it like Saturn devour its own children but like the Kilkenny cats it devours itself. In short, the stress laid on the completeness of the unity is fatal to the theory; for it turns the communion of different minds into a mere blank identity which is indistinguishable from a blank nothingness.

There are, I think, two answers to this question. We have already admitted elsewhere that every whole must be a whole of parts, and that all identity must therefore be an identity of differences. But if we look for the differences in this identity, they appear in two different ways, one from the side of the subject and one from that of the object.

(*a*) It must not forgotten that the unity we have described is a unity of minds. Its very existence depends on the harmony between the minds; and if by means of the unity one mind ceased to exist, the possibility of the union would vanish with it. For this reason the identity of wills does not result in a Spinozistic determinism of the one substance; for the identity *consists in the fact that each wills the same thing;* it is an identity not existing as a fixed unchangeable fact but *depending for its existence on the continued harmony of the two persons.* It does not unite them in spite of themselves, but because they choose to be united.

Then the distinction is not absolutely cancelled, if the parties are free to dissolve it; and if so, they retain their exclusive individuality all the time.—This looks unanswerable at first sight; but I think that it is really a quibble. The argument involved is, that if a mind or society is capable of becoming something, that proves that it really is that something all the time. This seems to me to imply principles and consequences which I cannot accept. Because a good man may some day forget himself and commit a crime, that proves (says the argument) that he was not really good at all: it shows that he had in him the germ of the crime. Undoubtedly he had, if by the germ is meant the freedom of will which makes crime possible; but to describe that as a germ of crime is most misleading, since the same thing is equally the germ of virtue. If by "germ" is meant any more than this—if it means a tendency which irresistibly grows into crime—then one must boldly reply that minds are not made like that; what they do, they do not in virtue of irresistible "tendencies" but because they choose to do it.

So we should admit that because of its freedom a mind may forfeit the unity, whether with itself or another, to which it has attained. But that does not mean that it never attained it. For all the conquests of mind are made and held by its own freedom, held no longer than it has the strength to hold them; and it can only lose this strength by its own self-betrayal.

(*b*) The identity also includes differences from the side of the object. If the object of the two minds was an abstract, undifferentiated one, then the two minds would also be a blank unity without difference. But this is not the case, for such an undifferentiated unity nowhere exists. In a sense, no two people ever do, or ever could, think or will exactly the same thing. This is not because unity is impossible; it is not because under the conditions of this imperfect world we can never get more than an approximation to it. If an ideal were not fully attainable by us here and now it would not be a valid ideal for us here and now. There is never an obligation to achieve the impossible.

Any truth or ideal of conduct expresses itself under infinitely various aspects. A single truth never means quite the same thing to different minds; each person invests it with an emphasis, an application, peculiar to himself. This does not mean that it is not the same truth; the difference does not destroy the identity any more than identity destroys difference. It is only in the identity that the differences arise.

The same is true of conduct. My own duties are the duties dictated by my situation; no one else is in precisely my situation and therefore no one else can have the same duties. And for the same reason no one else can have exactly my desires. But there is a community of aims; and this community is not the barren transmission of unchanging ideals, good or bad, in which social life is sometimes thought to consist, nor yet the equally abstract identity of the categorical imperative, which only applies to everybody and every situation because it abstracts from all the intricacies of real life. The community of aims consists in the fact that what I want is something which I cannot have except with your help and that of everyone else. The object of my desire is one part of a whole which can only exist if the other parts exist; or, if that way of putting it is preferred, I desire the existence of a whole to which I can only contribute one among many parts. The other parts must be contributed by other people; and therefore in willing my part I will theirs also.

3. The unity whose possibility we are concerned to prove is the fully concrete identification, by their own free activity, of two or more personalities. This is not a universal condition, but an ideal; it is the goal, not the starting-point, of human endeavor. But every real advance is like the spiral tunnel of an Alpine railway; it ends, if not where it began, at least immediately above it. The end is not the antithesis of the beginning, but the same thing raised to a higher power. The end is a unity, and the beginning is also a unity; but they are not the same unity. There is one perfectly concrete identity which consists in the highest degree of co-operation and the freest interchange of activities, and is destroyed when these fail; and there is another, an abstract, irreducible, and indefeasible identity or union which subsists between any two parts of the same whole, and must continue to subsist as long as they remain parts. The whole, in each case alike, may equally be a society or a single person. We cannot maintain that a person is simply a necessary, indefeasible unity of those things which constitute his character, while a society is entirely dependent for its unity on the positive and conscious co-operation of its members, failing which it is no longer a society at all. A person is undoubtedly himself, and can never help being himself, whatever he does; but this merely abstract unity, this bare minimum of self-identity, is much less than what we usually call his character or personality. That is rather constituted by the definite and concrete system of his various activities or habits. When we say, "I know his character, I am sure he will do this and not that," we mean that there is this systematic relation [2] between the different things he does, so that we can argue from one of them to the others; that the connection between his various actions is not the purely

2. Not deterministic, because dependent for its very existence, as we said above, on his will, and therefore capable of being infringed by his will.

abstract connection that they happen all to have been done by the same person. If there were no more than this abstract unity, we could not say that a man had any positive "character" at all. To say "he is not himself today" appears, if we hold to the purely abstract sense of "self," merely ridiculous; but in the concrete sense of "self," the sense in which the self is conceived as a co-operating unity of purpose, it has a perfectly real meaning.

The same distinction applies to the unity of a society. In one sense, any kind of relation between two people produces a kind of social union and identification; in another sense, only the right kind of relation unifies them, and a different relation would destroy the unity. In the first case, their union is what I call the purely abstract unity; in the latter, it is the concrete unity that has to be maintained by positive and harmonious activity. We cannot therefore say that, of these two kinds of unity, one is the kind proper to a person, and the other the kind proper to a society; for each alike may apply to either. But, having examined the nature of the concrete unity, it is necessary that we should also examine, and indeed demonstrate the existence of, this abstract unity.

(*a*) But is unity the same as identity? There seems at first sight to be a very decided difference between saying that two things are part of the same whole, and saying that they are the same thing; the parts of one thing seem to be themselves quite separate and self-existent things, possibly depending on each other, but each being what it is itself, and not the others; while the whole is simply their sum.

We have already expressed doubts as to the strict truth of this conception. We said in the last chapter that if a whole was to be knowable, it must be of such a kind that the parts are not simply added in series to one another, but interconnected in such a way that we can somehow say that each part is the whole. In that case each part would also be in a sense the others. At the time this may have seemed highly fanciful, if not a counsel of despair. What right, it will be asked, have we to lay down *a priori* what must be the nature of reality merely on the ground that if it is not thus, it is not knowable? How do we know that reality is knowable? And even if we are assured on that point, and legitimately assured, is it not a monstrous inversion of the true order to argue from knowability to reality?

I am not sure that it is. Knowledge is as much a fact as any other; and if the business of a sound theory is to account for the facts, a theory which does not admit of the world's being completely known is, to say the least of it, incomplete. The modern impatience with such forms of argument may be partly based on their connection with false theories of what knowability means, but it is certainly due in part to the prejudice that the facts of the external world are certain, while the nature of knowledge and the processes of mind are unknown; so that to argue to the nature of the real world from the nature of the mind is arguing from the unknown to the known, attempting to lay down by insecure deductions from a discredited metaphysic things which could be easily ascertained by appealing to the natural sciences. This "positivistic" attitude is lamentably self-contradictory; for if we are not to believe in the full knowability of the world, what becomes of the facts of science? And if we are, why should we hush the matter up? We cannot pretend ignorance of the nature of knowing while we claim that science gives us real knowledg and philosophy only a sham.

I think therefore that we need not retract the argument. But as it stood it was incomplete; for it merely sketched the conditions of a satisfactory view of the relation of the whole to its parts, without explaining how they can be fulfilled.

Let us take as an instance any whole consisting of three parts, *x, y, z.* It makes no difference whether it is a machine with three working parts, a society of three members, a stanza of three lines, or a syllogism containing three propositions. Each part has its own nature, its own individuality, which is in the strictest sense unique; and apart from the contribution made by each several element the whole would not exist. Change one part, and the whole becomes a different whole. Not only does the whole change, but the apparently unchanged parts change too. Substitute, in a tragic stanza, a grotesque last word, and the opening lines become suddenly instinct with ridiculous possibilities. Substitute in the society a new third man, and not only is it now a different society but the social value and function of the unchanged members is altered.

On the other hand, the part that is removed is no longer what it was. A man may resign his place in a society because he feels that he is no longer what the society requires him to be; and in that case his resignation gives him a new freedom. If he leaves it with no such reason, his personality is mutilated by the separation; one side of his character is cut off and frustrated. The separation of the part from the whole destroys part and whole alike. The part survives only as something different from what it was; it has to readjust itself, if it can, and become something else. If it cannot do this, it dies outright. The whole must in the same way readjust itself to the new conditions and become a different whole; otherwise it also dies.

It follows from this closeness of interconnection between the whole and its parts that the question "what is *x*?" cannot be answered merely by saying "*x is x*." *X* only exists as *x* in relation to *y* and *z*. If *y* or *z* were removed, *x* would no longer be what it was; it would have to become something else, or failing that, cease to exist at all. Consequently if we ask for a definition or description of *x* the only true reply is to describe it in its full relations with *y* and *z*. That is to say, a definition of *x* can only take the form of a definition of the whole system *xyz*. To explain the nature of the part we have to explain the nature of the whole; there seems to be no distinction between the part and the whole, except that the part is the whole under one particular aspect, seen as it were from one point of view. In the same way and in the same sense *y* and *z* are identical each with the whole and with each other and *x*. Each part is the whole, and each part is all the other parts.

A distinction is sometimes drawn which avoids this conclusion. There is, we are told, a difference between what a thing is in itself and what it is in relation to its context or the whole of which it is a part. *X* as a thing in itself remains (it is said) the same; it is only its relations with other things that change, and these are merely external, and do not affect its real nature. It is true that nothing is really destroyed by depriving it of its context. But this is only because we cannot deprive it of all context. A lintel taken out of its place in a house and laid on the ground has a context, though not an architectural context; and Robinson Crusoe in his solitude has a perfectly definite environment, though not a human environment.

However much we try to remove all context from a thing, we can do no more than to invest the thing with a different context. Indeed, there is a sense in which we may still call the stone a lintel and Robinson Crusoe the member of a human society; for the history of a thing in the past and its capabilities for the future are as real as its present situation, though in a different way. The isolated stone lying on the ground may still be called a lintel; but this is so only on account of the house from which it came (strictly, it *is* a stone that *was* a lintel), or into which it will be built (it is a stone that *will be* a lintel), or even because of the imaginary house which we can, so to speak, construct round it now (it is a stone that *might be* a lintel).

The character or self of a thing, what it is, cannot be distinguished from its relation. Architecturally, the stone *is* a lintel; that is its own character. But this character only consists in the fact that it stands in a certain relation to other stones which together with it make up the doorway. Geologically, the description of the stone is identical with the description of its place in the geological series. Every characteristic of the thing turns out to consist in a relation in which it stands to something else; and similarly, if we began at the other end we should find that every relation consists in a quality of the thing itself. This double movement is only not a vicious circle because, of the two things which thus turn into one another, each is already identical with the other.

The inner nature of the part x, then, is entirely constituted by its relations to y and z. And therefore x is simply one way of looking at the whole xyz; and y and z are other aspects of the same whole. The part is not added to other parts in order to make the whole: it is already in itself the whole, and the whole has other parts only in the sense that it can be looked at from other points of view, seen in other aspects. But in each aspect the whole is entirely present.

If we take the case of a musical duet, we have a whole which is analyzable into two parts. At first sight, we might be tempted to describe the relation between them in some such way as this: there are two separate things, two musical compositions, one called the treble and the other the bass. Each is an independent reality, has a tune of its own, and can be played separately. On the other hand, they are so arranged that they can also be played both at once; and when this happens, they produce an esthetic value greater than either can produce by itself. The whole is the sum of its parts; and the parts in combination remain exactly what they were before.

This description seems at first sight reasonable; and it is familiar as underlying, for instance, the Wagnerian view of opera. If you take two arts and add them together—so that view runs—you produce a new art twice as great as either.

But is the esthetic value of a duet really equal to the sum of the value of its parts played separately? No such thing. The query of one instrument may indeed be in itself a beautiful phrase, independently of the answer given by the other; but as seen in relation to that answer it acquires a totally different emphasis, a meaning which we never suspected. The accompaniment part, or even the solo part, played by itself, is simply not the same thing that it is when played in its proper relation to the other. It is this relation between the two that constitutes the duet. The performers are not doing two different things, which combine as if by magic to make a harmonious whole; they are co-operating to produce one and the same thing, a thing not in any sense divisible into parts; for the "thing" itself is only a relation, an interchange, a *balance between* the elements which at first we mistook for its parts. The notes played by the piano are not the same notes as those played by the violin; and if the duet was a merely physical fact, we could divide it into these two elements. But the duet is an esthetic, not a physical whole. It consists not of atmospheric disturbances, which could be divided, but of a harmony between sounds, and a harmony cannot be divided into the sounds between which it subsists.

The same is true of any really organic whole. A scene of Shakespeare can be regarded as so much "words, words, words," and, when so regarded, it can be divided into what Hamlet says and what Polonius says. But the real scene is not mere words; it is the interplay of two characters. It is one thing, not two. To subdivide it would be not to halve but to destroy its value. Even a baby can be cut in two, if it is regarded as a mere piece of flesh; but the resulting portions would be the halves not of a baby but of a corpse.

A unity of this kind exists not only in harmonious and fully co-operative wholes, but equally in everything that can be called a whole at all. Whatever the particular relation in which x stands to y and z, it is still true that each part is but an aspect of the whole and identical with the other parts. X, y, and z may be parties to a quarrel; but they are in that case just as much parts of the same whole, just as closely identified with one another, as if they were allies in a common cause. This kind of identity, therefore, is to be sharply distinguished from the contingent unity, the unity of co-operation, which we described at the beginning of this chapter. Upon this distinction turns the whole argument of this and the succeeding chapters.

(*b*) The universal and necessary identity, the abstract identity of mere coexistence, is often taken as supplying the key to all the difficulties with which the religious or philosophical mind feels itself beset when it deals with the problem of personality. All personalities are components of a whole, the universe; and therefore, by the above argument, they are all necessarily identified with each other and the whole, that is, with the universe considered as homogeneous with them, an absolute mind, God. The line of thought seems to be simple and impossible to refute; and if this is really so, it establishes at a blow the existence of God and his perfect immanence in humanity, and leaves nothing more to be achieved or desired.

To reject such an argument altogether would certainly be a mistake. It is true that, whether we like it or not, whether we live up to our position or deny our responsibilities, we are so intimately connected with each other and the divine mind that no act concerns the doer alone. This assumption is fundamental. But the error lies in mistaking this fundamental assumption for the final conclusion; in assuming that this elementary, abstract unity is the only one which concerns us. In point of fact, it concerns us, if at all, certainly in the very lowest possible degree. In practical matters, a constant which is always present and can never be altered is best ignored; and indeed this purely abstract identity is so shadowy a thing that it is hard to see what else to do. To call this formless and empty abstraction "the Absolute" is merely to abuse language; and to suppose that this is all philosophy has to offer in place of the concrete God of religion is completely to misunderstand the nature and aim of philosophy. There have been and no doubt still are people who claim the title of philosophers on the ground that they habitually amuse themselves with abstractions of this kind. But it is a pity that their claims have been and still are taken seriously.

The Absolute, as that word is used by any philosophy worthy of the name, is not a label for the bare residuum, blank existence, which is left when all discrepancies have been ignored and all irregularities planed away. An arbitrary smoothing-down of the world's wrinkled crust is not philosophy, but the vice against which all philosophy wages an unceasing war. A real philosophy builds its Absolute (for every philosophy has an Absolute) out of the differences of the world as it finds them, dealing individually with all contradictions and preserving every detail that can lend character to the whole.

Here as elsewhere the instinct of religion is the deliberate procedure of philosophy at its best. When religion demands a personal God, a God who has a definite character of his own and can, as the phrase goes, take sides in the battles of the world, it is really asserting the necessity for this concrete characterized Absolute, as against a sham "philosophy," the philosophy of abstractions, which assures it that since God is all, he cannot have any one attribute rather than its opposite; that since he is infinite, he cannot be a person; that since he is the strength of both sides, the slayer and the slain, he cannot himself fight on either side. In the Absolute, we are told, all contradictions are resolved, and therefore all distinctions vanish; good and evil are no more, for that of which each is a manifestation cannot itself be either. A personal God, creating the world and sustaining it by the might of his will, is a mythological fiction. A God who is in any sense transcendent and not purely immanent is inconceivable, and even imaginable only to the half-savage mind which anthropomorphizes everything it does not immediately understand.

So "philosophy" browbeats common sense till the latter for very shame yields the point; tries to recast its religion, if it still ventures to have one, on lines of pure immanence, and if it cannot make the immanent God seem as real and vivid as the transcendent, humbly puts the failure down to its own philosophical shortcomings. For "philosophy" has assured it that reality, properly faced and understood, will more than console it for its lost fairyland. There is little ground for surprise if after such experiences religion hates and despises the very name of philosophy. The formless and empty Absolute of this abstract metaphysic perished long ago in the fire of Hegel's sarcasm; and it is curious to find the very same pseudo-Absolute, the "night in which all cows are black," still regarded as being for good or evil the essence of philosophical thought.

(*c*) It is time to leave these abstractions and turn to the other kind of identity, the concrete identity of activity. A mind is self-identical in this sense if it thinks and wills the same things constantly; it is identical with another, if it thinks and wills the same things as that other. This might seem to imply that in the first case there was no possibility of change or process within the limits of the self-identity; and in the second case that the personal distinction between the two minds was reduced to a mere illusion. But, (1) so far is it from being true that a thing to be self-identical must not change, the very fact of change proves its continued identity; for only a thing which is still itself can be said to have changed. This however is abstract identity only, and it might be imagined that concrete identity was not compatible with change. But this is a mistake. It is the property of truth to present itself under the aspect of innumerable differences; and yet within these differences it is still one. If we reflect upon some particular fact, we can see it take under our eyes a hundred different forms, emphases, shades of meaning. In following out this process, it does in a quite concrete sense change; and the thinking of this change is a real mental process, in the only sense in which any thought can bear that name. (2) The identity of two minds which think the same thing does, as we have already seen, in one sense abolish the difference between them; but this very abolition is only possible through the free and independent activity of each separate mind. Difference is not simply absent; it is overcome.

Now these two cases are typical first of the self-identity of

God, and secondly of his identity with the human mind. God is not a mere abstract unity; he is a mind, and as such he can possess the higher unity of self-consistency. This attribute must necessarily belong to him if we are right in regarding him as omniscient and perfectly good. An omniscient mind is one whose beliefs are never false, and whose field of knowledge is not limited by any ignorance. This is the only type of mind which can be described as entirely consistent with itself. Any false belief, introduced into a system of judgments otherwise true, must breed contradiction; for its implications cannot be developed to infinity without coming into conflict with some other belief. Again, any limitation, any gap in one's knowledge, may have the same result; for different truths often seem to conflict until new knowledge explains them both and shows them to be harmonious. But two truths can never in reality contradict one another, and therefore a mind which believed all truths would have within itself no contradiction at all.

In the same way, we can conceive a mind which willed, not indeed all the actions, but all the good actions in existence. Of the different actions in the world, some are in antagonism to others, and therefore it is impossible for a mind to will both except at the cost of losing its concrete unity, its own positive nature, and becoming a formless something indistinguishable from nothing. A mind which willed all the good in existence would display this concrete unity to the full; for two duties, two good things, can no more conflict than two true things.

Each of these conflicts does often seem to take place. Two statements which contradict each other do very often seem to be, each from its own point of view and within its own limitations, true. And two people who are supporting opposed causes may seem to be both in the right. But in the former case we know that the conflict is only apparent; that if each disputant understood the other, it would in so far as each is right disappear. And similarly in the other case, though the fact is not such a universally recognized axiom in ethics as the "law of contradiction" is in logic, it is true that of the two opponents one, or possibly both, must be in the wrong; or, if that is not the case, the opposition between them must be illusory. Good is self-consistent just as truth is; and just as a mind which believes all truth is supremely self-consistent and self-identical, so it is with a mind which wills all good.

Further, this divine mind will become one with all other minds so far as they share its thought and volition; so far, that is, as they know any truth or will any good. And this unity between the two is not the merely abstract identity of coexistence, but the concrete identity of co-operation. The abstract unity would remain even in the case of a mind which (if that be possible) knew nothing true and did nothing right. There is a sense in which whether we will it or not we are indissolubly, by our very existence, one with God; that bond it is not in our power to break. But the highest and most real identity with him we can only possess in the knowledge of truth and the pursuit of goodness.

Thus God is at once immanent and transcendent; and man can be regarded as, on the one hand, a part of the universal divine spirit, and on the other, as a person separate from God and capable of opposition to him. God is immanent because all human knowledge and goodness are the very indwelling of his spirit in the mind of man; transcendent because, whether or not man attains to these things, God has attained to them; his being does not depend upon the success of human endeavor.

Such a mind as this, omniscient and perfectly good, is conceivable; but the conception may be called a mere hypothesis. I think it is more than this. Every good man, and every seeker after truth, is really, even if unconsciously, co-operating with every other in the ideal of a complete science or a perfect world; and if co-operating, then identified with the other and with an all-embracing purpose of perfection. There really is such a purpose, which lives in the lives of all good men wherever they are found, and unifies them all into a life of its own. This is God immanent; and it is no mere hypothesis. Is it equally certain that he also exists as transcendent, or does that remain a hypothesis, incapable of proof? Is God only existent as a spirit in our hearts, or is he also a real person with a life of his own, whether we know him or not?

The difficulty of answering this question is bound up with a well-known philosophical puzzle, the puzzle of how to prove the existence of anything except as present to the mind. If it is true that things cease to exist when we are not thinking of them, and that the people whom we generally suppose to be real independently of our dealings with them exist only as and when we are conscious of them, then it follows by the same argument that God is immanent only, and exists nowhere but in the minds of men. But we cannot really believe that these things are so. And to suppose that the spirit of goodness of which we are conscious in our hearts has its being there and there alone is no less fantastic than to suppose that the friends with whom we converse are only the projection upon nothingness of our own imagination. The arguments for pure immanence are at bottom identical with the philosophical creed of subjective idealism, and with that creed they stand or fall.

This conception of God as perfectly wise and good avoids at least the faults of an indefinite and empty abstraction. But is it any more than the other horn of an inevitable dilemma? God, as we have conceived his nature, is good indeed, but not omnipotent; wise, but unable entirely to control the world which he knows. He is the totality of truth and goodness, the Absolute of all the good there is; but the world's evil remains outside this totality, recalcitrant to the power of God and superior to his jurisdiction.

Here, it is sometimes said, lies the parting of the ways between religion and philosophy. Religion must at all costs have a God with a definite character of his own; philosophy must have an all-embracing totality, a rounded and complete universe. And when it is found that God, to be good, cannot be all, then religion and philosophy accept different horns of the dilemma, and from this point travel in different directions.

But such a solution really annihilates both philosophy and religion. The "universe" which philosophy is supposed to choose is again the empty abstraction of a something which is nothing definite; it is not an Absolute, but only the indication of an unsolved problem. And for religion too the problem is unsolved; for it refuses, and rightly refuses, to believe that a limited God is its last word. It cannot accept the antithesis between God and the world as final. Either it declares its faith in his ultimate omnipotence, in the final identification of the seemingly opposed terms, or it relapses into the pessimism of a forlorn hope which can do no more than hurl defiance at a world of evil which it cannot conquer. Of these alternatives, the highest religious faith unhesitatingly chooses the first, at the risk of being accused of a sentimental optimism. But the attitude so chosen is the only consistent one; for the pessimist's defiance of the world already achieves in some degree that very victory which he pronounces impossible.

Each solution, then, the undefined Absolute and the limited God, is provisional only, a working hypothesis and no more. An undefined Absolute is not an Absolute, and a limited God is not a God. Each alike can only be made satisfactory by acquiring the character of the other; and hence the problems of religion and philosophy are one and the same.

This brings us face to face with the question of evil. How can a world whose elements are at variance with one another be, except in a merely abstract sense, one world at all? How can the existence of a perfectly good God be reconciled with the reality of minds whose will is the very antithesis of his own?

GOD'S REDEMPTION OF MAN

1. WHATEVER else is involved in the doctrine of the Atonement, it includes at least this: that the sins of man are forgiven by God. And here at the very outset a difficulty arises which must be faced before the doctrine can be further developed. Forgiveness and punishment are generally conceived as two alternative ways of treating a wrongdoer. We may punish any particular criminal, or we may forgive him; and the question always is, which is the right course of action. On the other hand, however, punishment seems to be not a conditional but an absolute duty; and to neglect it is definitely wrong. Justice in man consists at least in punishing the guilty, and the conception of a just God similarly emphasizes his righteous infliction of penalties upon those who break his laws. The very idea of punishment is not that it is sometimes right and sometimes wrong or indifferent, but that its infliction is an inexorable demand of duty.

On the other hand, forgiveness is presented as an equally vital duty for man and an equally definite characteristic of God. This, again, is not conditional. The ideal of forgiveness is subject to no restrictions. The divine precept does not require us to forgive, say, seven times and then turn on the offender for reprisals. Forgiveness must be applied unequivocally to every offense alike.

Here, then, we have an absolute contradiction between two opposing ideals of conduct. And the result of applying the antithesis to the doctrine of Atonement is equally fatal whichever horn of the dilemma is accepted. Either punishment is right and forgiveness wrong, or forgiveness is right and punishment wrong. If punishment is right, then the doctrine that God forgives our sins is illusory and immoral; it ascribes to God the weakness of a doting father who spares the rod and spoils the child. If punishment is wrong, then the conception of a punishing God is a mere barbarism of

Reprinted from *Religion and Philosophy* (London: Macmillan & Co., 1916), pp. 169-193.

primitive theology, and atonement is no mystery, no divine grace, but simply the belated recognition by theology that its God is a moral being. Thus regarded, the Atonement becomes either a fallacy or a truism.

And it is common enough, in the abstract and hasty thought which in every age passes for modern, to find the conception of Atonement dismissed in this way. But such thought generally breaks down in two different directions. In its cavalier treatment of a doctrine, it ignores the real weight of thought and experience that has gone to the development of the theory, or broadly condemns it as illusion and dreams; and secondly, it proceeds without sufficient speculative analysis of its own conceptions, with a confidence based in the last resort upon ignorance. The historian of thought will develop the first of these objections; our aim is to consider the second.

The dilemma which has been applied to theology must, of course, equally apply to moral or political philosophy. In order to observe it at work, we must see what results it produces there. Punishment and forgiveness are things we find in our own human society; and unless we are to make an end of theology, religion, and philosophy by asserting that there is no relation between the human and the divine, we must try to explain each by what we know of the other.

(*a*) The first solution of the dilemma, then, might be to maintain that punishment is an absolute duty and forgiveness positively wrong. We cannot escape the rigor of this conclusion by supposing forgiveness to be "non-moral," for we cannot evade moral issues; the possibility of forgiveness only arises in cases where punishment is also an alternative, and if punishment is always right, then forgiveness must always be a crime.

Forgiveness, on this view, is a sentimental weakness, a mere neglect of the duty to punish. It is due to misguided partiality toward an offender; and instead of canceling or wiping out his crime, endorses it by committing another. Now this is a view which might conceivably be held; and if consistently held would be difficult to refute, without such a further examination of the conceptions involved as we shall undertake later. At this stage we can only point out that it does not deserve the name of an ethical theory, because it emphasizes one fact in the moral consciousness and arbitrarily ignores others. The fact is that people do forgive, and feel that they are acting morally in so doing. They distinguish quite clearly in their own minds between forgiving a crime and sentimentally overlooking or condoning it. Now the theory does not merely ignore this fact, but it implicitly or even, if pressed, explicitly denies it. To a person who protested, "But I am convinced that it is a duty to forgive," it would reply, "Then you are wrong; it is a crime." And if asked why it is a crime, the theory would explain, "Because it is inconsistent with the duty to punish." But the duty to punish rests on the same basis as the duty to forgive; it is a pronouncement of the moral consciousness. All the theory does is to assume quite uncritically that the moral consciousness is right in the one case and wrong in the other; whereas the reverse is equally possible. The two duties may be contradictory, but they rest on the same basis; and the argument which discredits one discredits the other too.

(*b*) The same difficulty applies to the other horn of the dilemma, according to which forgiveness is always right and punishment always wrong. Just as we cannot say that forgiveness is a crime because punishment is a duty, so we cannot say that punishment is a crime because forgiveness is a duty. But the theory of the immorality of punishment has been worked out rather more fully than is (I believe) the case with the theory of the immorality of forgiveness.

(1) Just as forgiveness was identified with sentimental condoning of an offense, so punishment has been equated with personal revenge. This view has been plausibly expressed in terms of evolution by the hypothesis that revenge for injuries has been gradually, in the progress of civilization, organized and centralized by state control; so that instead of a vendetta we nowadays have recourse to a lawsuit as our means of reprisal on those who have done us wrong. But such a statement overlooks the fact that punishment is not revenge in the simple and natural sense of that word. The difference is as plain as that between forgiveness and the neglect of the duty to punish. Revenge is a second crime which does nothing

to mitigate the first; punishment is not a crime but something which we feel to be a duty. The "state organization of revenge" really means the annihilation or supersession of revenge and the substitution for it of equitable punishment. And if we ask how this miracle has happened, the only answer is that people have come to see that revenge is wrong and so have given it up.

(2) A less crude theory of punishment as merely selfish is the view which describes it as deterrent, as a means of self-preservation on the part of society. We are told that crime in general is detrimental to social well-being (or, according to more thorough-going forms of the conception, what is found to be detrimental is arbitrarily called crime), and therefore society inflicts certain penalties on criminals in order to deter them and others from further anti-social acts. It is the function of "justice" to determine what amount of terror is necessary in order to prevent the crime.

Punishment so explained is not moral. We punish not because it is a duty but because it preserves us against certain dangers. A person has done us an injury, and we maltreat him, not out of a spirit of revenge, far from it, but in order to frighten others who may wish to imitate him. The condemned criminal is regarded as a marauder nailed *in terrorem* to the barn-door. One feels inclined to ask how such a combination of cruelty and selfishness can possibly be justified in civilized societies; and if the theory is still possessed by a lingering desire to justify punishment, it will perhaps reply that the criminal has "forfeited his right" to considerate treatment. Which means either that he has cut himself off from our society altogether (which he plainly has not) or that there is nothing wrong in being cruel to a criminal, which is monstrous. If society is trying to be moral at all, it has duties toward a criminal as much as toward anyone else. It may deny the duties, and have its criminals eaten by wild beasts for its amusement, or tortured for its increased security; perhaps the former is the less revolting practice; but in either case society is demonstrating its own corruption.

The deterrent theory, then, must not be used as a justification, but only as an impeachment, of punishment. But even if punishment is, as the theory maintains, a purely selfish activity, it must still be justified in a sense, not by its rightness but by its success. The question therefore is whether as a matter of fact punishment does deter. Now a "just" penalty, on this theory, is defined as one which is precisely sufficient to deter. If it does not deter, it is condemned as giving insufficient protection to society, and therefore unjust. Society will accordingly increase it, and this increase will continue till a balance is established and the crime is stamped out. Those crimes therefore happen oftenest whose statutable penalties are most in defect of this ideal balance. The fact that they happen proves that the penalty is inadequate. Therefore, if the deterrent view is correct, society must be anxious to increase these penalties. But we do not find that this is the case. If criminal statistics show an increase, we do not immediately increase the penalties. Still less do we go on increasing them further and further until the crime is no longer attractive. If we may argue from empirical evidence, such as the infliction of the death penalty for petty thefts, it is simply not the case that increased severity necessarily diminishes crime; and yet on the theory it ought to do so. On the contrary, it sometimes appears that higher penalties go with greater frequency. To reply to this that the frequency of crime is the cause, not the effect of the greater severity, would be to confess the failure of punishment as deterrent; for, on that view, severity ought to be the *cause* of *infrequency,* not the *effect* of *frequency.* The plea would amount to a confession that we cannot, as is supposed, control the amount of crime by the degree of punishment.

Thus the view that punishment is a selfish act of society to secure its own safety against crime breaks down. Its plausibility depends on the truth that the severity of punishments is somehow commensurate with the badness of the crime, that there is a connection of degree between the two. If we ask how this equation is brought about, the theory disappears at once. In punishment we do not try to hurt a man as much as he has hurt us, or even as much as may induce him not to hurt us. The "amount" of punishment is fixed by one standard only: what we suppose him to deserve. This is difficult to define exactly, and common practice represents only a very rough approximation to it; but it is that, not anything else, at which the approximation aims. And the conception of desert reintroduces into punishment the moral criterion which the theory tried to banish from it. To aim at giving a man the punishment he deserves implies that he does deserve it, and therefore that it is our duty to give it him.

(*c*) Both these escapes, therefore, have failed. We cannot say that either punishment or forgiveness is wrong, and thus vindicate the necessity of the other. Though contradictory they are both imperative. Nor can we make them apply to different cases; maintaining for instance that we should forgive the repentant and punish the obdurate. If we only forgive a man after he has repented, that is to say, put away his guilt and become good once more, the idea of forgiveness is a mockery. The very conception of forgiveness is that it should be our treatment of the guilty as guilty.

Nor can we escape by an abstraction distinguishing the sinner from the sin. We punish not the sin, but the sinner for his sin; and we forgive not the sinner distinguished from his sin, but identified with it and manifested in it. If we punish the sin, we must forgive the sin too: if we forgive the sinner, we must equally punish him.

2. This absolute contradiction between the two duties can only be soluble in one way. A contradiction of any kind is soluble either by discovering one member of it to be false, an expedient which has already been tried, or by showing that the two are not really, as we had supposed, incompatible. This is true, whether the contradiction is between two judgments of fact or between two duties or so-called "judgments of value"; for if it is axiomatic that two contradictory judgments cannot both be true, it is equally axiomatic that two incompatible courses of action cannot both be obligatory. This fact may be obscured by saying that on certain occasions we are faced with two alternatives of which each is a duty, but the question is which is the greater duty. But the "greater duty" is a phrase without meaning. In the supposed case the distinction is between this which we ought to do, and that which we ought not; the distinction between *ought* and *ought not* is not a matter of degree.

Granted, then, that in any given situation there can be only one duty, it follows necessarily that if of two actions each is really obligatory the two actions must be the same. We are therefore compelled to hold that punishment and forgiveness, so far from being incompatible duties, are really when properly understood identical.

This may seem impossible; but as yet we have defined neither conception, and this we must now proceed to do.

(*a*) Punishment consists in the infliction of deserved suffering on an offender. But it is not yet clear what suffering is inflicted, and how it is fixed, beyond the bare fact that it must be deserved. If we ask, "Why is that particular sort and amount of pain inflicted on this particular man?" the answer, "That is what he deserves," no doubt conveys the truth, but it does not fully explain it. It is not immediately clear without further thought that *this* must be the right punishment. Punishment is fixed not by a self-evident and inexplicable intuition, but by some motive or process of thought which we must try to analyze. The conception of desert proves that this motive is moral; and it remains to ask what is the moral attitude toward a crime or criminal.

If we take the case of a misdeed of our own and consider the attitude of our better moments toward it, we see that this attitude is one of condemnation. It is the act of a good will declaring its hostility to a bad one. This feeling of rejection, condemnation, or hostility is in fact the necessary attitude of all good wills toward all evil acts. The moral action of the person who punishes, therefore, consists primarily in this condemnation. Further, the condemnation, in our own case is the act in and through which we effect our liberation or alienation from the evil, and our adherence to the good. If a person is in a state of sin, that he should feel hostility toward his own sin is necessary to his moral salvation; he cannot become good except by condemning his own crime. The condemnation of the crime is not the *means* to goodness; it *is* the manifestation of the new good will.

The condemnation of evil is the necessary manifestation of all good wills. If A has committed a crime, B, if he is a moral person, condemns it. And this condemnation he will express to A if he is in social relations with him; for social relations consist of sharing thoughts and activities so far as possible. If B is successful in communicating his condemnation to A, A will thereupon share it; for A's knowledge that B condemns him, apart from his agreement in the condemnation, is not really a case of communication. But if A shares the condemnation he substitutes in that act a good will for an evil. The process is now complete: A's sin, B's condemnation, B's expression to A of his feelings, A's conversion and repentance. This is the inevitable result of social relations between the two persons, granting that A's will is good and that the relations are maintained.

Now this self-expression of a good will toward a bad is, I think, what we mean by the duty of punishment. It is no doubt the case that we describe many things as punishment in which we can hardly recognize these features at all. But examination of such cases shows that precisely so far as these facts are not present, so far as the punishment does not express moral feelings, and does not aim in some degree at the self-conviction of the criminal—so far, we are inclined to doubt whether it is a duty at all, and not a convention, a farce, or a crime. We conclude, therefore, that punishment—the only punishment we can attribute to God or to a good man—is the expression to a criminal of the punisher's moral attitude toward him. Hence punishment is an absolute duty, since not to feel that attitude would be to share his crime, and not to express it would be a denial of social relations, an act of hypocrisy.

(*b*) The pain inflicted on the criminal, then, is not the pain of evil consequences, recoiling from his action in the course of nature or by the design of God or man upon his own head; still less is it the mere regret for having done something which involves himself or others in such consequences. These things are not punishment at all, and ought never to be confused with it, though they may well be incidental to it. The pain of punishment is simply the pain of self-condemnation or moral repentance; the renunciation of one aim and the turning of the will to another. That is what we try to inflict upon him; and any other, incidental pains are merely the means by which we express to him our attitude and will. But why, it may be asked, should these incidental pains be necessary? Why should they be the only means of communicating such feelings? The answer is that they are not. The most perfect punishments involve no "incidental" pains at all. The condemnation is expressed simply and quietly in words, and goes straight home. The punishment consists in expression of condemnation and that alone; and to punish with a word instead of a blow is still punishment. It is, perhaps, a better and more civilized form of punishment; it indicates a higher degree of intelligence and a more delicate social organization. If a criminal is extremely coarsened and brutalized, we have to express our feelings in a crude way by cutting him off from the privileges of a society to whose moral aims he has shown himself hostile; but if we are punishing a child, the tongue is a much more efficient weapon than the stick.

Nor does the refinement of the penalty end there. It is possible to punish without the word of rebuke, to punish by saying nothing at all, or by an act of kindness. Here again, we cannot refuse the name of punishment because no "physical suffering" is inflicted. The expression of moral feelings, or the attitude of the good will to the bad, may take any form which the wrongdoer can understand. In fact, it is possible to hold that we often use "strong measures" when a word or a kind action would do just as well, or better. "If thine enemy hunger, feed him; for in so doing thou shalt heap coals of fire on his head." Sentimentalists have recoiled in horror from such a refinement of brutality, not realizing that to heap coals of fire, the fires of repentance, upon the head of the wrongdoer is the desire of all who wish to save his soul, not to perpetuate and endorse his crime.

But at this stage of the conception we should find it hard to discriminate between punishment and forgiveness. If punishment is to express condemnation, it must be the condemnation of a bad will by a good one. That is to say, it is the self-expression of a good will, and that good will is expressed as truly in the act of kindness as in the block and gallows. But if the punisher's will really is good, he continues, however severe his measures, to wish for the welfare and regeneration of the criminal. He punishes him not wholly with a view to "his good," because the punishment is not consciously undertaken as a means to an end, but as the spontaneous expression of a moral will; yet the aim of that will is not the criminal's mutilation or suffering as such but the awakening of his moral consciousness. And to treat the criminal as a fellow man capable of reformation, to feel still one's social relation and duty toward him, is surely the attitude which we call forgiveness.

If forgiveness means remission of the penalty, it is impossible to a moral will. For the penalty is simply the judgment; it is the expression of the moral will's own nature. If forgiveness means the remission of the more violent forms of self-expression on the part of the good will, then such restraint is not only still punishment but may be the most acute and effective form of it. But if forgiveness means—as it properly does—the wise and patient care for the criminal's welfare, for his regeneration and recovery into the life of a good society, then there is no distinction whatever between forgiveness and punishment.

(*c*) Punishment and forgiveness are thus not only compatible but identical; each is a name for the one and only right attitude of a good will toward a man of evil will. The details of the self-expression vary according to circumstances; and when we ask, "Shall we punish this man or forgive him?" we are really considering whether we shall use this or that method of expressing what is in either case equally punishment and forgiveness. The only important distinction we make between the two words is this: they refer to the same attitude of mind, but they serve to distinguish it from different ways of erring. When we describe an attitude as one of forgiveness, we mean to distinguish it, as right, from that brutality or unintelligent severity (punishment falsely so called) which inflicts pain either in mere wantonness or without considering the possibility of a milder expression. When we call it punishment, we distinguish it as right from that weakness or sentimentality (forgiveness falsely so called) which by shrinking from the infliction of pain amounts to condonation of the original offense.

3. The identity of punishment and forgiveness removes the preliminary difficulty in the way of any doctrine of atonement. So far as we can now understand God's attitude toward sin, it may be expressed thus.

God's attitude toward the sins of men must be one which combines condemnation of the sinful will with love and hope for it; these two being combined not as externally connected and internally inconsistent elements of a state of mind, but as being the single necessary expression of his perfect nature toward natures less perfect, but regarded as capable of perfection. This attitude on the part of God is, further, the means of man's redemption; for by understanding God's attitude toward sin man comes himself to share in that attitude, and is thus converted to a new life in harmony with God's good will.

Here we seem to have a relation involving two separate activities, the divine and the human. On the one hand there is the initiation of the repentance, the act of punishment or forgiveness on the part of God; and on the other, the response to God's act, the repentance of man in virtue of the original self-expression of God.

These two are inseparable aspects of one and the same process; the tendency to lay exclusive emphasis on one or the other leads to two main types of theory, each equally unsatisfactory because each, while really one-sided, claims to be an account of the whole truth. These views I call the objective and subjective theories respectively.

(*a*) The objective theory of atonement points out that whatever change takes place in the human will is due to the free gift of the Spirit of God. Man can do nothing good except by virtue of God's grace, and therefore if the evil will of a man is converted into a good will, the whole process is an act of God. The Atonement, the redemption of man, is a fact entirely on the side of God, not at all on the side of man; for without God's help and inspiration there would be nothing good in man at all.

This view lays the emphasis on God's attitude to the world, and concerns itself chiefly with the question, what change did the Incarnation mark in the development of God's plans? We cannot suppose that there was no change at all, that it merely put a new ideal before man, because man always had high ideals; he had Moses and the prophets, and had not listened to them. The divine grace of the Atonement consists in the imparting not of a new ideal but of a new power and energy to live up to the ideal. Man, in a word, cannot redeem himself; his redemption comes from God and is God's alone.

Now this "objective" view is exposed to the danger of forgetting that redemption must be the redemption of a will, the change of a will; and that in the last resort a will can only be changed by itself. If this is forgotten, the objective theory lapses into an abstract legalism according to which grace becomes a fictitious and conventional restoration to favor without any corresponding renovation of character. These two things must never be allowed to fall apart in such a way that the Atonement consists in one to the exclusion of the other; for unless the grace of God awakes a response in the will of man there is no true atonement. But this response is just the fact which this type of theory tends either to overlook or at least to describe with insufficient accuracy.

In examining actual theories of the Atonement, however, we must bear in mind that a verbal statement which appears to be one-sided does not necessarily either neglect or exclude the other side. The objective view is perfectly true so far as it goes; and the criticism often directed against it, on the ground that redemption is a matter of the individual will alone and must arise entirely from within, is due to a fallacious theory of personality.

(*b*) The "subjective" theory insists on the attitude of man to God, and lays down that since redemption involves an attitude or state of the subject's will it cannot without violence to his freedom be brought about by the act of another person, even if that other person be God. Grace as something merely proceeding from God is not only a hypothesis, but a useless hypothesis; the fact to be explained is the change, repentance, reformation of the individual, and this fact cannot be explained by reference to another's actions. Nobody can change my mind for me except myself. The question in short is not, what change has occurred in God?—since God is and always was long-suffering and merciful. It is rather, what difference has the life of Christ made in me? How has his example fired me to imitate him, his life challenged me to new effort, his love called forth love in me?

This view is attended by a parallel danger. It insists on the reality and inviolability of the individual; and the least overemphasis on this truth leads to the theory that no real help, no real stimulus, can pass over from one individual to another. In short, it brings us to the exclusive or individualistic theory of personality for which every person is a law to himself, supplies himself with his own standards of right and wrong, and draws upon his own resources in order to live up to them; for which the influence of one person on another is either impossible or—inconsistently with the theory—possible, but an "infringement of the rights" of the individual.

From such a point of view it might be replied to one who spoke of Christ's life on earth, "What good can it do? He lived nobly, you say, and died a martyr; but why should you tell me these things? I can only do what lies in my power; I cannot behave like a hero, being the man I am. It is useless for you to set up an ideal before me unless you can give me strength to live up to it. And the strength that I do not possess nobody can give me." And if the instructor goes on to expound the doctrine of grace and the indwelling of the Spirit of the Lord in his Church, the reply will be that these things are dreams, impossible from the very nature of personality, which is such that "one consciousness"—that of the Holy Spirit—"cannot include another"—that of an individual human being; or else that if these things are possible they involve an intolerable swamping of one's own personality, a surrender of one's freedom and individuality which can only be a morbid and unhealthy state of mind.

We have dealt with this individualistic theory elsewhere, and shall now only repeat that it implies the negation not merely of atonement in the sense of redemption of man whether by man, Christ, or God, but also of social life as a whole; and therefore it destroys by implication the very individual whose reality it hoped to vindicate. It presents us with the portrait of an ideal man who stands in no need of any external stimulus or assistance in working out his own salvation. If such a person existed, he would be independent of God and man alike, and would justly feel insulted by the offer of an atonement. But the portrait is untrue, not simply because no actual man ever attains this complete self-dependence, but rather because it is a false ideal; the perfect life for man is a life not of absolute isolation but of absolute communion. A man shows his greatness not in ignoring his surroundings but in understanding and assimilating them; and his debt to his environment is no loss to his individuality but a gain.

(*c*) It must be obvious by now that of the two theories sketched above, each is an abstraction; each emphasizes one side of a reality in which both sides are present and in which, as a matter of fact, both sides are one. The two sides must be united; but this cannot be effected by a compromise. A compromise is a middle path between two extremes, and includes neither. The combination at which we must aim will assert both theories to the full while avoiding the errors which alone keep them apart. As often happens in such cases, the two opposing theories are based on the same error, and a little further analysis will show wherein this error consists.

The danger of objectivism was to assume that grace could pass from God to man leaving man's inmost will untouched. The legalistic conception of grace depended on the separation of the human personality from the divine as two vessels, one of which might receive "content" from the other while its nature remained unaltered. The theory clings to the omnipotence of God and the fact that from him comes man's salvation, but conceives this omnipotence as God's power of imposing his own good will upon man. But this is no true redemption; the man's own will is merely superseded by, not unified with, the will of God. That is to say the good will which is manifested is solely God's and not in any sense man's. The human will is not redeemed but annihilated.

In order to avoid this conclusion subjectivism lays stress on the point which the above theory was led to deny, namely the fact that redemption is a free state of man's own will. It rightly asserts that whatever reform takes place in the character must be the work of the character itself, and cannot be thrust upon it by the operation of another. But it goes on to deny that redemption is in any sense the work of God, and to maintain that no act of God can have any influence on the moral destiny of man. Thus the conception of a divine will disappears altogether from the world of human morality.

The implication in each case seems to be the same; for to assert the will of God and deny man's inner redemption, or to assert man's redemption and deny the will of God, equally implies conceiving God's power and man's freedom to be inconsistent. This is the fallacy common to the two views. Each alike holds that a given action may be done either by God or by man, in either case the other being inactive. This separation of the will of God from that of man is fatal to any theory of the Atonement, where the fact to be explained is that man is redeemed not merely by his own act but also and essentially by God's.

A satisfactory theory of the Atonement seems to demand that the infusion of grace from God does not forcibly and artificially bring about but actually is a change of mind in man. It is an event which only co-operation of the various wills involved can effect at all. The error of the objective theory (or rather the error into which that way of stating the truth is most liable to fall) is to regard God as wholly active, man as wholly passive; and to forget that God's purpose of redemption is powerless apart from man's will to be redeemed.

The tendency of subjectivism on the other hand is to assume that the righteousness of man is independent of his relation to God; that man's will is sanctified by his own effort whether he is justified in the eyes of God or not. Here again the fault lies in the absolute separation of man from God. God is not realized as the one and only source of goodness; it is not understood that to will the right is to unify one's will with God's. The two things—righteousness and reconciliation with God—are really one and the same, and to represent one as means to the other or *vice versa,* or to insist on one and neglect the other, implies forgetting their identity and making an arbitrary and false separation of the two.

Neither is it enough merely to combine the two sides which the foregoing theories have separated. That would be to make the Atonement a combination of two different acts—God's forgiveness and man's repentance—of which each is peculiar to its own agent; it would fail to account for the essential unity of the whole process, and, taking the two sides as co-ordinate and equally vital, would substitute an unintelligible dualism for what is really one fact. In other words, any theory must show exactly how the forgiveness of God is related to the repentance of man, how it is possible for the one to bring about the other; and the dualistic view would be nothing more than a restatement of this central difficulty.

The failure of the theories hitherto examined has been in every case due to this distinction within the Atonement of two sides, God's and man's. Each agent, it is supposed, makes his own individual contribution to the whole process, God's contribution being the act of forgiveness, man's that of repentance. Now our previous analysis of the idea of co-operation suggests that this distinction needs revising. We found in a former chapter that in the co-operation of two wills we could only disentangle the respective contribution to the whole of each separate personality by an act of forcible and arbitrary abstraction; that in point of fact the two minds became identified in a common experience of which each willed the whole and neither a mere part. If we mean to apply this principle to the present difficulty, we must find a statement of the case which will no longer distinguish God's contribution from man's; which will enable us to say that God's punishment of man is man's own self-punishment, and that man's repentance is God's repentance too. If we can hold such a view we shall have identified the part played by God in redemption with that played by man; and we shall be able to define the Atonement, in terms consistent with our general theory, as the re-indwelling of the divine spirit in a man who has previously been alienated from it.

4. We have to make two identifications; first to show that God's punishment of man is man's punishment of himself, and second that man's repentance is God's repentance also.

The first point causes little difficulty after our examination of the meaning of punishment. We have already seen that the essence of punishment is the communication to the offender of our condemnation of his act; and that therefore all punishment consists in trying to make a criminal punish himself, that is inflict on himself the pain of remorse and conversion from his evil past to a better present. It is clear therefore without further explanation that in God's punishment of sin the sinner, through repentance, punishes his own sin. God's activity is shared by man too; man co-operates with God in punishing himself. And just as he punishes himself, he forgives himself, for he displays in repentance just that combination of severity toward the past and hope toward the future in which true forgiveness consists.

(*a*) The conception of divine repentance is at first sight less easy to grasp; but this is because we have not yet asked what is the precise nature of the experience to which we attach the name. We are in the habit of defining repentance as the conversion of an evil will to good; a condition only possible to one who has been sinful and is in process of renouncing his own sin. And if we accept this definition as final, we can only say that the conception of divine penitence is self-contradictory. Repentance is peculiar to a sinner; God is not a sinner, therefore he cannot feel repentance.

But we must ask whether the account offered of repentance is really satisfactory. Repentance is a particular state of mind, a feeling of a quite individual kind; and it is notoriously difficult to define a feeling in so many words. In point of fact, we generally give up the attempt, and substitute for a definition of the thing itself a description of the circumstances in which we feel it. If we are asked what we mean by the feelings of triumph, sorrow, indignation and so on, we reply as a rule by explaining the kind of occasion which excites them: "triumph is what you feel when you have succeeded in spite of opposition." But this is quite a different thing from stating what triumph feels like. This method of description is very common. We apply it for instance to such things as smells, for which we have practically no descriptive vocabulary. We generally define a scent not by its individual nature but by its associations; we state not what sort of smell it is but what it is the smell of.

Definition by circumstances (as we may call it) is apt to mislead us seriously in any attempt to describe our feelings. We think we have described the feeling when we have only described the occasions on which it arises; and since in consequence of this habit we apply names to feelings rather in virtue of their occasions than because of their own characters, we are often ready to assert *a priori* who can and who cannot experience a given emotion, merely on the ground that if such and such a person felt it we should call it something else.

In the case of repentance we are being misled by words if we argue that repentance is the conversion of a sinful will and therefore impossible to God. Repentance is a perfectly definite feeling with a perfectly definite character of its own: when we experience it, we recognize it as we recognize a smell, not because of any external circumstances but simply because of something which we may call its own peculiar flavor. In asking whether a sinless person feels repentance we must try to fix our minds on this flavor, not on its external associations.

We must notice that even the occasion of repentance has not

been very well described. Its occasion is not the mere abstract point of junction, so to speak, between two states, a bad state and a good state. We do not cease to repent when our will becomes good. Indeed if that were the case we should never repent at all; for the moment of transition from a bad will to a good is not a positive experience; it is the mere chink or joint between two experiences. Conversion is not a neutral moment between being bad and being good; it is a feeling set up by the inrush of positive goodness. Repentance, then, must be redefined by its circumstances as the peculiar feeling of a converted person toward his own evil past. A person only repents in so far as he is now good; repentance is necessarily the attitude of a good will. It does not precede conversion; it is the spirit of conversion.

If repentance is the feeling with which a person contemplates the evil past he has left behind him, the problem is to distinguish it from the feeling with which he, or any good person, contemplates the misdeeds of another. If we can maintain such a distinction, we cannot admit the reality of divine penitence.

Now if we look at the matter solely from the psychological point of view, if we simply reflect on the feeling with which we look at the sins we have ourselves committed, and compare it with our feeling toward the sins of others, we shall, I think, only find a difference in so far as one or other of these feelings is vitiated by our own limitations of knowledge or errors of attitude. In an ideal case, when we have struck the true balance between harshness and laxity of judgment, we feel to our own sins exactly as we feel to those of any other person. We do not feel sorry for our own sins and indignant at other people's; the sorrow and the indignation are both present in each case. A good man's feeling toward the sins of others is exactly the same kind of emotion as that which he feels toward his own. The fact that we call this feeling one of penitence when it regards himself and one of forgiveness (or punishment) when it regards others must not mislead us; for this is merely an example of the distinction according to circumstances of two emotions which when considered in themselves are seen to be one and the same.

But, it may be asked, can we really abstract emotions in this way from their circumstances? Is not any emotion simply the attitude of a will toward a particular event or reality? And if this is so, we are right in defining emotions by reference to their circumstances, because where circumstances differ there must be some difference in the state of mind which they evoke. The objection is perfectly sound; and our merely psychological argument must be reinforced by asking whether the circumstances in the two cases really are different. In the one case we have a good man's attitude toward the actions of his own evil past; in the other, his attitude toward another man who is doing evil now. The difference of time is plainly unimportant; we do not think differently of an action merely as it is present or past. The real question is the difference of person.

We must remember that, since a will is what it does, we cannot maintain that this good man is in every sense the same man who was bad. The bad will has been swept out of existence and its place taken by a good will; the man is, as we say, a new man; a new motive force lives in him and directs his actions. This does not mean that he is not "responsible" in his present state for the actions of his past. It means, if we must press the conclusion, not that he can shirk the responsibility for his own actions, but that he is bound to accept the responsibility for those of others; and this is no paradox if we rid the word of its legal associations and ask what moral meaning it can have. For to call a man responsible means that he ought to be punished, and the punishment, the sorrow, that a good man undergoes for his own sins he does certainly undergo for the sins of other men.

Thus God, who is perfectly good, must feel repentance for the sins of men; he bears in his own person the punishment which is their due, and by the communication to them of the spirit of his own penitence he leads them to repent, and so in self-punishment to work their own redemption. The divine and human sides, the objective and subjective, completely coincide. What God does man also does, and what man feels, God feels also.

(*b*) All human redemption thus comes from God, and is the rebirth in man's will of the original divine penitence. But in this immediate communication to man of the spirit of God, mediation is not excluded. In one sense, all right acting and true knowing involves utterly unmediated communion of the soul with God. As Elisha lay upon the dead child, his mouth upon his mouth, and his eyes upon his eyes, and his hands upon his hands, till the child came to life again, so the soul is quickened by complete, immediate contact with God, every part at once with every part. But though we know God directly or not at all, we yet know him only as revealed to us through various channels of illumination and means of grace. The mystic who dwells alone with God is only a mystic through social influences and the stimulus of his surroundings, and in his union with the divine mind he is united no less with all the community of living spirits.

So repentance comes not only from God but through paths which in a sense we distinguish from the activity of God. Every truth is reached through some stimulus or instruction which comes from a source in the world around us; and in the same way repentance reaches us through human channels, and we repent of our sins because we see others repent of them. This is human vicarious penitence; others suffer for our sins, the suffering being not a mere "natural consequence" of the sin but specifically sorrow, penitence, that is, punishment for it; and their suffering is literally the means of grace for us, the influence by which we come to our own repentance.

But this universal fact of human life is, like all others, summed up and expressed most completely in the divine manhood of the Christ. He alone is always and perfectly penitent; for a sinful man cannot, while sinful, repent for his own sins or any others; permanent penitence is only possible for a permanently sinless mind. And this repentance of Christ is not only subjectively complete, that is, unbroken by sins of his own, but objectively perfect also; it is incapable of supplement or addition, sufficient to atone for the sins of the whole world, to convert all sinners by the spectacle of God's suffering. No further example could add anything to its force. There is only one way of destroying sin; namely, to convert the sinner. And there is only one way of converting the sinner; namely, to express to him, in such a way that he cannot but realize it, the attitude toward himself of a good will, the attitude which unites condemnation and forgiveness in the concrete reality of vicarious repentance.

Thus the supreme example of sinless suffering is the salvation of the world; final in the sense that nothing can be added to it, that every new repentance is identical with it; not final, but only initial, in the sense that by itself it is nothing without the response it should awake, the infinite reproduction of itself in the consciousness of all mankind. It is not merely an example set up for our imitation; not merely a guarantee of the possibilities of human life. It is an unfailing source and fountain of spiritual energy; it gives to those who would imitate it the strength to work miracles, to cast aside their old selves and to enter upon a new life prepared from the beginning of the world; for out of it power goes forth to draw all men to itself.

THE DEVIL

"From the crafts and assaults of the Devil, good Lord, deliver us." So we pray; and the prayer certainly answers our need. We feel ourselves surrounded by powers of evil, from which we want to be defended, and the desire expresses itself in the form of a petition for help against the Devil. But most people who have responded to the prayer must have asked themselves how much more than this they meant; whether they believed in a Devil at all, and if so what they imagined him to be like. There is no doubt that common belief has long been tending more and more to discard the idea of a Devil; and yet the idea is orthodox. Does this mean that modern thought is drifting away from orthodox Christianity? Is the disbelief in a Devil only part of that vague optimism, that disinclination to believe in anything evil, that blind conviction of the stability of its own virtue and the perfection of its own civilization, which seems at times to be the chief vice of the modern world?

In part this is so. And a world rudely awakened once more to the conviction that evil is real may come again to believe in a Devil. But if it returns to the same belief which it has gradually been relinquishing, the step will be retrograde. For that belief was neither fully orthodox nor fully true. Orthodox Christianity believes in a Devil who is, as it were, the bad child in God's family; the "Devil" in whom people of today are coming to disbelieve owes much if not all of his character to the Manichaean fiction of an evil power over against God and struggling with Him for the dominion over man's soul. It may seem surprising that popular thought should confuse Manichaeism with orthodoxy; and it certainly is surprising that theologians should so seldom come forward to correct the mistake. But it is hard for the uninstructed to follow technical theology, and it is perhaps equally hard for the theologian to follow the obscure workings of the uninstructed mind.

Reprinted from B. F. Streeter, ed., *Concerning Prayer* (London: Macmillan & Co., 1916).

It is clear then that the vital question is not, does the Devil exist? but rather, what conception have we of the Devil? Unless we first answer this question it will not be certain whether the spirit into whose existence we are enquiring is the orthodox or Manichaean or indeed any other devil. Further, it is important to determine in what sense we believe in him. A man may, for instance, believe in Our Lord in the sense of believing what history tells us about Him, but yet not believe in Him, in the sense of not believing in His spiritual presence in the Church. So one might believe in the Devil in the sense that one accepts the story of Lucifer as historical, or in the sense that one believes in Lucifer as an evil force now present in the world, and so forth.

This way of proceeding may be called the critical method; and it is this which will be adopted in the present essay. But much popular thought on the subject is of a different kind. It concerns itself immediately with the question, does the devil exist? without first asking these other questions; and the method it adopts is "scientific" in the popular sense of the word, that is, inductive. It proceeds by searching for "evidence" of the Devil's existence; and this evidence is nowadays drawn chiefly from psychology. As the eighteenth century found the evidences of religion chiefly in the world of nature, so the present generation tends to seek them in the mind of man; but the argument is in each case of the same kind.

This psychological argument plays such an important part in popular thought that we must begin by reviewing it; otherwise every step in our criticism will be impeded by the protest that an ounce of fact is worth a ton of theory, and that, however we may theorize, there are facts, positive facts, which prove the existence of the Devil.

Let us then begin by considering these facts; not *in extenso,* for they would fill many volumes and could only be collected by much labor, but in a few typical instances, in order to see what kind of conclusion they yield. The evidence is no doubt cumulative, like all evidence; but a sample will show in what direction, if any, the accumulation tends.

The two most striking groups of evidence may be described as obsessions and visions. By "obsession" I mean not the morbid phenemena of demoniacal possession, or the *"idée fixe"* of mania, but the sense of the merging of one's own personality in a greater and more powerful self, the feeling that one is overwhelmed and carried away not by impulses within but by the resistless force of another will. This feeling is extremely common in all religious experience. The saint feels himself passive in the hands of God. "This is a trait" (says Höffding, *Philosophy of Religion,* § 28) "very frequently found in mystics and pietists; the more they retain (or believe themselves to retain) their powers of thought and will, the more they tend to attribute to their inmost experiences a divine origin." Höffding's parenthesis looks almost like a suggestion that the feeling only occurs in persons whose will is really in process of decay. But if the suggestion is intended, it is quite indefensible. The weak man, like Shakespeare's Henry VI, may have this feeling; but St. Paul had it even more strongly, and he was certainly not a weak man.

This feeling of obsession by a divine power is in fact only an extreme form of the sensation, which everybody knows, that we are surrounded by spiritual forces which by suggestion or other means influence our wills for good. And the same feeling, both in its rudimentary and extreme forms, exists with regard to evil forces. Children come quite naturally to believe in good and bad angels which draw them in different directions; and this belief may pass through all stages of intensity until we think of our own personality, not as a free will balancing and choosing between suggestions presented to it by angels of light and darkness, but as shrunk to a vanishing point, the moment of impact between two gigantic and opposed forces. Man becomes the merely sentient battlefield of God and Satan.

The case which immediately concerns us is that of the soul overwhelmed by a spirit of evil; and this is equally familiar to psychology. As the saint represents himself the passive instrument of God, so the sinner feels that he is the passive instrument of the Devil. The saint says with St. Paul: "I live, and yet not I but Christ liveth in me." The sinner replies, from the same source: "It is no more I that do it, but Sin that dwelleth in me."

Here, then, is the first group of evidence for the existence of the Devil; and we must try to determine what it is worth. It will be noticed that the same type of experience serves as evidence in one case for the existence of the Devil, and in the other for the existence of God. We believe in the Devil (it is suggested) because we immediately experience his power over our hearts; and we believe in God for the same kind of reason. But psychology itself, which collects for us the evidence, warns us against this uncritical use of it. It may be that the whole feeling is a morbid and unhealthy one; or it may be that in one case it is natural and healthy, and in the other unnatural and morbid. Psychology can describe the feelings which people actually do have; but it cannot tell us whether the feelings are good or bad, trustworthy or misleading, sanity or mania. Telepathy, self-hypnotism, subconscious cerebration, force of education or environment—these and a thousand other explanations are from time to time adopted; and each is, within the limits of psychology, possible, none certain. In point of fact, the psychologist takes whichever view for the moment suits him as a working hypothesis, but the supposed explanation is never more than this, and is generally much less. So the really vital point in the argument is a gap which can only be bridged by the gossamers of flimsiest speculation.

The second group of evidence appears at first sight more conclusive. The visions of God, of Our Lord, of angels and of saints which are found in all types of Christianity (and similar visions seem to occur in all other religions) are parallel to visions, no less authentic, of fiends and demons and of the Devil himself.[1] These

1. It is not necessary to encumber the text with instances of such familiar experiences; but I should like to refer here, since it has only appeared in a review, to the case of a Roman Catholic priest, described in a series of his own letters in the *British Review,* I, No. 2 (April 1913), 71-95. "On one occasion, when I had retired for the night, a being appeared who addressed me using the most vile language and rehearsing for me in a terrible manner many incidents in my past life. . . . I jumped up and ran at it, making a large Cross in the air, when the figure melted away like smoke, leaving a smell as if a gun had been discharged. . . . When it reappeared I began to recite sentences of the exorcism, and it seemed to me that when I came to the more forcible portions of it the voice grew less distinct. As I proceeded and also made use of holy water the voice died away in a sort of moan. . . . The voice claimed to be that of Lucifer."

sensational forms of religious experience often seem to carry special weight as evidence of the reality of spirits other than our own; but here too the whole argument turns on their interpretation. Are they, in the language of popular philosophy, "subjective" or "objective"?

In order to analyze this question, an attempt is sometimes made to analyze them with a view to discovering what they owe to tradition, to the education or surroundings of the person who sees them. Thus it is found that a vision of the Devil is accompanied by a smell of brimstone, and that one's patron saint appears in the clothes which he wears in the window of one's parish church. But these details prove exactly what the interpreter chooses to make them prove. To the simple, they are corroborative; they prove that the apparition is genuine. To the subtler critic they are suspicious; they suggest that the alleged vision is a merely "subjective" reproduction of traditional images. But the critic is at least no better off than the simple believer. For if my patron saint wishes to appear to me, why should he not choose to appear in a form in which I can recognize him? And if I see the Devil and smell brimstone, may not the coincidence with tradition be due to the fact that when the Devil appears he really does smell of brimstone?

Thus the discussion as to the subjective or objective nature of these visions is involved in an endless obscurity, and whatever answer is given depends on a private interpretation of the facts, which is at once challenged by the opponent. Psychology can collect accounts of visions; but to decide whether they are real or illusory is outside its power. Such a decision can only be reached in the light of critical principles which psychology itself cannot establish. There is nothing in a vision itself, and therefore there is nothing in a thousand visions, to guarantee its truth or falsity; and therefore the uncritical use of such things as evidence is no more than a delusion.

There is, however, a second and less crude method of using psychological data. How, it is asked, do we account for the existence of all the world's evil? We are conscious in ourselves of solicitations and temptations to sin; and even if we are not in these temptations directly conscious of the personal presence of a tempter, we cannot account for their existence except by assuming that he is real. We do not, according to this argument, claim direct personal knowledge of the Devil, but we argue to his reality from the facts of life. There must be a Devil, because there is so much evil in the world. We know that our own sins make others sin, and it seems only reasonable to suppose that our sins may in turn be due to an arch-sinner, whose primal sin propagates itself in the wills of those who come under his malign influence.

Everything, we believe, must have a cause; and in assigning it to its cause we have, so far as we can ever hope to do so, explained it. A thing whose cause we have not discovered is, we say, unexplained, and one which has no cause is inexplicable; but we refuse to believe that anything is in the long run inexplicable. Evil then—so we argue—must have a cause; and the cause of evil in me can only be some other evil outside myself. And therefore we postulate a Devil as the First Cause of all evil, just as we postulate a God as the First Cause of all good.

But the parallel here suggested is entirely misleading. God and the Devil are not twin hypotheses which stand or fall together. God, as present to the religious mind, is not a hypothesis at all; He is not a far-fetched explanation of phenomena. He is about our path and about our bed; we do not search the world for traces of His passing by, or render His existence more probable by scientific inductions. Philosophy may demand a proof of His existence, as it may demand a proof of the existence of this paper, of the philosopher's friends or of the philosopher himself; but the kind of certainty which the religious mind has of God is of the same kind as that which we have of ourselves and of other people, and not in any way similar to the gradually strengthening belief in a hypothesis. The two kinds of belief must not be confused. I do not consider the existence of another mind like my own as a highly probable explanation of the voice I hear in conversation with a friend; to describe my belief in such terms would be entirely to misrepresent its real nature. The Devil may be a hypothesis, but God is not; and if we find reason for rejecting the above argument for the reality of the Devil we have not thereby thrown any doubt on the reality of God.

The belief in a Devil is supposed to be a hypothesis. But is it a good hypothesis? Does it explain the facts?

There are two questions to which we may require an answer. First, how do I come to think of this sin as a possible thing to do? Secondly, why do I desire to do it? To the first question the hypothesis does supply an answer: but no answer is really needed. My own faculties are sufficient, without any diabolical instruction, to discover that on a given occasion I might do wrong if I would.

To the second and much more important question the hypothesis of a Devil supplies no answer at all; and to conceal this deficiency it raises two other questions, each equally hard, and each in point of fact only a new form of the original problem. If evil can only be explained by postulating a Devil, in the first place, what explains the sins of the Devil himself? Secondly, granted that there is a Devil, why do people do what he wants them to do? The first of these questions is not answered by saying that the Devil's sin is a First Cause and needs no explanation; that is, that it was the uncaused act of a free being. The same is obviously true of our own actions; and it was only because this account of them seemed insufficient that we felt compelled to postulate a Devil. But if it is insufficient in our case, how can we guarantee its sufficiency in his?

The other question is even more unanswerable. If the Devil, by some compulsive power, forces us to act in certain ways, then these acts are not our acts, and therefore not our sins; and if he only induces us to act, the question is, why do we let ourselves be induced? If there is a Devil who wants me to do something wrong, his desire is impotent until I choose to fall in with it. And therefore his existence does nothing whatever to explain my sin. The hypothesis of a Devil explains nothing; and if the fact which it is meant to explain, the fact of evil, requires an explanation, then the Devil himself requires an explanation of the same kind.

The truth is that evil neither requires nor admits any explanation whatever. To the question, "Why do people do wrong?" the only answer is, "Because they choose to." To a mind obsessed by the idea of causation, the idea that everything must be explained by something else, this answer seems inadequate. But action is precisely that which is not caused; the will of a person acting determines itself and is not determined by anything outside itself. Causation has doubtless its proper sphere. In certain studies it may be true, or true enough for scientific purposes, to describe one event as entirely due to another. But if the Law of Causation is a good servant, it is a bad master. It cannot be applied to the activity of the will without explicitly falsifying the whole nature of that activity. An act of the will is its own cause and its own explanation; to seek its explanation in something else is to treat it not as an act but as a mechanical event. It is hardly surprising that such a quest should end in a confusion greater than that in which it began. Evil, like every other activity of free beings, has its source and its explanation within itself alone. It neither needs nor can be explained by the invocation of a fictitious entity such as the Devil.

In the absence of any results from the method of evidence and hypothesis, we must turn to the only other alternative, the simpler though perhaps more difficult method described above as the method of criticism. Instead of asking whether or not the Devil exists, we must ask what we understand by the Devil, and whether that conception is itself a possible and reasonable one. When we have answered these questions we shall perhaps find that the other has answered itself.

To this critical procedure it may be objected at the outset that the method is illegitimate; for it implies the claim to conceive things which in their very nature are inconceivable. Infinite good and infinite evil are, it is said, beyond the grasp of our finite minds; we cannot conceive God, and therefore neither can we conceive the Devil. To limit infinity within the circle of a definition is necessarily to falsify it; any attempt at conception can only lead to misconception.

Even if this objection were justified, instead of being based on a false theory of knowledge, it would not really affect our question. If the Devil is inconceivable, then we have no conception of him, or only a false one; and there is an end of the matter. But anyone who maintains his existence does claim to have a conception of him;

he uses the word Devil and presumably means something by it. The objection, if used on behalf of a believer in the Devil, would be no more than a confession that he attaches no meaning to the word and therefore does not believe in a Devil at all. So far as he does believe, his belief is a conception and can therefore be criticized.

Now the idea of God as an omnipotent and entirely good being is certainly conceivable. It is possible to imagine a person who possessed all the power in existence, who could do everything there was to be done, and who did everything well. Whether this conception can be so easily reconciled with others, we do not ask; we are only examining the idea itself. Further, it is an essential element in the conception of God that He should be not perfectly good alone, but also the sole and absolute source of goodness; that He should will not only good but all the good there is. Now it is essential to grasp the fact that whether such a will as this is conceivable or not depends on whether good things are all compatible with one another, or whether one good thing may exclude, contradict, or compete with another good thing. If they are all compatible, if the "Law of Contradiction," that no truth can contradict another truth, applies *mutatis mutandis* to the sphere of morality, then all individual good things are parts of one harmonious scheme of good which might be the aim of a single perfectly good will. If, on the other hand, one good thing is incompatible with another, it follows that they are not parts of a single whole, but essentially in conflict with one another, and that therefore the same will cannot include, that is cannot choose, all at once. For instance, granted that A and B cannot both have a thing, if it is right that A should have it and also right that B should have it, God cannot will all that is good; for one mind can only choose one of two contradictory things.

It seems to be a necessary axiom of ethics that on any given occasion there can only be one duty. For duty means that which a man ought to do; and it cannot conceivably be a duty to do something impossible.[2] Therefore if I have two duties at the same time,

2. It is sometimes perhaps a duty to *try* to do an impossible thing. But in that case the claims of duty are satisfied by the attempt; and to attempt the impossible is not necessarily itself impossible.

it must be possible for me to do both. They cannot contradict one another, for then one would be impossible and therefore not obligatory. There can be a "conflict of duties" only in the sense that from two different points of view each of two incompatible things seems to be my duty; the conflict disappears when I determine which point of view ought to be for the moment supreme. This does not mean that there is a greater duty which overrides the less; for the distinction between doing and not doing, and between "ought to do" and "ought not to do," is not a question of degree. The one is simply my duty, and the other not my duty. No doubt the latter might have been my duty in a different situation; and it is often distressing to see what good things we might have done if the situation, created perhaps by our own or another's folly, had not demanded something else. But here again there are not two duties; there is one and only one, together with the knowledge that in other conditions some other duty would have taken its place.

If it is true that my duty can never contradict itself, it is equally true that my duty cannot contradict anyone else's. A may feel it is his duty to promote a cause which B feels it right to resist; but clearly in this case one must be mistaken. Their countries may be at war, and they may be called upon by the voice of duty to fight each other; but one country—perhaps both—must be in the wrong. It is possibly a duty to fight for one's country in a wrongful cause; but if that is so it is one's duty not to win but to atone in some degree for the national sin by one's own death.

A real duty, and therefore a real good, is a good not for this or that man, but for the whole world. If it is good, morally good, that A should have a thing, it is good for B that A should have it. Thus all moral goods are compatible, and they are therefore capable of being all simultaneously willed by a single mind. So far, then, the idea of God seems to be a consistent and conceivable notion. Is the same true of the idea of the Devil?

The Devil is generally regarded as being not only entirely bad, but the cause of all evil: the absolute evil will, as God is the absolute good will. But a very little reflection shows that this is impossible. Good cannot contradict good, just as truth cannot contradict truth; but two errors may conflict, and so may two crimes. Two good men can only quarrel in so far as their goodness is fragmentary and incomplete; but there is no security that two absolutely bad men would agree. The reverse is true; they can only agree so far as they set a limit to their badness, and each undertakes not to thwart and cheat the other. Every really good thing in the world harmonizes with every other; but evil is at variance not only with good but with other evils. If two thieves quarrel over their plunder, a wrong is done whichever gets it, but no one Devil can will both these wrongs. The idea of a Devil as a person who wills all actual and possible evil, then, contradicts itself, and no amount of psychological evidence or mythological explanation can make it a conceivable idea.

Our first notion of the Devil must be given up. But we might modify it by suggesting that the Devil does not will that either thief should get the plunder; he desires not our success in evil projects, but simply our badness. He incites the two to fight out of pure malice, not with any constructive purpose but simply in order to make mischief. That one thief should succeed prevents the other thief from succeeding; but there is nothing in the mere badness of the one incompatible with the mere badness of the other. And the badness of each is quite sufficiently shown in the attempt, whether successful or not, to defraud the other.

This brings us to a different conception of the Devil as a person who does, not all the evil there is, but all the evil he can. He is an opportunist; when thieves can do most harm by agreeing, he leads them to agree; when by quarreling, he incites them to quarrel. He may not be omnipotent in evil; whatever evil he brings about is at the expense of other possible ills; but at least he is consistently wicked and never does anything good. Is this second idea more conceivable than the first? In order to answer this question we must enquire briefly into the character and conditions of the evil will.

There are two well-established and popular accounts of evil, neither of which is entirely satisfactory. Sometimes evil is said to be the mere negation of good; nothing positive, but rather a deficiency of that which alone is positive, namely goodness; more commonly good and evil are represented as different and opposed forces.

The first view contains elements of real truth, and is supported by such great names as that of Augustine, who was led, in his reaction from Manichaeism, to adopt it as expressing the distinctively Christian attitude toward evil.

This view is generally criticized by pointing out that as evil is the negation of good, so good is the negation of evil; either is positive in itself but negative in relation to the other. This criticism is valid as against the verbal expression of the theory, though it does not touch the inner meaning which the theory aims at expressing. But unless this inner meaning is thought out and developed with much more care than is generally the case, the view of evil as merely negative expresses nothing but a superficial optimism, implying that any activity is good if only there is enough of it, that only small and trivial things can be bad, and (in extreme forms of the theory) that evil is only evil from a limited and human point of view, whereas to a fuller and more comprehensive view it would be non-existent. These sophistical conclusions are so plainly untenable that they force the mind to take refuge in the opposite view.

Good and evil, according to this view, are different and opposed forces. If the opposition is imagined as existing between an absolute good will and an absolute bad (as for instance in Manichaeism) we have already shown that it cannot be maintained, for an absolute bad will is inconceivable. The crude antithesis of Manichaeism therefore gives place to a different kind of opposition, such as that between body and soul, desire and reason, matter and spirit, egoism and altruism, and so on *ad infinitum*. To criticize these in detail would be tedious; it is perhaps enough to point out the fallacy which underlies all alike. That which acts is never one part of the self; it is the whole self. It is impossible to split up a man into two parts and ascribe his good actions to one part—his soul, his reason, his spirit, his altruistic impulses—and his bad actions to another. Each action is done by him, by his one indivisible will. Call that will anything you like; say that his self is desire, and you must distinguish between right desires and wrong desires; say that it is spirit, and you must add that spirit may be good or bad. The essence of his good acts is that he might have done a bad one: the essence of his bad, that he—the same he—might have done a good. It is impossible to distinguish between any two categories one of which is necessarily bad and the other necessarily good. We constantly try to do so; we say, for instance, that it is wrong to yield to passion and right to act on principle. But either we beg the question by surreptitiously identifying passion with that which is wrong and principle with that which is right, or we must confess that passions may well be right and that principles are very often wrong. The moral struggle is not a struggle between two different elements in our personality; for two different elements, just so far as they are different, cannot ever cross each other's path. What opposes desires for evil is not reason, but desires for good. What opposes egoism—a false valuation of oneself—is not altruism, but, as Butler long ago pointed out, a higher egoism, a true valuation of oneself.

Evil, and therefore the Devil, is not a mere negation, not the shadow cast by the light of goodness. Nor is it identical with matter, body, desire, or any other single term of a quasi-Manichaean antithesis. It is something homogeneous with good, and yet not good; neither the mere absence of goodness nor the mere presence of its opposite. We do evil not through lack of positive will, nor yet because we will something definitely and obviously different from good. The first alternative breaks down because doing wrong is a real activity of the will; the second because doing wrong for the sake of wrong, if it happens at all, is a very small part of the evil that actually exists.

It is surely the case that the immense majority of crimes are done under a kind of self-deception. We persuade ourselves that this act, which is generally considered a crime, is really when properly understood, or when seen in the light of our peculiar circumstances, a fine and praiseworthy act. Such a plea is not in itself wrong. It is a duty, indeed it is the spring of all moral advance, to criticize current standards of morality and to ask whether this may not be a case where the current rule fails to apply. But though this criticism is not necessarily wrong but is the very essence of right action, it is not necessarily right but is the very essence of evil. To set oneself against current beliefs and practices is the central characteristic of all heroes, and it is equally the central characteristic of all criminals; of Christ and of Lucifer. The difference is not psychological; it is not that the hero has noble and exalted sentiments while the criminal gives way to ignoble and debased passions. The essence of crime is the pride of Lucifer, the feeling of nobility and exaltation, of superiority to convention and vulgar prejudice. When we do wrong, we believe, or persuade ourselves, that the opinion which is really the right one, really the expression of moral truth, is a mere fiction or convention; and we represent ourselves as rebels and martyrs for a noble cause.

It may be that some crimes have not this characteristic. At times, perhaps, we act wrongly in the clear understanding that we are doing wrong, while still attaching the right meaning to that word. But when we say, "I know it is wrong, but I intend to do it," we generally mean by "wrong" that which is commonly called wrong; wrong in public opinion, but to our own superior understanding right. Or, what is really the same thing, we admit that it is "morally wrong" but hold that it has a value other than, and transcending, that of morality; a meaningless phrase if we recollect that morality is simply that kind of value which actions possess, so that to judge them by another standard is impossible. Any other standard we apply is morality under another name.[3]

The essence of evil, then, is that it should set itself up not in opposition, open and proclaimed, to good as good; but that it should set itself up to be the good, standing where it ought not in the holy place and demanding that worship which is due to good alone. Evil is not the absence of good nor yet the opposite of good; it is the counterfeit of good.[4]

3. People say, for instance, "So-and-so ought to think less about morality, and more about his neighbors' happiness," or the like. But this language means that to consult his neighbors' happiness is a moral duty which So-and-so has been neglecting. Here, as in the similar case of polemics against "morality," the word is misused for "that which people wrongly imagine to be morality." Those writers who expect or exhort mankind to develop into a life beyond good and evil do not quite realize that they regard it as a *good* thing to be "beyond good and evil." To believe that any standard is the right one to act upon implies believing, or rather is believing, that it is a moral standard.

4. It goes without saying that counterfeit goods or false ideals, like true ones, are seldom the peculiar property of any one individual; they are often,

Now if this is so, it follows that nobody can be entirely and deliberately bad. To be enslaved by a counterfeit of goodness we must know goodness itself; there must be an element of real good in a will before it can ever become evil. And that element of good persists throughout, and is the basis of all hopes of redemption. The force and life of evil comes from the positive experience of good which underlies the evil, which alone makes evil possible. Therefore the Devil, just as he cannot will all the evil there is, cannot be fundamentally and perfectly wicked; he is not a wicked angel but a fallen angel, preserving in his fall the tattered remnants of the glory that was his, to be at once the foundation and the abatement of his badness. It is this contradiction in the nature of the evil will that Dante has in mind when, coming to the center and heart of the Inferno, he finds its lord not triumphant, not proud and happy in his kingdom, but inconsolably wretched.

> Con sei occhi piangeva, e per tre menti
> Gocciava 'l pianto e sanguinosa bava.[5]

And Milton knows that Satan's mind, in the thought of lost

---

though of course not necessarily, common to a family or class or sex or nation. This fact has, however, no bearing on the point at issue, and is only quoted here because of a false value very often attached to it. The ideals I act on are, wherever I get them from, mine; that they should happen to be shared by others is irrelevant. But, it is said, I get them as a matter of fact from others; I have them because others have them; the influence of a corrupt public opinion is of the utmost importance in any concrete account of the evil will. This language is so common that it is worthwhile to point out the fallacy it contains. It is another instance of a fictitious entity (in this case "Society") posing as the "explanation" of evil. The alleged explanation contains (1) a vicious circle and (2) a fatal gap. (1) "Society" consists of Tom, Dick, and Harry: if I "get my ideals" from them, where do they "get" theirs from? Presumably from me, unless it is supposed that ideals never change at all, but are simply transmitted *en bloc* from generation to generation. (2) If other people's ideals are bad, they may on that account equally well reproduce themselves in me, or rouse me to reject them. Man's relation to his moral environment is just as much negative as affirmative; and therefore no detail of his moral character can ever be explained by reference to such environment.

5. *Inferno,* canto xxxiv, lines 53-54. "With six eyes he wept, and down three chins trickled his tears and blood-stained slaver." Stained, that is, with the blood of the traitors whose limbs he was mangling.

happiness and lasting pain, was filled with torments of huge affliction and dismay, confounded though immortal.[6]

In these and kindred accounts of the Devil we recognize a very real and profound truth. But of what kind is this truth? Is it a true portrait of an actual, historical person called Lucifer or Satan who at some time in the remote past rose against God and set himself up as leader of an angelic rebellion? Or is it the true description of a real spirit who, whatever his past history, lives and rules the forces of evil now? Or lastly, is its truth mythical truth? Is Satan simply the type of all evil wills?

In answer to the first of these questions we can only say that such a thing may well have happened. There may have been, at some definite time in the past, war in heaven, Michael and his angels fighting against the dragon and his angels. We know of countless people who have at various times set up false ideals of truth and of right, and have worshipped those false gods, instead of the true God. And it may be that there was once a person, not a human being but a being of some kind, whose rebellion was of surpassing magnitude and weight, like Arianism among the Christian heresies; and that his name has somehow come down to us as Lucifer. If this is presented as mere history it is not possible to prove or disprove it. But in speaking of the fall of Lucifer do we really mean this, and only this?

It would appear that we mean both more and less. Less, because we hardly believe that Lucifer's fall took place at any actual date. It was "before the beginning of the world"; it has no definite place in our time series. To ask its date seems incongruous, not because we have no evidence for dating it, but because we do not regard it as quite an event in history. But we also mean more; for we regard Lucifer or the Devil not as a character in past history only, a pretender like Perkin Warbeck, but as a spiritual force about us here and now. His fall is somehow repeated and represented, not merely imitated, in the apparition and collapse of any great force working for evil. There may have been a historical Lucifer,

6. *Paradise Lost,* Book I.

but it is not he, it is no historical person simply as such, of whom we speak as the Devil.

Is he then the supreme evil power? Is he the Manichaean anti-God whose spirit informs the communion of sinners as the Holy Spirit informs the communion of saints? No, for we have already seen that there can be no supreme power which directs and controls all the forces of evil. That army is one without discipline, without a leader; the throne of the kingdom of evil is empty, and its government is anarchy. Evil wills exist, but they owe no allegiance to any supreme spirit. They worship evil, they worship the Devil; but their worship is idolatry because they themselves create its god. If the Devil were a real ruler, then worship of him would be within its limits a true religion; but it is false religion, the worship of a phantom.

It remains that we should regard the Devil as a myth. This does not mean that the descriptions of him are untrue, or that they are the product of that fancy whose creations are neither true nor false but merely imaginary. A myth is capable of, and is judged by, a certain kind of truth. Mythology is to the naïve consciousness a form of history; the myth of Herakles to a simple-minded Greek was the biography of a real person. But, as such, it was false. Mythology does not contain historical truth, though it presents itself in a historical form. The truth it contains may perhaps be described as typical truth. Herakles is the type of all strong men who devote their strength to the bettering of human life; and the truth of the myth lies precisely in this, that the story truly presents the real character of the type. This is the difference between mythology and art, the work of the imagination. The mythical person is never quite an individual. He is always something of an abstraction, a type rather than a person. In art, on the other hand, the person is not a type but an individual. Hamlet is not typical of any class of men, as Herakles is; he is simply his unique self. An art which forgets the individual and presents the type, an art which generalizes, has forgotten its artistic mission and has become mythology.

The Devil is in this sense a myth. He rebels against God and sets himself up for worship, because all evil is rebellion against the true good and the worship of false ideals, of counterfeit goods, of idols. He rules over the kingdom of darkness, and yet his rule is only a mockery, because there is no real unity in evil, though there is a fictitious and spurious unity. He is a laughing-stock to the saints, because evil once seen as evil has no more power over the mind; it only controls those who worship it, who reverence it as good. He torments souls in hell, and is himself tormented, because the evil will is divided against itself and can never reach the unity and harmony which alone characterize the good. His strength lies in his infinite disguises; he comes in countless alluring forms, which at the word of power vanish leaving his own naked horror of impotent rage, because evil is never seen as evil by its worshipers; they clothe it in all the forms of beauty and sincerity and virtue, which must be torn away by the wind of truth leaving the idolater face to face with the reality of the thing he has worshiped till he turns from it in loathing. Christian demonology is a storehouse of observations, not as to the life history of a single Devil or even of many devils, but as to the nature, growth, and development of the evil will.

Are there, then, no spiritual forces which influence man for evil? Are the malign spirits which surround us with temptations a mere mythological description of our own inner wickedness?

There certainly are spiritual forces of evil. But by "spiritual" we do not necessarily mean other than human; still less do we refer to a class of ambiguous beings sometimes physical and sometimes "dematerialized"; the "spirits" of vulgar superstition. There may be personal minds other than those we know as God, man, and the lower animals; and if so, they are doubtless good or bad. But, as we saw, no such beings need be postulated to account for human sin; nor would they account for it, if they existed. The spirits whose evil we know are human spirits; and the forces of evil with which we are surrounded are the sins of this human world. The Devil is an immanent spirit of evil in the heart of man, as God is an immanent spirit of goodness. But there is this great difference, that God is transcendent also, a real mind with a life of His own, while the Devil is purely immanent, that is, considered as a person, non-existent.

Nor is it even entirely true to say that the Devil is immanent.

For that would imply that evil is a principle one and the same in all evil acts; and this it cannot be, for while good acts all form part of one whole of goodness, evil acts have no parallel unity. There is no communion of sinners; they live not in communion with one another, but in mutual strife. There is not one immanent Devil, but countless immanent devils, born in a moment and each in a moment dying to give place to one another, or else to that re-entering spirit of good which is always one and the same.

The devils within us are our own evil selves. But this does not mean that they cannot come, in a sense, from without. When one man infects another with his own badness, it is quite literal truth to say that a devil goes from one to the other; and there may be a kind of unity, a kind of momentary kingdom of evil, when the same devil seizes upon a large number of people and they do in a crowd things which no man would do by himself. There may even be a more lasting kingdom where an institution or a class keeps alive for generations a false ideal. And since evil influences may affect us from books, from places, from the weather, we tend naturally to think of devils as inhabiting these things. Are we here back again in mythology? There really is a devil—a spirit of evil—in a bad person; is there one, in the same sense, in a wood or in the east wind?

It is a difficult question to answer, since it depends on how far each of these things has a self, and how far the selfhood which to us it seems to have is really conferred upon it by our own thought. To us the east wind is a definite thing; and so to us it can be a devil. But is it a definite thing to itself? Is the influence it exerts upon us its own influence, or is it only the reflection of our own nature? Perhaps it is best to leave the question open. There may be devils in places and in things which we generally regard as inanimate; but those which we know exist in the human mind. Of these the Devil of orthodoxy is a type or myth; a myth not in the colloquial sense in which the word means a fiction or illusion, but in the proper sense which we have explained above. And the truth of the orthodox belief consists in the fact that it does with perfect accuracy describe the real nature of the evil will. But as soon as the mythical nature of the belief is forgotten, as soon as the Devil is taken not as a type of all evil wills but as their actual supreme ruler, then the step has been taken from truth to superstition, from Christianity to Manichaeism.

How does all this affect the theory and practice of prayer? "The Devil" in any given case is simply the person who is sinning; the wickedness into which he has made himself. Therefore devil-worship is first and primarily self-worship. Self-worship is not necessarily bad; the "religion of humanity" may mean the worship of God as revealed in and through human goodness. But in that case it is not mere self-worship, but the worship of the God immanent in ourselves. Worship of the self pure and simple must always be devil-worship, for it is only the bad self that can be called self pure and simple. The good self is always something more than self; it is self informed and directed by the spirit of God. Man is only alone in the world when he has expelled the spirit of God from his heart and lives a life of evil; for there is no great central power of evil upon which he can then depend as in the alternative case he depends on God. The vacant sanctuary can only be filled with an idol created by man for his own worship; and this idol is the Brocken-specter on the fog, the gigantic shadow of man himself when he turns away from the sunlight.

Idolatry, self-worship, and devil-worship are one and the same thing; and they are identical with evil in general. For that false ideal which, in evil, takes the place due to the true ideal or God, is always our self, or rather a magnified reflection of our self. Intellectual evil consists in setting up that which I believe as the standard of truth, whereas I ought rather to test and if necessary reject my beliefs by comparing them with reality. Moral evil consists not so much in yielding to desires which I know to be wrong as in erecting my moral standards and judgments into the sole test of rightness. In every case alike evil arises when man takes himself, exactly as he stands, for the measure of all things; for in that case he is setting up a god in his own image and worshiping idols.

True religion lies not in making God in our image, but in

making ourselves in God's image; for God alone exists, and man is only struggling into existence for good or evil. In order to attain to any existence worth having, we must bear in mind that truth, reality, God, are real things existing quite independently of our individual life and private opinions; and an opinion is no less private if it happens to be shared by the whole human race. The type of all false religion is to believe what we will to believe, instead of what we have ascertained to be true; supposing that reality must be such as to satisfy our desires, and if not, go to, let us alter it. This is no ultimate, inexplicable fact; it follows necessarily from the truth that man's nature is as yet unformed, incomplete; it is, in the great phrase of an English philosopher,[7] "in process of being communicated to him"; and in that incomplete shape it is incapable of being the standard of anything. It is itself in need of a standard, and that standard, which for science is reality, for religion is God.

Man's life is a becoming; and not only becoming, but self-creation. He does not grow under the direction and control of irresistible forces. The force that shapes him is his own will. All his life is an effort to attain to real human nature. But human nature, since man is at bottom spirit, is only exemplified in the absolute spirit of God. Hence man must shape himself in God's image, or he ceases to be even human and becomes diabolical. This self-creation must also be self-knowledge; not the self-knowledge of introspection, the examination of the self that is, but the knowledge of God, the self that is to be. Knowledge of God is the beginning, the center, and end, of human life.

A painter makes his picture perfect by looking back from moment to moment at the vision which he is trying to reproduce. A scientist perfects his theory by testing it at every point by the facts of nature. So the religious life must come back again and again to the contemplation of its ideal in God. But God is a person, not a thing; a mind, not an object. We contemplate objects, but we do not contemplate persons. The attitude of one mind to another is not contemplation but communion; and communion with God is

7. T. H. Green.

prayer. Prayer may not be the whole of religion, but it is the touchstone of it. All religion must come to the test of prayer; for in prayer the soul maps out the course it has taken and the journey it has yet to make, reviewing the past and the future in the light of the presence of God.

Part Four. Religion and Absolute Spirit: The Metaphysics of Absolute Self-Making

INTRODUCTION

THE readings collected together in this section deal with what Collingwood regarded as the central doctrine of the Christian faith, the doctrine of the Incarnation or Atonement. In *Religion and Philosophy* the emphasis is placed not only on the dialectic of man's redemption through his experience of the transcendence of God but also on the meaning of God's self-expression through humanity (RP, 147; 251). The purely philosophical dimensions of this phenomenon are further explored in *Speculum Mentis,* which deals with the relation between finite and absolute mind, and in the essay, "Can the New Idealism Dispense with Mysticism?" which locates the basis of transcendental philosophy in the theory of mind as "pure act." Just as religion maintains that it is possible for man to be identified with God without losing his autonomy as man and without sacrificing his freedom, so finite historical consciousness can be shown to be identical with absolute mind without losing its autonomy.

In *Religion and Philosophy* Collingwood concentrates on the implications for man of God's omniscience and omnipotence. There are many who believe that because of God's omniscience the future of man is secure. Not only do we live in the best of all possible worlds, but as time unfolds the world becomes better and better, progressing ever and ever closer to perfection. But, Collingwood explains, just as a composer sees his symphony complete and perfect but cannot know beforehand every mistake of the performers, so God has an idea of the world which excludes those eruptions of evil which are no part of God's plan. Man, in other words, is free to will his own imperfections.

It has been argued, of course, that this very admission undermines God's omnipotence. But God's omnipotence can never be compromised by man's capacity to will evil. The source of the omniscience and omnipotence of God is the ontological fact that his essence, what he is *per* se in himself, coincides with his existence.

In the case of man, however, no such coincidence is possible. As the existentialists have emphasized, man is the being whose very being is to be self-alienated. This is what it means to be man, that he is always in the process of striving (but without success) to overcome the discrepancy between his essence and his existence. But, again to use the language of existentialism, man is also the being whose being is to transcend himself. To the extent to which he submits his will to the will of God he overcomes his self-alienation and fulfills the conditions of his inherent rationality. This is the source of man's transcendence. To the extent to which he wills evil, whether by choice, or through error, he only deepens his alienation and negates his inherent rationality. Since the negation of his rationality is not itself rational and can never be justified, it can never be traced to God, nor can God in any way be held responsible for it. Sin is the price man pays for being human.

But just as man relates to God through his own choice, so reason faces truth. That there is a truth to be sought does not guarantee the inevitability of its being captured. Nor does failure to capture it necessarily imply that it is in principle inaccessible or untruthful. Neither truth nor God can be compromised by the freedom of consciousness to sin and fall into error (RP, 157; 260). And lest one deceive himself into believing otherwise, let no man think that in spite of his sin God will yet redeem him. The omnipotence of God is fulfilled by the mere fact of his existence, and by the immanence of that existence in the consciousness of man. Beyond that God is not required to go. In the end, as Schelling once said, "man's freedom is essentially *his own deed.*" [1]

Collingwood therefore argues that God's identity with man neither confirms pantheism nor endorses the often-cited argument that since man and God are one, and since man is inherently evil, God is evil as well as imperfect. For to say that God is identical with the world is not to say that he is every part of the world. The

1. *Of Human Freedom* (Chicago: Open Court, 1936), p. 64. Schelling also writes, however: "The act which determines man's life in time does not itself belong in time but in eternity. Moreover it does not precede life in time but occurs throughout time . . . as an act eternal by its own nature (63-64).

world, like every finite being, is characterized by a discrepancy between essence and existence. Or, to put it another way, the world in its *wholeness* is ontologically distinct from the world in its *parts*. In its wholeness the world is an ordered, consistent, and rational system; and it is only with the world as good and as rational that God is equated. Thus God is directly revealed through that which is good, while that which is evil reveals him, indirectly perhaps, but no less demonstrably, through its relations with good (RP, 162; 264). That is why even in sin and error man possesses a criterion for dissolving his error and hence redeeming himself. Refusal to follow that criterion is an act of will which signifies corruption; it is an act of bad faith. Just as freedom is man's own prerogative, so man's pathology is his own deed.

There is another argument to the effect that any truth or reality which becomes an object of knowledge is itself subject to the conditions under which it is known. Since these conditions are historically and culturally relative, truth itself is relative. This argument, by implication, once again compromises the omnipotence of God. For just as the nature of truth varies with the conditions under which it is known, so God's nature is likewise dependent upon the conditions under which he is experienced. But Collingwood contends that even though the attainment of truth and the knowledge of God is an event in time and subject, therefore, to the conditions of historicity, "the truth itself is not historically circumscribed" (RP, 167; 268). Whether or not men come to know truth—or experience God—does not affect the essence of God as God. If being known by man makes a difference to God, this difference relates to God's existence as man. The paradox of divine existence is that God is both infinite and finite; his essence both transcends and is expressed through the finitude of man. It is because of God's identity with man that man's knowledge of God constitutes God's knowledge of himself (God's self-expression in man) and that man's obligation to himself as man is at the same time an infinite obligation. Man's knowledge of God means then, so far as God is concerned, that God's existence *qua* God is transcended by being deepened when God as man takes on the dimension of human freedom. It is human to strive for freedom; it is divine to succeed.

On the side of man, then, knowledge of God means that man comes into touch with something out of time, something to which time makes no difference. This is the mark of finite self-transcendence. And since knowledge of God is union with God, in this act of transcendence man does not merely *see* an extra-temporal reality, he does not merely "*glance* through breaking mists at the battlements of eternity, as Moses saw the promised land from the hill of renunciation." By his knowledge of eternity he is *one with eternity;* he has entered into the life of God, and in becoming one with God, "he is already beyond the shadow of changing and the bitterness of death" (RP, 167; 268). This is the source of man's immortality; that because God is omniscient and omnipotent, once man's life has become a part of God, it can never cease to be, but must live always within the center of divine existence. Through devotion to God man's life becomes something that in its very nature cannot pass away *except by desertion of the achieved ideal* (RP, 168; 269).

1. PHILOSOPHY AS IMMANENCE-TRANSCENDENCE

Collingwood's account of the relation of God to man parallels the metaphysical doctrine of immanence-transcendence which underlies the theory of absolute mind. Since this aspect of Collingwood's thought has never been properly attended to, and since its understanding is crucial to the interpretation of Collingwood's philosophical development, it is pertinent at this point to go into some detail. And since the theory of absolute mind is, by Collingwood's own admission, an expression of the Christian faith, perhaps we can illustrate the way in which one religion, at least, has expressed itself when dealing with ultimate questions. It will also show how the religious experience which Christianity makes possible can be expressed philosophically as the dialectical drama of absolute mind.

Philosophy is the reflective moment of each particular standpoint or form of life and for this reason is subject to the conditions of historicity. This is the source of the immanence of philosophy. At the same time, however, philosophy is itself a standpoint—that standpoint, namely, from which the other standpoints can be made intelligible. This is the source of its transcendence.

But philosophy is not transcendent in the sense that it is the mind's knowledge of its own pure and unchanging nature:

> In an immediate and direct way, the mind can never know itself: it can only know itself through the mediation of an external world, know that what it sees in the external world is its own reflection. Hence the construction of external worlds—works of art, religions, sciences, structures of historical fact, codes of law, systems of philosophy and so forth *ad infinitum*—is the only way by which the mind can come to that self-knowledge which is its end (SM, 315; 290).

This means of course that not only the mind but the truth to which mind aspires is itself only a system of appearances, and the conclusions of philosophy (*philosophia quaedam perennis*) are "not a body of truth revealed once for all, but a living thought whose content never discovered for the first time is progressively determined and clarified by every genuine thinker" (SM, 13 and 296; 297). The transcendence of philosophy, then, is a transcendence which is intrinsic to the process of change, and this transcendence consists in the fact that not only is the concrete life of philosophy a ceaseless act of achieving balance, but philosophy knows itself to be so changing and understands the basis of this change. This understanding is not only the source of the transcendence of philosophy (SM, 301; 301), it is also the source of self-making. The conscious effort to understand its own change is the condition under which the mind both discovers what it is and makes itself what it is, not only as finite but as infinite mind (SM, 296; 297):

> Man recognizes himself as finite and knows that, if he really is finite, he is thereby debarred from that infinity to which he aspires. But just as a being really limited in time could not know of its own limitation—for it could have no conception of a past and a future if it lived wholly in the present—so a

being really finite could not know itself as finite. The self-knowledge of man as finite is already his assertion of himself as infinite (SM, 302; 301-302).

But how is it possible for the mind to be both in and out of change at the same time? The answer lies in Collingwood's interpretation of absolute mind as "pure act" (NL; 61). As pure act, mind is a self-making activity the very essence of which is to change by discovering that its commitments are founded on error. But this is to introduce a new truth which transcends all previous errors. In its moment of transcendence, then, philosophy is the conscious insight into the untruth of phenomenal or finite historical knowledge.[2] This insight is also a form of action. The philosopher cannot so know himself without at the same time creating himself. The discovery of each error is the occasion upon which philosophy asserts a new truth.

This process may be likened to the process of aesthetic creation. As in the case of art neither philosophy nor its object pre-exists to the concrete process of experience itself. The pure idea, or notion, in other words, both transcends experience and is contingent upon it:

> Art as a whole, we saw, is the pure act of imagination, and this act has its life in a process of self-differentiation and self-concentration, diastole and systole, which generates the various forms and phases of aesthetic activity within the unity of imagination itself, and having generated them treats them as so much material by the mastery of which it vindicates this unity. The act does not find a material, given from without, to unify which is the problem of its life; it generates the material out of itself and thus sets itself the problems which it lives by solving. In the same way the life of the spirit differentiates itself into art, religion, and the rest in order that it may exhibit its own unity in this diversity; or rather, that it may through this diversity bring into existence a unity which is not the

2. Hegel, *The Phenomenology of Mind* (London: Allen and Unwin, 1949), p. 136.

> bare unity with which it began but a unity enriched by all the differentiations through which it has passed (OPA, 94).

When Collingwood describes this process which takes place in time as "eternal," he is referring not to a static, unchanging eternity, but to a dynamic, self-making eternity:

> . . . it is always beginning, it has always reached any given point, and it has always arrived at its conclusion, somewhat as —to revert to a previous simile—a river is always rising at its source, always flowing over each part of its course, and always discharging itself into the sea (OPA, 94-95).

But because this process is a conscious process, like a river which should be aware of itself throughout its course, Collingwood denies that it merely travels through a fixed cycle of changes; rather, it finds itself at every stage altered in significance by the consciousness of what has gone before. The unity of the spiritual life is therefore characterized as "the unity of an infinitely increasing spiral rather than the unity of a rotating circle" (OPA, 95). Finally, the "energy which causes the spiral to expand" (or, to put it another way the fundamental presupposition of this life of the spirit so defined) is simply the "pure activity which is the spirit" (OPA, 94). It is this act, which, in comprehending its own change, rises above and transcends that change.

2. THE THEORY OF THE MIND AS PURE ACT

The theory of the mind as pure act is further discussed in "Can the New Idealism Dispense with Mysticism?" (1923). The ostensible purpose of this paper is to discuss the philosophy of Giovanni Gentile and defend it against the charge that it dissolves into mysticism. Gentile cannot be charged with mysticism because his thought is grounded in a transcendental philosophy, which Collingwood refers to as "the common ground of all idealism" (CNI, 169; 277), a doctrine which bears a striking resemblance to the position of *Speculum Mentis*.

Collingwood begins by pointing out that according to Gentile the essence of mind is historicity. But historicity must not be confused with radical pluralism. Historical change is change initiated by self-knowledge. Only a mind that knows itself to be changing can give rise to historical change. Unless change is known as a process, it can never be a genuine process. For a genuine process to exist at all it must occur against the background of a continuity without which change would be unintelligible. Transcendence, in other words, is a necessary condition of the possibility of change and hence of the possibility of mind as such. The very essence of mind, in other words, is to be both in and out of change at the same time. But how is this apparent contradiction to be accounted for?

Gentile's answer, according to Collingwood, is that the mind not only suffers change which it later comprehends but indeed *initiates change in itself*. This change is initiated in a variety of ways such as through aesthetic, religious, and moral acts. In religion, for example, change is initiated by man's effort to fulfill the will of God to which he has chosen to submit his own finite will. But unless God's will were already implicit in the finite will of man, the two could never coincide. Yet it cannot be present *in toto;* otherwise it would not have to be sought after. This double aspect of the mind as active and passive, as seeking for that which both is and yet is not already implicit, is the very heart of both Gentile's and Collingwood's philosophy (CNI, 166-167; 275).

But if man's freedom consists in his capacity to initiate change, what makes this freedom creative is the fact that the direction of change is governed by truth, by a reality which is already immanent in the very process of change itself:

> If the permanent and changing principle is called God and the changing creation is called the world, we thus reach the formula that it is only the presence of God in the world that makes the world real, and only his self-expression in the act of creating the world that makes God actual (CNI, 167; 275).

Thus, according to Gentile, the immanence of truth is celebrated in art, while the transcendence of truth is made possible by religion.

The aesthetic experience is the attempt to create meaning out of the tension of finite existence; religion is an experience of the continuity of the force which sustains the creative process.[3]

The standpoint from which Collingwood discusses and defends Gentile bears a striking resemblance to the theory of mind which is expounded in *Speculum Mentis*. The notions of "God" and the "World," for example, which Collingwood uses to explicate Gentile's distinction between the "pure act" and the products of creation have their origins in Collingwood's own system—the latter in the dialectical scale of forms constituted by the partial and erroneous worlds of art, religion, science, history, and philosophy; the former in the notion of absolute mind itself, which Collingwood defines as an activity of conscious creation, as both creative act (SM, 296; 297) and historical fact (SM, 298; 298). Following Gentile, Collingwood places the significance of the creative act in the fact that it is not only conscious but self-conscious—which for Collingwood is the ground of its permanence or transhistoricity. At the same time, because its creativity is an act of self-creation, it is also immanent, and as such expresses itself in the construction and destruction of external worlds or historical world views.

Collingwood departs from Gentile, however, by conceiving the notion of the pure act (or absolute mind) as the logic of the overlap of classes. So conceived, the pure act is the source of each particular form or category of experience as well. Through works of art and acts of faith the mind brings itself into existence *qua* imagination; through scientific observation and perception it brings itself into existence *qua* understanding (whose object is the abstract universal), while through history and philosophy the mind brings itself into existence *qua* reason (whose object is the concrete universal) (SM, 195 ff.).

3. Cf. Hegel's account of the tension between the historicity of finite thought and the transhistoricity of absolute thought: "In thinking I lift myself up to the absolute above all that is finite, and am infinite consciousness, while I am at the same time finite consciousness, and indeed am such in accordance with my whole empirical character. Both sides, as well as their relation, exist for me. Both sides seek each other, and both flee from each other . . . I am the conflict . . . I am not *one* of those taking part in the strife, but I am both the combatants, and am the strife itself." *Lectures on the Philosophy of Religion* (London, 1895), I, 63-64.

The theory of the mind as pure act, or immanence-transcendence, is the foundation of Collingwood's entire philosophy and the basis upon which the rapprochement between philosophy and the other forms of knowledge and experience is finally achieved. It is also the basis of the theory of absolute mind in *Speculum Mentis* and is regarded by Collingwood as "the solution of all those problems concerning finitude and infinity which have so vexed abstract thought" (SM, 302; 301). Philosophy as absolute knowledge is the concrete life of mind. As such it is implicit in all other standpoints and is therefore the basis upon which each standpoint comes to self-consciousness. In this form philosophy is subject to its own historical development, a development which has its ground in the logical development of mind itself. At the same time philosophy is transcendental knowledge of the structure of mind as pure act—as it is revealed and only revealed in the history of thought. Philosophy discovers what it is doing by doing it, and in so doing, it creates its own laws.

Collingwood makes it quite clear that this conception of philosophy—a conception which is obviously at the center of *Speculum Mentis*—does not reduce philosophy to a mere intuition or to mysticism, if by the latter is meant a noncognitive, nonrational, nondiscursive apprehension of ultimate truths. On the contrary, according to Collingwood, the philosophical tradition in which the above conception of philosophy arose, namely the tradition of idealism, has always maintained "that ultimate truth is to be reached, if at all, only by hard thinking, by critical development of rational theory, and not by any kind of intellectual intuition" (CNI, 171; 279). If it is true, Collingwood continues, that ultimate truths are to be reached by the path of intuition and not by the labor of the notion, then certainly all scientific and historical thinking is futile, and modern philosophy is indeed bankrupt.[4] "It can only be a

4. Cf. Hegel on the "scientific" character of philosophy. Philosophy according to Hegel, can reach truth "only by the inherent life of the notion" (*Phenomenology, op. cit.*, 111). We must reject, he says, all interpretations of philosophy which place the emphasis on the feeling and intuition of truth, on unreflective and emotional knowledge. On such a view, philosophy is regarded as aiming not so much at insight as edification (*nicht sowohl Einsicht als Erbauung gewähren*) (*ibid.*, 72). But, warns Hegel, "philosophy must beware of wishing to

non-existent way of apprehending the non-existent" (CNI, 171; 279).

> ... the only thing left for the person who wants to get at the truth is to return like Nebuchadnezzar to the level of the instinctive animals and *s'installer dans le mouvement,* instead of trying to raise himself above it in order to understand it. (CNI, 171; 279).

The truth is, asserts Collingwood, that what often passes (under the name of mysticism) for supra-cognitive intuition, is in fact a mediation which, while actually present, is not wholly explicit. The mind reaches truths but does not know how it has reached them. It is the business of scientific or philosophical thought "to lay bare this concealed process, to render explicit the mediation which in the mystical experience itself was only implicit" (CNI, 173; 281). This is precisely the role of philosophy in *Speculum Mentis.* In the essay on Gentile, Collingwood cites Hegel's remark that "truth is not dependent for its first revelation upon philosophy" (CNI, 173-174; 281). In the mystical or religious experience (as indeed in every other experience) truth is actually attained, and it remains for philosophy to explain how it was attained. The necessity for the mystical experience, writes Collingwood:

> lies in the principle that we discover new truths neither by the inference of the logic books nor by the intuition of Aristotle, but by an act of mind which reaches out beyond the given, grasps the new thought as it were in the dark, and

---

be edifying" (*ibid.,* 74). The fact is, he declares, the search for truth can never escape from "the toil of science" (*ibid.,* 133) and the need for "measurable precision and definiteness" (*ibid.,* 74). Indeed, he writes: "Philosophic utterances about right, morality, and ethical life from those who would banish thought and have recourse instead to feeling, enthusiasm, the heart and the breast, are expressive of the utterly contemptible position into which thought and philosophic science have fallen, because what this amounts to is that even philosophic science itself, plunged in self-despair and extreme exhaustion, is taking as its principle barbarity and absence of thought, and would do its best to rob mankind of all truth, worth, and dignity." *Philosophy of Right* (Oxford, 1942), p. 30.

> only after that consolidates its new conquest by building up to it a bridge of reasoned proof (CNI, 174; 281).

But the building of this bridge, which is the task of reflection, is "nothing but the implicitness of thought in the mystical experience" (CNI, 174; 281):

> . . . the bringing out into visibility on the sensitive plate of what has already been recorded upon it, the rendering explicit of a mediation or proof which was already there implicitly (CNI, 174; 281).

This view of the rapprochement between philosophy and mysticism is, of course, an early formulation of the rapprochement between faith and reason. What is even more significant is the fact that in 1923 Collingwood presented it as an example of how "a modern idealistic philosophy" might achieve this rapprochement. It is tempting to suspect that the phrase "a modern idealistic philosophy" is a direct reference to Collingwood's own views in *Speculum Mentis.*

3. THE DRAMA OF ABSOLUTE MIND

If Collingwood's rapprochement between philosophy and religion seems unnecessarily obscure, it is only because like all great metaphysicians, he is wrestling with a formidable God, a God, perhaps, whose only adequate means of communication is a language charged with metaphor and imagery. To communicate the results of the encounter with the absolute in the language of rational discourse is perhaps the greatest challenge which finite mind can set itself. And at times, in its search for clarity and in order to enrich its own rational insights, reason, which is after all only faith and imagination cultivating itself, must return with proven humility to the language of metaphor and imagery, seeking more the mood than the logical anatomy of absolute truth. Collingwood, in keeping with his own convictions on this matter, resorts at times to such imagery. And in one particular passage, which sums up the essence of his philosophical achievement, he depicts the plight and drama of absolute mind in the language of religious imagery:

> God is here conceived as the absolute spirit, alpha and omega, the beginning and the end. Behind him, beyond him, apart from him, there is nothing: neither matter nor law, neither earth nor heaven, neither space nor time. In the beginning, by an absolute act which was not itself subject to any determination of time or space, God created the heavens and the earth; the visible world, with all its order and furniture, even the very space in which it floats and the time in which it endures and changes, is the work of this absolute act. But this world is no mere toy shaped by God and thrown off from himself in contemptuous alienation. His spirit moves upon the face of the waters, even the waters of chaos, and this same breath becomes the soul of life in the man whom he creates in his own image. Man is one with God, no mere part of the whole but informed by the indwelling of the divine spirit. Now man by his misguided thirst for knowledge, partakes of that knowledge which is forbidden, namely error, or the human wisdom which negates God's wisdom. This error deforms his own true, that is divine, nature, and the deformation takes the shape of banishment from the presence of God into the wilderness of the visible world. Having thus lost even the sight of God, the knowledge of what he himself ought to be, he cannot recover his lost perfection until he comes to know himself as he actually is. But not knowing himself as he ought to be, he cannot know himself as he is. His error is implicit just because it is complete. It can only become explicit if God reveals himself afresh, if the true ideal breaks in upon the soul clouded by error. This, in the fulness of time, is granted. Human nature sunk in error is confronted by the confutation of its own error, and thus, through a fresh dialectical process, redeemed.

Now in this imagery there is one flaw, namely the transcendence of God; God standing aloof from the drama of human sin and redemption, a mere stage manager, is no true symbol of the absolute mind in its concreteness. But this is exactly where the truth of our religious imagery shines most brilliantly. It is God who accepts the burden of error, takes upon himself the moral responsibility for the fall, and so redeems not his creature but himself (SM, 302-303; 302-303).

The absolute mind, which I have attempted to explicate in terms of the philosophical doctrine of immanence-transcendence, can never, for Collingwood, be more profoundly or impressively pictured than in this religious drama of the fall and redemption of man.

THE SELF-EXPRESSION OF GOD IN MAN

In this . . . part we shall attempt to use the results of the foregoing chapters as an approach to some of the more technical problems of theology. We shall take what I suppose to be the central doctrine of the Christian faith, and ask what light is thrown upon it by the conclusions we have reached as to the relation between God, man, and the world on the one hand, and between good and evil on the other. By the central doctrine of Christianity I mean that taking-up of humanity into God which is called the Incarnation or the Atonement, according as the emphasis is laid on God's self-expression through humanity or man's redemption through the spirit of God.

It must be understood that I approach this subject from a single definite point of view. I shall make no attempt to state in detail the beliefs of the Church, or of any other body. Some initial statement is necessary, but this may be very brief and can perhaps be presented in a form to which no school of Christian thought would very strongly object. The details will then be developed by applying to these statements the general principles set forth in the second part. It follows that these chapters aim not at orthodoxy but at the faithful translation into theological terms of the philosophy already expressed in the preceding pages. I might, no doubt, have gone on to consider whether the ultimate theological results were in agreement with the beliefs of orthodox Christianity. But I have not done this; not through any indifference to the question, for it would be hypocritical to conceal my hope that the conclusions here advanced may really agree with the deepest interpretation of the Christian creed, but because the task involved in

Reprinted from *Religion and Philosophy* (London: Macmillan & Co., 1916), pp. 147-168.

such a comparison would take me far beyond the limits of this volume.

1. The doctrine of the Incarnation, in its most central characteristics, may perhaps be outlined in some such way as this. There was a certain historical person who was both divine and human. He was truly and actually divine with the full characteristics of Godhead, and fully and completely human in all the individuality of manhood. He was not, however, a compound of two different personalities, but one single personality.

This statement of two natures in one person may be taken as our starting-point. It represents approximately the "formula of Chalcedon"; and it must be noticed in passing that this formula is no more than a starting-point. As stated, it puts the problem without offering any solution at all. It is our task to discover how such a problem can be solved. The problem, more precisely, is not for us, "Was such and such a person both divine and human?" but, "How is it possible for a person to be both?" That is to say, we are setting aside all questions as to the "historical Jesus" and attending merely to the necessary implications of the doctrine. Our answer will be in the form, "if any man fulfilled such and such conditions, he was perfectly divine as well as perfectly human; but it is not our purpose to inquire whether the conditions have been fulfilled."

(*a*) How can there be an identity between a human being and God? There are two types of answer to this question. The first type runs thus: Man, simply as man, is already divine. Man is spirit, and God is spirit, and between the two there is no sharp line of demarcation. This truth, the divinity of man, the fatherhood of God, is the message of Jesus and the creed of Christendom.

The second type of answer lays stress not on the nature of mankind as a whole, but on the nature of the one man who alone is believed to have been truly and fully divine. He, and no other, has lived a perfect life; he and no other has set before the world in his own person an example of love and power which it cannot choose but worship.

These two answers seem not only different, but utterly and radically hostile; representative of points of view between which there can be no truce. The first is the purest immanent Pantheism, the second an absolutely transcendent Theism. If all men are equally divine by their very manhood, then the claim of one to be especially so is indefensible. The claim, then, must be explained away or boldly pronounced a mistake. Perhaps, it is sometimes suggested, "the divine man" means no more than "the man who first discovered the divinity of man." On the other hand, if one man alone is divine, it cannot for a moment be admitted that the same is true of all other men; for that would be to sacrifice the whole value of the one unique life.

It is clear that if the first type of answer is adopted, the original question falls to the ground. We need no longer ask, how is it possible for a man to be divine? because no man is anything else. But we are left with two difficulties. In the first place, can such a view be made to square with the words or the spirit of the New Testament narratives? and secondly, is the view itself a sound and reasonable one?

With the first difficulty we have nothing to do. We have to ask whether it is reasonable to hold that all men are divine in such a way that no one is more divine than any other. And here we may recall the two senses in which the word identity was found to be used. There is, it will be remembered, a purely abstract identity, an identity which cannot be diminished or increased, which subsists merely in virtue of the continued existence, in whatever relation, of the things identified. There is also another identity, not abstract but concrete, subsisting in virtue of an identity of thought or purpose between the persons concerned, and existing only so long as that identity is maintained.

Now in the first sense every man must be, so far as he exists, identical with every other and with God. There must be some relation between God and any man, even a man ignorant of God or hostile to him. And where there is some relation there is some identity. Not indeed a low degree or small amount of identity, for identity only exists absolutely: it is either complete or non-existent. According to this kind of identity, then, every man is already and fully divine, and it is not possible that any one man should be more so than any other.

But the other kind of identity depends not on bare existence but on the kind of existence which a free being chooses to have. According to this kind of identity, it is clear that any man who fully knew the mind of God, and whose will was bent on the same ends as the divine will, would be himself both man and God in one, completely human and completely divine. In this sense not every man is divine; indeed it is rather to be doubted whether any man ever has been or ever could be. This question we shall raise later.

The position which we described as Pantheism, then, namely that every man is necessarily and unchangeably divine, is very far from being false; but is equally far from being the whole truth, and to represent it as the whole truth is to make a serious mistake. The divinity of every man, simply as man, is no more than an abstract divinity, the guarantee of a fuller and more concrete union. And this concrete union is only to be attained in and by the identification of the self in all its aspects with the perfect mind of God.

The kind of identity which we are to consider is the latter kind only. Of the former, there is indeed nothing more to say; it is a pure abstraction, and of an abstraction we can say no more than that—in its own abstract way—it exists. The divinity for the possession of which we reverence the Founder of Christianity, the union with God which we ourselves desire to attain, is no abstraction; it is a concrete and living activity, and therefore it depends on, or rather consists in, not the bare unchangeable nature of man as man, but the positive character of his life, his individual thoughts and actions.

God and man are identified in one person, concretely identified, that is identified not only fully but also in the highest possible sense, when a human being has an individuality of his own, identified with that of God in the unity of all his thought and action with the divine knowledge and the divine purpose. This ideal person, in whom Godhead and manhood not only coexist but coincide, I shall call the Christ; but without, for the purposes of this chapter, assuming his identity with the Jesus of history, or indeed assuming that such a person has ever lived at all.

(*b*) It may be objected to such a conception, that the supposed union is impossible because no one man—no single individual—can comprehend completely the nature, and identify himself with the purpose, of God the absolute mind. The knowledge and manifestation of God are, it may be said, attained little by little, through an infinite process of historical growth and development. Not one man, but the whole of humanity is necessary to reveal God, and not humanity only, since in any one class of facts God can only reveal as much of his nature as that kind of fact will express. A single man can only express one very limited side of the divine character, which is too large to be confined within the circle of a finite personality.

This objection carries great weight and seems very convincing; and it has often led to the adoption of a view according to which the revelation in Jesus is only one of an infinite number of revelations, each and all contributing something to the total knowledge of the infinite God. And yet if God is infinite and each manifestation of him is finite, how can any number of manifestations come any nearer to expressing his full nature? A large number of units is no nearer infinity than a single one. Again, is it really justifiable to describe a human personality as finite at all? We saw reason to maintain in a former chapter that a mind was only definable in terms of the object of which it was conscious; and if God is infinite and man is really conscious of God, it seems to follow that man thereby becomes infinite. It is sometimes said that for this very reason man can never know God; but to lay down *a priori* what a given mind can and what it cannot know in virtue of its own constitution is to begin at the wrong end. The mind is what it makes itself; and its finitude or infinity (if the words mean anything) consists merely in its failure or success in the attainment of its desire.

The objection in fact is precisely an instance of the materialistic type of thought which we criticized in a former chapter. It represents God as a whole composed of separate and mutually-exclusive parts, one of which is handled at a time; when humanity has examined one part, it goes on to another; and so on. Whereas God is not subdivisible; he is a true whole, with no separable parts; each part is an aspect of the whole, and to know one "part" is to know implicitly all. The idea of progressive revelation is only a new materialism.

(*c*) Another objection of the same kind asserts that a man whose knowledge and will were divine in content would be himself only God-like, not actually one with God. He would be not identical but similar. This again depends on principles which we have already criticized. It is based on abstracting the personality of a mind from its content; I am I, whatever I do and say and think, and on the same terms you are you. The individual self-identity of the particular mind is unchangeable and underlies all changes of activity; and therefore since A's ideas happen in A's mind and B's ideas in B's mind, A and B cannot have the same consciousness but only a similar one.

We have, as I said, already considered this view in detail. Our objection to it may be put shortly by saying that it admits at once too much and too little. If A's consciousness is only very like B's instead of being identical, there is no real communion between them; for that requires an identity. But even this inadequate similarity cannot be maintained; the same argument which destroyed the identity is fatal to it also. In fact this view is a compromise with materialism (in the form of psychological individualism or abstract pluralism), and any such compromise must be fatal to the whole truth.

(*d*) We must maintain, then, that it is possible for a human being to be identified with God in the concrete sense, as having a full and real intuition of the divine nature in its completeness, not of one side of it only, and a full harmony and agreement with the divine will; not abandoning his own will and adopting the false negativity of quietism, but acting in complete union with God, so that where there might be two wills there is one, not by the annihilation of one but by the activity of both at once in a single purpose. Such a man would be rightly described as perfect God and perfect man, for the distinction would in his personality have no further meaning. He would therefore show in completion the powers of God in thought and in action.

This last statement may cause difficulty. It seems that the very fact of human life limits and circumscribes the man, and makes it impossible for him to exercise the full powers of the infinite mind of God. A particular man, it appears, cannot be omnipotent or omniscient, though he might be entirely sinless; and therefore theories have arisen to the effect that in becoming man God would find it necessary to abandon certain of his attributes. Such a self-sacrifice seems to be an additional and very strong proof of the love of God toward humanity.

But it is not easy to see what can be meant by the renunciation of some of the divine attributes. The life of the mind is whole, without seam, woven from the top throughout; the only sense in which we can separate one attribute from the others is that we may abstract it, that is, have a false theory that is separate; we can never actually employ one faculty alone. The conception of the self-limitation of a will may in fact mean two things; either volition itself, which by accepting one end involves renunciation of another, or a volition in which it is determined not to will at all. Now in the thing else. Thus the temptation of Jesus, for instance, represents a former sense, self-limitation or self-sacrifice is the negative side of all acting; nothing can be done at all without the sacrifice of some-true self-limitation; he decides not to adopt certain courses of action, not as a mere act of abstract self-sacrifice but because he is determined on a course with which these others are incompatible. In the second sense, self-limitation cannot exist at all; for every act of will is the will to do something, and a will whose sole end was the abstract decision not to will cannot be imagined. We never, strictly speaking, decide "not to do anything"; when we use that phrase we always mean that we decide not to do some definite thing A or B, but to go on doing C.

The self-limitation of God, then, cannot be interpreted in this abstract way as the mere renunciation of certain faculties. And it is not true that such things as omniscience and omnipotence are "faculties" at all, distinguishable from the faculties of knowing and acting in general. The question is whether human life as such is incompatible with the exercise of the divine attributes, wisdom and goodness, at all. No impassable gulf separates divine knowledge from human; God has not, in addition to his power of knowing, another power denied to man and called omniscience. Omniscience is merely the name for the complete and unremitting employment of the faculty of knowing. This faculty man certainly possesses. If it were not so, the possibility of a divine-human life would doubtless be at an end. Man could neither know God nor obey his will; and the divine spirit could only operate in man by losing all its essential character. All human thought would be illusion, and all human activity sin, and to make it otherwise would be beyond the power of God himself. Rather than accept such conclusions, we shall do right in maintaining that all God's nature, without any reservation or abatement, is expressible in human form.

The human being in whom God is fully manifested, then, must have God's powers and faculties fully developed, and if fully developed then fully employed, since an unemployed faculty has no real existence at all. He must be omnipotent and omniscient. Whatever God can know and do, he also can know and do. This is a grave difficulty if we think of omnipotence and omniscience in an utterly abstract way, involving such things as the power to make twice two into five or the knowledge of an action which has not yet been decided upon. But omnipotence does not mean power to do absurdities. The compulsion of another's will is such an absurdity; and therefore no real omnipotence could force such a compulsion. Omnipotence is spiritual, and spirit acts not by brute compulsion but by knowledge and inspiration. The omnipotence of God, his kingdom over men's minds, consists in their allegiance to his purposes, their answer to his love, their repentance and return from sin to his side. And this omnipotence—the universal kingdom which is planted in the hearts of men—can indeed be wielded by God in human form. To say that God cannot compel is not to deny him omnipotence; it is to assert his positive nature as spirit. But since spirit is self-creative and makes its own nature, this absence of compulsion is in one sense a self-limitation of the will of God. But (1) it is a self-limitation of God as God, not of God as incarnate in man; (2) it is only self-limitation in the sense in which any determination, *e.g.* of a good man to abstain from taking mean advantages, is a self-limitation.

In the category of knowledge we must also hold that the omniscience of God is shared by the Christ in whom his nature is manifested. It might be thought that this was unnecessary; that the divine man would know God as he is, but would not know the things God knows. But such a plea is based on the false distinction between the mind and its content, the individual consciousness and the knowledge of which it is conscious. To know someone's mind is nothing more nor less than to see eye to eye with him, to look at reality as he looks at it, to know what he knows. His mind is not an object in itself; it is an attitude toward the real world, and to know his mind is to know and share that attitude. The Christ, then, must be as omniscient as God is.

This again is a serious difficulty. How can an individual man, whose consciousness is bounded by his age and time, be omniscient or even approximate to such a state? Is not that a fallacy now happily exploded and consigned to the theological rubbish-heap? Omniscient in a quite abstract sense the Christ cannot be, just as he cannot be in the same sense omnipotent. That is to say, looking at history as a succession of detached events temporally distinct, he cannot know the future; future history, actions, and events generally he cannot foretell. But this is simply because, taking history in this abstract way, the future is positively undetermined, non-existent as yet, unknowable; God himself cannot know it. On the other hand, if history means the discovery of absolute truth and the development of God's purposes, the divine man will stand at the center of it and know it, past and future, from within, not as a process but as a whole. This means not that he will be acquainted with details of scholarship and history, but that he will know as from its source the essential truth at which wise men have aimed, so that whatever is of permanent value in knowledge, ancient or modern, is already summed up in his view of the world.

If God's purposes can be—as we have said—really hindered and blocked by evil wills, then God himself cannot know in advance their detailed history. He knows their ultimate fate; he sees them as a composer sees his symphony complete and perfect; but he cannot know beforehand every mistake of the performers. Those irruptions of the evil will into God's plans are no part of the unity of the world, no part of the plan; it is only by destroying them, wiping them out of existence, that God's purposes can be fulfilled. God himself strives against evil, does not merely look down from heaven upon our conflict; and if he does not blast the wicked with the breath of his mouth, neither does he set them up as mere puppets, targets for virtue's archery. The existence of evil, if it can be called a real abatement of God's omnipotence, is equally so of his omniscience; not merely of that of his human manifestation. But as we said in a former chapter that evil does not truly limit God's omnipotence, because he conquers it in his own way, so the freedom of the future is not truly a detriment to his omniscience.

So far, then, it seems that the expression of deity in a human being is definitely possible, because in whatever sense we can conceive God to be omnipotent and omniscient, in the same sense it is conceivable that his human incarnation should be so. There will be no failure to express in bodily form the whole fullness of God's nature; every aspect, every potentiality of his being will be included in the life of the perfect man who is also perfect God.

2. But if these are the relations of the Christ to God, how shall we describe his relations with humanity? In what sense can he be called perfect man, and what is the relation of his life and consciousness to those of the human race in general?

(*a*) The first point is the reality of his manhood. There is a real difficulty in this point owing to the vaguess of the term "manhood." Many Christological discussions suffer from lack of reflection on this point. The conception of deity is thought to be a difficult and abstruse one, to elucidate which no pains are sufficient; that of humanity, on the other hand, is often passed over as too simple to need investigation. Yet if we ask, does a man who is identical with God thereby cease to be a man? it is clear that he does or does not according to different senses of the word. Many people are ready to say that the notion of finitude, fallibility, sinfulness, is "contained in the very idea of manhood." If that is really so, then the perfect man cannot be called a man; and any man becomes less and less human as he becomes better and better. If, on the other hand, we mean by man nothing more than a person living in human relations, then the perfect man is clearly a man among his fellowmen; a better man, but a man. The question is what name we give to manhood purged of its imperfections; and so far, it is a merely verbal question.

But the point at issue is not entirely verbal. Granted his divinity, his perfection and absoluteness, it may be said, he cannot be the member of a society in which every part is limited by and dovetailed into every other. He will burst the bonds of any society into which he is put; and inasmuch as he is anti-social in this way he cannot be called a man among men. After what we have already said, this argument need not detain us long. It is true that he will certainly burst the bonds of any society, that his appearance heralds the overthrow of the world's powers, that he comes to bring a sword. But it is society that is anti-social, and not he; he destroys it because of his humanity and its inhuman mechanisms and deadnesses. Destruction must always be the effect of any new truth or new impulse; but what it destroys is man's idolatries, not man himself.

The most important difficulty in the way of conceiving the Christ as truly human is in the last resort identical with that which formed the subject of our last section (§1, *d*). As long as human and divine nature are regarded simply as different sets or groups of qualities, to assert their inherence in one individual is really meaningless, as if we should assert the existence of a geometrical figure which was both a square and a circle. This does not mean that those who asserted "two natures in one person" were wrong; but it does mean that they were trying to express a truth in terms that simply would not express it. If anyone said that he did not see how such a union of natures could take place, he was necessarily told that it was a mystery past understanding. But the mystery, the element which baffles the intellect, lies not at all in the truth to be expressed, but solely in its expression by improper language; that is to say, the combination with it of presuppositions which contradict it. We start by assuming human nature to be one definite thing and divine nature another; and the language which is framed on such a basis can never serve to express intelligibly the fact which it implicitly denies, namely the union of the two. This assumption we have by now criticized and found to be inadequate; we have rejected the idea of a mind as having a "nature" of its own in distinction from what it does; and by doing so we have removed in advance the abstract argument that a divine person, by his very nature, cannot be truly and completely human.

(*b*) But the impulse of the divine spirit is not exhausted by any one man. His followers, so far as they attain discipleship, share his spirit and his life; his knowledge of God becomes theirs, and his identification of God's will with his own is also theirs. To this extent they have precisely the relation to him which he has to God; and through him they attain the same relation to God in which he lives. That is to say, their mind actually becomes one with his mind, his mind lives in them and they in him. This must be true of every one who learns from him and follows him. The union with God which he enjoys is imparted to them; they become he, and in so doing they equally with him become God.

Here again, we do not ask whether anybody has ever attained discipleship in this absolute degree; we merely say that if any one did truly follow the light given by the divine incarnation he would live literally in God and God in him; there would be no more "division of substance" than there is between the Father and the Son. Thus the Christ appears as Mediator of the divine life; he enjoys that life to the full himself, and imparts it fully to his disciples. Through learning of him and following him it is possible to attain, by his mediation, the same divine life which we see in him.

(*c*) But such a union of life with life can hardly be confined to the definite disciples of any historical person. Among the countless numbers who know nothing of his life as a historical fact, to whom his words and example have never penetrated, are certainly many who have true knowledge of reality and the real attainment of a good life. What is the relation of these to the divine incarnation?

The spirit of truth is not circumscribed by the limits of space and time. If a real community of life is possible between two men who share each other's outward presence and inward thoughts, it is possible no less between two who have never met; between the ancient poet and his modern reader, or the dead scientist and the living man who continues his work. The earlier in point of time lives on in the life of the later; each deriving the benefit from such intercourse. Even if we did not suppose the individual consciousness of the dead to remain with us, we should at least admit that all that was left of them—their work—profits by our carrying it on; and we profit by using it as our starting-point. In this sense there is a real community between the Christ and the predecessors whose lives have, historically speaking, led up to and made possible his own.

Again, there is a union of mind between persons who are in the order of history unaware of each other's existence, between Hebrew prophet and Greek philosopher, between two scientists who cannot read each other's language. This union consists in the fact that both are dealing with the same problems; for in so far as any two minds are conscious of the same reality, they are the same mind. Thus there is a certain spiritual intercourse between men who have no outward point of contact whatever; and even if it is true, as Aristotle says, that bodily presence is the fulfilment of friendship, men may still be friends when neither knows the other's name.

The life of the Christ then is shared not only by his professed disciples but by all who know truth and lead a good life; all such participate in the life of God and in that of his human incarnation. But whereas we say that his disciples enjoy the divine life through his mediation, it seems at first sight that we cannot speak of mediation in this other case. If mediation means simply example and instruction of one historical person by another, that is true. But there is no ultimate difference between the two cases. In each case the spirit of God, whose presence in the heart is truth, is shared by men as it was shared by the Christ; and to speak of reaching him through God or God through him is to introduce a conception of process or transition which is really indefensible. As the disciple finds God in the Christ, so the non-disciple finds the Christ in God; in the fact that he knows God he is already one with the Christ whom, "according to the flesh," he does not know.

The conception of mediation, then, does not stand in the last resort. The experience which it designates is perfectly real; but the word itself implies a division of the indivisible. We speak of reaching God *through* Christ when we rather mean that we find him *in*

Christ. And therefore the relation of the Christ to those who do not know him as a historical man is as intimate, granted that in their ignorance they do lead a life of truth and endeavor, as his union with those who call themselves his followers. In the language of religion, he saves not only his disciples but those who lived before his birth and those who never knew his name.

3. Whether such an incarnation has ever happened at all is, we repeat, a question for history. And if so, it is equally for history to decide whether it has happened once or many times. But on this question certain *a priori* points must be considered. There are certain arguments which seem to prove the plurality of incarnations.

(*a*) The first is the pantheistic argument. God is exemplified not simply in one man but in everything. There is no fact which does not reveal God to anyone who is able to see him there. And consequently it is idle to talk of one final revelation. There are countless revelations.

This is almost a restatement of the view in § 1, *b,* which required an infinite number of revelations to express the infinite aspects of God's character. It springs from the thought that since God is all, every individual reality has an equal right to stand as a revelation of him. This is the view which we define as Pantheism. Our answer to that general position is that God is not every isolated thing, but only that which is good and true; or, which comes, as we have seen, to the same thing, reality as a whole, in an ordered and coherent system. That which is good reveals God directly; that which is evil reveals him indeed no less, but only indirectly, through its relations with the good. A wicked man does not, by his wickedness, reveal the nature of God; but if we understood the whole history, the beginning and end, of his sins, we should realize that he, no less than the good, stands as an example of God's dealings with the world.

(*b*) Secondly, there is a logical argument. God is regarded from this point of view as the universal, and man as the particular. Now every particular expresses the universal, and each expresses it completely. The whole universal is expressed in each particular, and the whole of the particular expresses the universal and nothing

else. Every particular number is equally an example of number, and nothing but number. Therefore every man really expresses the universal, God, equally well. It may be that one particular expresses it to us more clearly than another by reason of certain conventionalities and habits of our mind; as for instance a schoolboy might be unable to prove of a cardboard triangle what he can perfectly well prove of one in chalk on the blackboard. But this is a fault of the schoolboy, and no merit in the chalk triangle. One particular may seem to represent the universal in so uniquely perfect a way that it and it alone may be taken as the full representation of it; but this error.
is never really a justifiable proceeding. It is a prejudice and an

On the other hand, the universal itself, which as a matter of fact exists only in various particulars, is sometimes falsely conceived as if it were itself another particular; and thus arises the notion of an archetype or ideal specimen of a class, to which every less perfect member is an approximation. These two tendencies of false logic, the tendency to elevate one particular into the standard and only real instance of a universal, and the tendency to hypostasize the universal into a perfect and ideal particular, together give (it is supposed) the *rationale* of the process by which one man has been elevated into the sole and perfect revelation of the divine. The truth rather is (according to this view) that every man, as a particular instance of the nature of spirit, whose universal is God, is equally an instance of that nature and a manifestation of the essence of God.

This view is based on assuming that God is the universal of which man is the particular. But this can hardly be the case; for God and man would then be as inseparable as triangularity from a given triangle. The fact of evil, that is to say, the alienation of man from God, becomes on such a view mere nonsense, as if one should talk of the de-triangularizing of triangles. The assumption involved, that every man as such is completely and in the fullest sense divine, begs the question at issue. Indeed it is an unwarranted assumption that because we call a given set of individuals men therefore they equally well manifest even the nature of men. If human nature means virtues—what man ought to be—it is not common to every man equally. Some men in that sense are human and others inhuman. And if it merely means the bare qualities which every man has in common, such qualities considered in abstraction are nothing definite at all; for the quality which one man makes a means to crime another may use as a means to virtue; and the crime or the virtue are the really important things, the character of the individual men. But these are not common to all men, and therefore not "human nature" in this sense. In fact there is no such thing as human nature in the sense of a definite body of characteristics common to everyone, and if there were it would not be by any means the same thing as God.

If the universal is a quality or attribute exemplified by individuals which are called its particulars, according to the doctrine of logic, then the relation between God and men is not one of universal and particular. If God were considered as simply the quality goodness instead of being a person, then he would be the universal of all good actions; but on that account he would not be the universal of bad ones, and since bad actions are real acts of will, God would not be the universal of minds as such. The ordinary logical conception of the universal, the one quality of many things, is in fact inapplicable to the relation between God and other minds. And therefore we cannot argue that any particular mind shows the nature of God as well as any other. The question to be asked about mind is not what it is, but what it does, a question with which the logic of things and qualities does not deal.

(*c*) Beyond these objections the question of Christ's uniqueness passes into the region of history. It is only necessary to add one warning: that if he is the means of communicating the divine life to man and raising man into union with God, the very success of his mission will in one sense destroy his uniqueness. Anyone who fully learns his teacher's lesson has become spiritually one with his teacher; and therefore the teacher's experience of the truth is no longer unique. The teacher remains unique only as the first discoverer of the truth in the order of time, or as the mediator of it in the order of education; in the completion of his life this uniqueness disappears into absolute unity with his disciples. If therefore we try to define the uniqueness of the Christ in such a way as to make his experience incapable of real communication to man, we shall be preserving his divinity at the expense of his humanity, and making the supposed manifestation of God to man an illusion. The revelation—any revelation—sets before us an ideal; if the ideal is not literally and completely capable of attainment, it is not an ideal at all. It is an *ignis fatuus*.

But if this is so, it will be asked, why does history tell us of one and only one life in which it has been fully attained? Does not the isolated position of Jesus Christ in history, his infinite moral superiority to all the saints, prove that there was in his nature some element that is denied to us; and are we not driven by the facts to suppose that his uniqueness lay not so much in the use he made of human faculties as in the possession of superhuman?

To this we must reply that the possession by any person of faculties inherently different, whether in nature or integrity, from our own, makes our attempts to live his life not merely vain but unreasonable; as if a man should emulate the strength of an elephant or a hereditary consumptive the physique of his untainted ancestors. If it is answered that these higher faculties can indeed be possessed by man, but only as bestowed by divine grace, we shall reply that this is exactly the position we have been maintaining: for we believe that a man's human nature consists in no definite and circumscribed group of qualities, but precisely in those achievements to which the divine grace may lead him, or those sins into which he may fall by the rejection of such guidance. But to explain why one man attains and another fails is no part of our task.

(*d*) The Christ has absolute experience of the nature of God and lives in absolute free obedience to his will. So far as anybody attains these ideals in the pursuit of truth and duty, he shares the experience with Christ in absolute union with him, that is, with God. Such moments of attainment, in even the greatest men, are no doubt rare; but they are the metal of life which, when the reckoning is made, is separated from the dross and is alone worth calling life at all. Separate out from the total of experience all errors, all failures, all sins; and the gold that is left will be entirely one with the Christ-life. We thus see from a new point of view the absolute unity of Christ and God; for, as we said earlier, God is the reality of the world conceived as a whole which in its self-realization and impulse toward unity purges out of itself all evil and error. History regarded in that way—not as a mere bundle of events but as a process of the solution of problems and the overcoming of difficulties—is altogether summed up in the infinite personality of God; and we can now see that it is equally summed up in the infinite personality of the God-Man.

If Christ is thus the epitome, the summary and ordered whole, of history, the same is true of every man in his degree. The attainment of any real truth is an event, doubtless, in time, and capable of being catalogued in the chronologies of abstract history; but the truth itself is not historically circumscribed. A man may come to know God through a sudden "revelation" or "conversion"; but God is the same now and forever. In the knowledge of God, then, which means in all true knowledge, man comes into touch with something out of time, something to which time makes no difference. And since knowledge of God is union with God, he does not merely see an extra-temporal reality; he does not merely glance through breaking mists at the battlements of eternity, as Moses saw the promised land from the hill of renunciation. By his knowledge of eternity he is one with eternity; he has set himself in the center of all time and all existence, free from the changes and the flux of things. He has entered into the life of God, and in becoming one with God he is already beyond the shadow of changing and the bitterness of death.

There is a faint analogue to this immortality in the work by which a man leaves something of himself visibly present on earth. The workman in a cathedral sets his own mark upon the whole and leaves his monument in the work of his hands. He passes away, but his work—his expressed thought, his testimony to the glory of God—remains enshrined in stone. Even that is liable to decay, and in time such earthly immortality is as if it had never been. But if a man has won his union with the mind of God, has known God's thought and served God's purpose in any of the countless ways in which it can be served, his monument is not something that stands for an age when he is dead. It is his own new and perfected life; something that in its very nature cannot pass away, except by desertion of the achieved ideal. This is the statue of the perfect man, more perennial than bronze; the life in a house not made with hands, eternal in the heavens.

CAN THE NEW IDEALISM DISPENSE WITH MYSTICISM?

BY the "new idealism" Miss Underhill seems to mean the philosophy of Croce and Gentile. Her thesis is therefore a criticism of these writers, and I shall try to discover how far they are really open to her criticisms. This is a question of fact, and is solely concerned with the actual content of their philosophy, and especially that of Gentile, for reasons stated below.

By "mysticism" I take her to mean an intuitive or immediate consciousness of the supreme reality as one, eternal, and spiritual. The question therefore arises whether these philosophers differ from mysticism in content, *i.e.,* in having a different view of the nature of reality, or in form, *i.e.,* in not regarding the ultimate reality as capable of being apprehended intuitively. I am not certain what she means by "dispense with," but she might mean (1) ignore, leave out of the picture of human life, or (2) dissociate oneself from, decline to identify oneself with. Thus a philosophy which denied that mysticism was a necessary element in human life would dispense with it, or try to, in the first sense; a philosophy which held that the proper method of philosophical thought was distinct from the method followed by mysticism would dispense with it, or try to, in the second.

The first sense may be at once dismissed. No philosopher worthy of the name ignores religion or tries to construct a view of human life in which it has no part whatever: and both Croce and Gentile identify mysticism with religion. Croce, it is true, does not in his systematic philosophy represent religion as one of the "necessary forms of the spirit," but he certainly tries to give us, even here, a philosophical account of religion, though a slight and not altogether satisfactory one. The only necessary forms of the spirit which

Reprinted from *Proceedings of the Aristotelian Society,* Supp. Vol. III (1923).

he recognizes are art, history regarded as identical with philosophy, economic action, and moral action. Religion, in that case, is not a pure form of the spirit but a mixed form, a compound of elements drawn from various sources, and therefore unstable, because these elements are liable to separate out and pursue each its own way, and confused, because the different elements impose conflicting claims on the mind and this gives rise to a division of the mind against itself. This is not by any means altogether false as an account of certain characteristics of religion. For instance, religion is not wholly unconcerned with philosophy, like art; for it always contains a philosophical element. But it cannot allow this philosophical element to have its head and take command, for then what was religion would simply become philosophy. Thus religion has not that singleness of aim which marks a true form of the spirit: it contains a number of conflicting tendencies, to each of which it must say, *nec tecum possum vivere, nec sine te.*

This is the view of religion expressed in Croce's earlier works, and it evidently belongs to that rigid and abstract formalism which has given us the doctrine of the four "Forms of the Spirit." This doctrine represents not the vital and fertile element of Croce's philosophy, but its barren and mechanical side; and the greatness both of Croce himself and of his followers is shown by the extent to which they extricate themselves from its blighting influence. Croce himself, in his later works, partly modifies and partly ignores it: his abler successors break away from it altogether. But when this doctrine is no longer treated as a philosophical first principle, the depreciatory view of religion which is its corollary vanishes. For that view was only adopted because there was no room for religion in the formal scheme of the philosophy of the spirit.

This happens in Croce himself in such passages as the following. "Religion is nothing but the need for an orientation toward the concept and the value of life and reality as a whole. Without religion, without this orientation, no one can live; or at least one lives in division and perplexity of spirit, lives unhappily. A religion which coincides with philosophical truth is no doubt better than a mythological religion; but any religion, however mythological, is better than none." (*Cultura e vita morale,* p. 37.) Here, in a work written without special reference to the writer's formal philosophical views, we reach the germ of a new attitude to religion, which those views had suppressed.

This hint of a new attitude to religion is in Croce no more than a hint; but in Gentile it blossoms into a complete new philosophy of religion.[1] This is best expressed in the essay *Le Forme assolute dello Spirito,* in the volume *Il Modernismo e i Rapporti tra Religione e Filosofia* (1909). Religion, in this view, is a permanent and necessary form of the spirit. In so far as the spirit simply asserts itself, careless of the existence and the nature of any object for its thought, it expresses itself as art. Art is thus purely subjective and free imagination. In so far as it renounces this freedom of caprice and imagination and surrenders itself to its object, this object being of course the absolute object, the supreme reality, it expresses itself as religion. To art belong all the virtues of self-assertion, to religion those of loyalty, humility, self-denial. But neither of these forms exists by itself. Each as described is an abstraction, a limiting case, represents not anything that really exists but something that would exist if its opposite could (*per impossibile*) be annihilated. Actual human life is always a synthesis of art and religion, and so far as this synthesis is really effected and the two elements co-exist harmoniously in the mind, their combined functioning is philosophy. Hence the concrete life of religion is properly called not religion merely but religion and art at once, that is, philosophy. And the same is true of the concrete life of art. So far as any human being succeeds in living and in satisfying somehow the various needs of his mind, so far as he at all finds peace and salvation, he is, certainly, in possession of religion; but not of religion alone. He is, though he may not call himself by that name, a philosopher. His religion is not the only force at work within him: it is supplemented and compensated by the force of art. If he were solely religious, if religion were the only thing he cared for, his personality would be simply swallowed up in the object of his worship. This, Miss Underhill reminds us, does not

1. Not altogether new, in so far as it only restates the fundamental doctrine of Hegel's *Philosophie des Geistes.*

happen to the mystic.[2] Certainly it does not, and Gentile never suggests that it does. But the reason why it does not is that the religious impulse to lose oneself in God is balanced by the artistic impulse to assert and express oneself, to find oneself in the very act of self-surrender.

So far, the difference between Gentile's view and that for which Miss Underhill is contending is a mere matter of words. Each is agreed that there is one single and whole spiritual life, which is the true life of man and is actually achieved by human beings in this world; each is agreed that in this life we at once lose ourselves in the contemplation of an absolute object and in that self-surrender find ourselves. Gentile calls this life philosophy, and Miss Underhill calls it mysticism. That is not in itself an important difference. For Gentile does not mean that this life is a privilege of those who have taken a University degree in philosophy, nor does Miss Underhill mean that it is confined to people who get their names mentioned in learned works on mysticism.

What then is the point on which they differ? It appears from Miss Underhill's opening paragraphs to be this. Gentile's philosophy, she thinks, denies outright the existence of any such absolute object of thought as that which the mystics contemplate. This absolute object is one, eternal, and unchanging: Gentile's philosophy, she tells us, is a philosophy of change. It agrees here, she says, with that of Bergson. Its absolute reality is an absolute flux. Hence it stands in the sharpest opposition to all mysticism, whose insistence that its own object is lifted above the flux of things cannot be lightly passed over or explained away.

In this matter I am heartily at one with Miss Underhill. I do think that if we accept a philosophy of change we must describe the experience of the mystics as a peculiar form of hallucination, and it is a hallucination whose origin we shall find it very difficult to explain. But I venture to accuse her of a radical misunderstanding of Gentile's philosophy when she identifies it with the philosophies of change. I know that the same view was lately expressed by

2. She seems even to deny that there is in mysticism a *tendency* for it to happen; but she would no doubt disclaim any intention of denying this.

Dr. Bosanquet, and it is just because of my deep respect and affection for his memory that I welcome the opportunity of clearing up a question on which I believe him to have made a mistake, without being forced to engage in controversy with one who can no longer reply. For the point is one of some importance and concerns our whole valuation of a philosophy which, whatever its shortcomings, is one of the most remarkable of the present day. And I confine myself to Gentile, because it is in his hands that the tendency common to him and Croce reveals its features most clearly, and that this tendency first gives rise to a considered and consistent philosophy of religion.

Reality, for Gentile, is history. Now history is not, as Miss Underhill assumes, a synonym for change. Change is, if I may put it this way, a realistic concept, history an idealistic. That which changes is a mere object, which need not know that it is changing, and indeed which no one need know to be changing. The philosophy of change is a "metaphysic of being," that is, a philosophy which tries to describe the world as a thing in itself without raising the question how it comes to be known. And there can be little doubt that the philosophy of change makes the world unknowable. That which has a history, on the other hand, is a mind, for matter may change but it cannot be said to have a history. And this mind knows its own history. It is simply by knowing its own history that, in Gentile's view, it comes to have a history at all. Hence Gentile's philosophy is a "metaphysic of knowledge," that is to say, a philosophy which never loses sight of the question "how do we come to know what we know?"

History is thus by definition something known. It is not merely a process, it is a known process. But the mind which knows a process can only do so by somehow detaching itself from and rising above this process. If it were wholly immersed in the process, it would, perhaps, *be* changing, but it could never know that it was changing. And this unknowable process would therefore not really be a process at all; it would not be a change *in* the mind, for the mind would no longer possess that continuity without which no change can take place. One mind would perish at every instant and another would come into being; and that is not change in a mind.

Hence change *in* a mind must be change *for* that mind, a change of which that mind is conscious; and to be conscious of it, the mind must somehow be raised above it. How is this apparent contradiction to be realized? How is the mind to be at once in change and out of change? Only if the mind *originates change in itself*. For then, as the source and ground of change, it will not be *subject* to change; while on the other hand, as undergoing change through its own free act, it will exhibit change. This double aspect of the mind as active and passive is the very heart of Gentile's philosophy. It is his favorite distinction of *act* and *fact*. The act is out of time in the sense that it creates time, just as it is supernatural in the sense that it creates nature; the fact is temporal, natural, subject to all those laws which constitute its finiteness. But between the act and the fact there is no division: the distinction is only an ideal distinction. In creating the fact, the act realizes itself, and does not live apart in a heaven of its own from which it issues mandates for the creation of facts; it lives in the facts which it creates, and can say to the fact, "Thou art my son, this day have I begotten thee." [3]

This identity of act and fact, which is the immanence of which so much is said by Croce, is necessary for the following reason. If the active or creative mind were *merely* active and creative, if what it created were something other than itself, then this other, this created object, would be a mere flux of appearances without permanence, solidity, or substance. Only the permanent can change; and therefore the principle of permanence, the unchanging reality, must be immanent in the very process of change, or this process could not take place. If the changing were one thing and the unchanging another, if that which changed were not also permanent and that which is permanent were not also changing, then both the permanent and the changing would be illusory. If the permanent and creative principle is called God and the changing creation is called the World, we thus reach the formula that it is only the presence of God in the world that makes the world real, and only his self-expression in the act of creating the world that makes God actual. Whether formulae of this kind, so notoriously common in mystical

3. *Autoctisi,* "self-creation," is one of Gentile's favorite words for this "pure act."

writings, are really at variance with the spirit of mysticism, I do not take upon myself to say. But they are of the essence of Gentile's philosophy.

Miss Underhill says, however, that mysticism also requires transcendence, and that Gentile denies all transcendence, and hence denies a fundamental principle of mysticism. Her paper suggests that she regards transcendence and mysticism as synonymous, but we all know from her works that this is not her view, and that she really regards transcendence as one aspect of mysticism, complementary to immanence. Now here again there is some danger of a quarrel about words. Gentile gives the name religion or mysticism to the element of transcendence or the losing of the mind in its object, an element, as he tells us, of all human life but not the only element. To the element of immanence he gives the name of art. And these two elements are always actually found together in the synthesis which is philosophy. In this synthesis, therefore, transcendence is always present, but is never the last word; it is dialectically present as one of the two elements whose tension constitutes the life of the whole, but the last word lies with the synthesis which is neither mere transcendence nor mere immanence, but the principle called by De Ruggiero *absolute* immanence. Here the word absolute is not loosely used for "pure," as Miss Underhill seems to think: it is used in a well-defined technical sense. The absolute, in this sense, is that which has reconciled its own opposite to itself, and therefore no longer stands in opposition to it. This usage is quite common in the Italian idealists, especially in De Ruggiero. But it goes back to a very respectable antiquity. Thus the metaphysic of *absolute* immanence is the philosophy whose primary principle, that of immanence, has overcome its own abstractness by including in itself its own opposite, namely, the principle of transcendence. And the only sense in which Gentile ever denies all transcendence is that he denies *in toto* its right to be considered as the ultimate solution of the problem of philosophy. Thus Gentile is as convinced of the necessity of transcendence as Miss Underhill herself, and differs from her, here again, in the use of words only. That reconciliation of the opposing principles of immanence and transcendence which both regard as possible, necessary, and indeed actual, she calls mysticism, and he calls it philosophy.

This broad agreement between Gentile and his critic is recognized by Miss Underhill herself when she comes to mention Hegel. Hegel's Absolute Spirit, she says, is all that mysticism requires; though she takes this back by adding that, so far as Hegel identifies reality with history and becoming, he falls into the modern error of regarding time as ultimately real. This is an accusation which would surprise Hegel as much as it would Gentile. For both alike, reality is the absolute spirit; so far there is no difference between them. For both alike, time is created by this absolute spirit in the process of its own activity; it is a product of that activity, not its condition. Here again, Hegel and Gentile are in perfect agreement. Bergsonism is as repugnant to Hegel as it can possibly be to Gentile; and how repugnant it is to *him* can be judged from De Ruggiero's strong remarks on its spiritual emptiness in *Modern Philosophy* (E.T.), p. 370. Here, as usual, the views of Gentile are pretty well in agreement with those expressed by De Ruggiero. Miss Underhill, in fact, seems anxious to detect differences between the idealism of Hegel and that of the modern Italians where in fact none exist. I do not mean that there are no differences; but the views to which she takes exception in the Italians are really not "new"—the Italians would be indignant at being labeled "new idealists," as if their philosophy were something different from the well-established tradition of post-Kantian idealism—but are the commonplaces of the post-Kantian tradition. It is indeed simply because they are commonplaces that she has not quite understood them; for Gentile's books are written for the student who is presumed to have been already well drilled in the philosophy of Kant and his successors. Hence the argument which I have set forth and described as the heart of Gentile's philosophy is for the most part rather assumed than stated by himself. It is the common ground of all idealism, and he takes for granted the reader's knowledge of it. Had he not done so, had he written a philosophical book for the untrained reader, he would have laid upon it an emphasis which he nowhere actually gives it. Thus his books are easy for the non-

Italian reader to misunderstand: and this is especially the case if the reader approaches them with Bergson in his mind. Gentile never takes it into his head to point out his own divergences from Bergson; he evidently sees no reason why he should do so, because he rightly thinks that there is between them no common ground. Hence I do not know that he even mentions the French philosopher in the whole course of his works.

The only divergence of view which I have so far been able to find between Miss Underhill and Gentile is that, for Gentile, the absolute spirit which is the ground of time and change subjects *itself* to these laws and does not impose them upon a reality outside itself; whereas I gather that Miss Underhill wants an absolute which is not merely the creator of time and change, but is not itself bound by the laws of its own making and is therefore to be described as *unchanging*. This negative qualification of the absolute goes beyond the positive qualification by which it is described as the author and ground of change. But I may be wrong in thinking that Miss Underhill would insist on this negative term; and if she does, I feel bound to remind her that she has (rightly, I think) denounced those philosophies which claim to say what the universe *is not*.

But I suspect that there may be graver differences not yet brought to light. In the first place, when she asks whether this or that philosophy can dispense with mysticism, the phrase conveys to my mind the following suggestion. I do not know whether Miss Underhill would endorse the suggestion or not. It is that philosophy, by its very nature as discursive thinking, is incapable of reaching ultimate truths, since these can only be reached by a kind of intellectual intuition; and this disability on the part of philosophy attaches with especial force to those philosophies which most emphatically renounce all claim to the possession of such intuition. Now it is notorious that all idealism since Kant has maintained that ultimate truth is to be reached, if at all, only by hard thinking, by the critical development of rational theory, and not by any kind of intellectual intuition. There are today philosophies which still claim such an intuition, but none of these are idealistic, and Miss Underhill's selection of an object for attack suggests that she thinks the intuition of the mystic to be a revelation of ultimate truth which the modern idealist misses by his own fault; while the intuitionist like Bergson stands a chance of achieving it.

Now if it is true that ultimate truths are to be reached by the path of intuition, and not by the "labor of the notion," then certainly all idealism is futile. So is all scientific and historical thinking. And the only thing left for the person who wants to get at the truth is to return like Nebuchadnezzar to the level of the instinctive animals and *s'installer dans le mouvement,* instead of trying to raise himself above it in order to understand it. I do not know if Miss Underhill means to recommend the example of Nebuchadnezzar, but such counsel is a good deal in fashion today. If on the other hand she means to recommend not the instinctive or infra-rational intuition of a Bergson but some supra-rational intuition, I can only reply that I want further particulars of it. Is it the intuitive νοῦς of Aristotle; and does she really mean us to go back to that as an ideal of knowledge? If so, then modern philosophy is indeed bankrupt. But if not, what is it? Whatever it is, it is intuitive; and that means that it cannot explain or indeed express itself; and so it is perhaps useless for us to demand a description of it. It is as indescribable in itself as it is unable to describe the truths it apprehends. It can only be the non-existent way of apprehending the non-existent.

But, I may be told, this intuitive thought is actually enjoyed by the mystics. It is non-existent; it is a quite familiar experience, and its object is the ultimate reality. To this I should reply that I have no doubt either of the existence or of the validity of the mystical experience. But I have the gravest doubts about its intuitive or immediate character. It is a common thing that people who have certain experiences should be unable to give an account of them, and it is hardly less common that they should give a wrong account. If you ask an artist how he composes his works of art, you may get for answer, "I don't know"; or you may, and often do, get a description which is demonstrably false, and recognizably derived not from genuine introspection but from some philosophy or psychology in fashion at the moment. I suggest that this, which is so flagrantly true of artists, may perhaps be true of mystics also; and that we ought carefully to distinguish between the real mystical experience and the account of that experience which the mystic himself gives when asked for one. Now Christian mysticism—I am not entitled to express an opinion about other kinds—grew up in close contact with a theory of knowledge derived from Greek sources and culminating in the theory of intuitive νοῦς as the method of apprehending ultimate realities. This being the theory accepted by all psychologists of the period, there was every inducement for the mystic, when trying to give an account of the psychology of his own mystical experience, to describe it as an intellectual intuition. And this does not prove that it really was an intellectual intuition, any more than the way in which artists describe their own psychology in terms of Schopenhauer proves that Schopenhauer's philosophy is the true account of the esthetic experience. Nor on the other hand does the fact that the theory of νοῦς is discredited, as it certainly is, prove that the mystical experience is an illusion. All it proves is that the mystical experience is not really immediate.

We need then to distinguish between mystical experiences and descriptive theories of them. The mystics of history have commonly described their experiences in terms of a philosophy now out of date, a philosophy which no competent person now accepts. This need not induce us to throw mysticism overboard as an illusion, but it saddles us with the serious duty of redescribing it in terms of our own philosophy. Modern idealism maintains that all experience is mediate, and therefore it is bound to show that mystical experience is mediate too, and that the traditional account of it as intuitive mutilates and distorts it. I do not think that this is a difficult task. It is easy to show that all sorts of processes of thought have been going on in the mystic's mind, and that the only reason why he overlooked their presence was that he tried his utmost to bring his experience within the narrow frame of the intuitive theory of knowledge. That theory once destroyed, mysticism is easier, not harder, to welcome as a genuine form of experience.

I ought perhaps to close with a rough sketch of the way in which a modern idealistic philosophy might carry out this program. I am aware that in doing so I recklessly expose myself to criticism; but criticism is what I want. Mysticism, then, is a thing which an idealistic philosophy cannot dispense with, in the sense that it cannot frame a view of human life without including it. The function of mysticism in such a view will be not to take the place of scientific or philosophical thought but to have a place of its own. Its peculiarity is perhaps to be sought in the fact that in it the mediation which is actually present is not wholly explicit: the mind reaches truths, but does not know how it has reached them. It may even think that it has not reached them by *any* path, that is by any describable process of thinking; but this, if it is believed, is wrongly believed. The truths in question are reached somehow, and it is the business of scientific or philosophical thought to lay bare this concealed process, to render explicit the mediation which in the mystical experience itself was only implicit. "Substantial truth," said Hegel, and every idealist will agree, "is not dependent for its first revelation upon philosophy." In the mystical experience substantial truth is actually attained, and it remains for philosophy to explain how it was attained. If the mystic likes to hug the idea that his truths were revealed to him by a miracle which no philosophy can explain or describe, such a self-deception is his own affair. That is not mysticism, but a superstitious belief about mysticism. The necessity of mystical experience lies in the principle that we discover new truths neither by the inference of the logic-books nor by the intuition of Aristotle, but by an act of mind which reaches out beyond the given, grasps the new thought as it were in the dark, and only after that consolidates its new conquest by building up to it a bridge of reasoned proof. But the building of this bridge, which is the task of reflection, is only the bringing out into visibility on the sensitive plate of what has already been recorded upon it, the rendering explicit of a mediation or proof which was already there implicitly. The darkness and obscurity which all mystics recognize as a feature of their own experience, by whatever name they call it (inexpressible, ineffable, etc.), is nothing but the implicitness of thought in the mystical experience. Thus the mystical experience is never complete in itself, it always requires to be explicated and tested by philosophical reflection, which alone can say what it is that in our mystical experience we have discovered, and indeed whether we have discovered anything at all, and have not been merely the victims of an illusion. For taken by itself, the mystical experience may always be illusory, and this is fully admitted by Miss Underhill when she speaks of "the excesses to which it has always been liable." To check these excesses something other than mysticism is obviously necessary, and this we find in the discipline, without which mysticism would be mere vaporing, of conscious critical thought. This thought is philosophy, and it is the business of philosophy to criticize mysticism, not the business of mysticism to criticize philosophy. But, as the old verse has it, which is philosopher and which is mystic, "God bless us all, that's quite another thing." [4]

4. Miss Underhill appeals for an explanation of the saying that reality is not (does not exist) but creates itself. The word "exist" here means to exist in a perfectly pure undifferentiated and unchanging self-identity. This is the technical sense of the word fixed by Hegel in the first category of his logic. When Gentile says that reality does not exist he is only saying that it is not a mere empty undifferentiated *one,* but that it has within it articulations, processes, activities. He is denying rather the adequacy of the category than its abstract applicability.

SPECULUM SPECULI: THE UNITY OF LIFE AND MIND

WE set out to construct a map of knowledge on which every legitimate form of human experience should be laid down, its boundaries determined, and its relations with its neighbors set forth. We assumed that such a map could be made: imperfect and abstract, like all maps, but none the less valuable to those whose task it is to explore and cultivate the country of the mind. We assumed, that is to say, the real existence of art, religion, and so forth as distinct forms of experience, forms not wholly separable or independent, but at least mutually exclusive, relatively autonomous and capable of some kind of delimitation.

Such a map of knowledge is impossible; and our trouble is well spent if it produces no other result than the recognition that this is so. There are no autonomous and mutually exclusive forms of experience, and, what is more, it is in no one's interest to assume that there are.

The artist does not want a map of knowledge: he only wants a map of art, and this map is art itself. For him art and life are the same thing: art is long and life is short, his own actual span of work lies wholly within the all-embracing universe of art. The religious man, again, just in so far as he is really religious, in his truly religious moments, knows that nothing but religion exists. All experience is religious experience, even that of the heathen and the atheist. He does not ask for a holiday from his religion: his holiday would be to dwell in the house of the Lord forever. The moralist, again, sees the whole of life as duty. Every claim is for him the claim of duty, and he is not to be deceived when the devil offers him a "moral holiday" or poses him with sophistries about the relation of morality to art. For him, art, when it ought to be pur-

Reprinted from *Speculum Mentis* (Oxford: Clarendon Press, 1924), pp. 306-317.

sued, is a duty: when it ought not, it is a crime. That is all. The scientist again is by the principles of his own thought compelled to interpret everything in scientific terms, as the working of abstract and iron laws. Anyone who pleads for the least little bit of backlash in the working of his machine, an *exiguum clinamen,* at certain moments and at certain points *une certaine élasticité,* is simply as a publican and a sinner: a stink in the nostrils of the scientific conscience. The scientist does not want a map of the forms of knowledge. There is for him only one legitimate form, science; and that is its own map. All other forms are not other territories but false maps of the same territory.

Every person who is actually absorbed in any given form of experience is by this very absorption committed to the opinion that no other form is valid, that his form is the only one adequate to the comprehension of reality. Hence arise discords; for when artists and scientists, who after all do inhabit a common world of fact, meet and discuss their aims, each is apt to accuse the other of wasting his life on a world of illusions. The "ancient quarrel between poetry and philosophy" is only one of a whole series of such quarrels in a ceaseless international war in which every country on our map is eternally embroiled with every other; for all, "because of their independency, are in continual jealousies and in the state and posture of gladiators, having their weapons pointing, and their eyes fixed on one another . . . which is a posture of war." This war is complete even down to the existence of pacifists of the mind, getting between the legs of the combatants and kindly offering to explain to "religion and science," or whatever the combatants may be, that they are fighting about nothing.

On this scene of international warfare the philosopher pictures himself as looking down calmly, enthroned on a cloud *audessus de la mêlée,* seeing perhaps that it is God's will for these deluded mortals to fly at one another's throats, or perhaps, in a voice of authority, bidding them be still, with a result suggestive rather of Canute than of Christ. For they, poor things, do not recognize the philosopher's superhuman status: they actually think he is one of the combatants. "Philosophers," wrote a great historian to a young friend appointed to a philosophical tutorship, "are my natural enemies." And this is perfectly just; for the philosopher asserts philosophy as the only legitimate form of experience, and not only condemns the others as illusory but adds insult to injury by giving reasons for his condemnation, which goes against all the maxims of civilized warfare. Philosophers are justly, therefore, the objects of universal dislike. They fight their own professional battle and claim to be defending the ark of God.

This, roughly speaking, is the situation with which we began. We hoped that the proper construction of a map of knowledge, by a kind of international boundary commission, might do something to stop the fighting. It was a vain hope. Plenty of such maps have been made already, in the form of philosophies of the human mind and so forth, and they only arouse suspicion, because they are not international documents but the propaganda of one combatant.

Beginning, then, with our assumption of the separateness and autonomy of the various forms of experience, we have found that this separateness is an illusion. Each form is at bottom identical with all the others. It is only an error that makes some people ignore one element of their experience and others ignore another, and thus come to the conclusion that their experiences are of a fundamentally different kind. They are different, but it is only the error of thinking they are different that makes them different. Artists and scientists must fight; it is their nature to; but they have acquired this nature by committing themselves to the error of regarding art and science as independent things.

The various countries on our initial map, then, turn up to be variously-distorted versions of one and the same country. No one accustomed to maps compiled from travelers' reports will be surprised at that. What, then, is this one country? It is the world of historical fact, seen as the mind's knowledge of itself. Can we, then, sketch this country's features in outline?

We cannot. To explore that country is the endless task of the mind; and it only exists in being explored. Of such a country there is no map, for it is itself its own map. The explorer, the country explored, and the map are one and the same thing.

There is and can be no map of knowledge, for a map means an abstract of the main features of a country, laid before the traveler in advance of his experience of the country itself. Now no one can describe life to a person who stands on the threshold of life. The maxims given by age to youth are valueless not because age means nothing by them but because what it means is just its own past life. To youth they are empty words. The life of the spirit cannot be described except by repeating it: an account of it would just be itself. This is equally the case whether we present our map in the form of a group of categories or concepts which are supposed to reappear as units of thought in the texture of experience; or a group of laws somehow suspended above it which govern its course; or a group of presuppositions which lie beyond and behind its very beginning, and condition, through its beginning, its whole development; or a world of objects over against it, in beating itself against which it comes to the use of its own powers; or a series of stages through which, as along a railway line, it necessarily runs. All these assertions of something other than the absolute mind itself are versions of a single error: the error of abstraction, of failing to realize that subject and object, condition and conditioned, ground and consequence, particular and universal, can only be distinctions which fall within one and the same whole, and that this whole can only be the infinite fact which is the absolute mind. A fact which has anything outside it is not the concrete fact. If that which falls outside it is its own law or nature, we have fallen into the abstraction which tears apart the individual into particular and universal; if another fact, we have torn apart the individual into two individuals unrelated and therefore both fictitious.

Our inquiry has not only abolished the notion of a map of knowledge distinct from knowledge itself: it has also abolished the notion of an external world other than the mind. It has not, of course, abolished the distinction between subject and object: on the contrary, it has established our right to use that distinction by showing its necessity in the life of thought. It is no more abolished than are the distinctions between truth and error, good and evil, particular and universal: these distinctions are only abolished by the *coincidentia oppositorum* which is the suicide of abstract thought, and conserved by the synthesis of opposites which is the life of concrete thought. Just as we began by assuming a map of knowledge, so we began by assuming an external world, a world of which we could say with the realists that it really is what, errors apart, we think it to be: a world of which we could even say that it was what it was quite irrespective of any ignorance or error of our own about it. Our position at the start was wholly realistic, and there is a sense in which it is realistic to the end. But we did not—and this is where realists tend to go wrong—assume that "errors apart" is a clause which need not be taken too seriously. We did not assume that any one form of experience could be accepted as already, in its main lines, wholly free from error. Led by this principle, we found that the real world was implied, but not asserted, in art; asserted, but not thought out, in religion; thought out, but only subject to fictitious assumptions, in science; and therefore in all these we found an ostensible object—the work of art, God, the material universe—which was confessedly a figment and not the real object. The real object is the mind itself, as we now know.

But in abolishing the notion of an external world other than the mind we do not assert any of the silly nonsense usually described by unintelligent critics as idealism. We do not assert that the trees and hills and people of our world are "unreal" or "mere ideas in my mind," still less that matter is nothing but a swarm of mind-particles. The very essence of trees and hills and people is that they should be not myself but my objects in perception: they are not subjective but objective, not states of myself but facts that I know. None the less, my knowing them is organic to them: it is because they are what they are that I can know them, because I know them that they can be what to me they really are. They and I alike are members of one whole, a whole which the destruction of one part would in a sense destroy throughout, as the death of our dearest friend darkens for us the very light of the sun.

A philosopher once refuted idealism by begging his audience to watch his desk and see whether, when he left the room, it continued to exist or not. It was a pretty piece of buffoonery, whose chief merit was to show that he imagined them to see in his desk everything that he saw in it himself: in other words, that he took his stand firmly on the abstract point of view which cannot see that any given fact makes any difference to the whole. Now such an act of abstraction, error though it is, really creates its own world, though not a wholly rational world. To dispose of this world by calling it a mere idea is no more intelligent than to call a temptation to sin, or a nightmare, or a toothache, a mere idea in the hope of dispelling it. The world of abstract concepts—the material world—is an objective world called into existence indeed by an error of the mind, but by that very error *asserted as real*. Hence to make the abstraction and to regard the reality of its object as self-evident are one and the same thing, and these farcical refutations of idealism are only successful as showing, what nobody doubts, that it is as possible to put your blind eye to a microscope as to a telescope.

Now the construction of such an abstract world is not a pointless or purposeless waste of energy on the part of the mind. To suppose that this is so, that religion is *only* a fiction and science *only* an arbitrary play of abstractions, is the error of those critics, whether of religion or science, who unintelligently praise one by unintelligently condemning the other. In the toil of art, the agony of religion, and the relentless labor of science, actual truth is being won and the mind is coming to its own true stature. This is simply because the ostensible object whose apparent articulations are being so patiently traced is not the real object, and because every new touch given to the determination of the former does not obscure, but rather illustrates, the latter. For the true object is not concealed behind the ostensible as behind a veil. Had that been so, the elaboration of the veil could but make its density deeper, and religion or science would be the prison-house of a self-frustrated mind whose very effort to see the world only resulted in its enclosure within a thicker and thicker crust of illusion. But the true object is not

> our great roof, its gilt carving and groining,
> Under yon spider-webs lying.

It is the mind itself. And thus the external world is not a veil between it and its object, but a picture of itself, drawn to aid its own self-vision; a picture which as it grows firmer and harder, takes surface and polish and steadiness, becomes the Mirror of the

Mind; and all the detail visible in it is seen by the mind to be the reflection of its own face.

Knowledge polarizes itself into abstract or erroneous and concrete or true. Abstract knowledge is the same as error, because, separating what is thought to be from what is, it erects that which it thinks into a false object over against itself, an external world. To err, and believe in an external world over against the mind, are one and the same thing. Now if error were mere error, the mind would merely assert the external object, which is what it thinks itself to be, and thereby deny itself, and resolve the dualism. But all error contains an element of truth, and the conflict between the truth and the error appears as the externality of the object, its otherness with respect to the mind. Because these two are really one, all knowledge of the external object is really the mind's knowledge of itself. But all this knowledge, however true it may be, is affected by the fact that it is projected upon an external world: it is, so to speak, reversed like the face we see in the glass. This reversal constitutes its falsity; as long as we do not know that we are looking at our own reflection, we see not ourselves but a distorted caricature of ourselves, in some ways strangely like, in some ways opposite. Hence we can never resolve the doubt whether nature is our tender mother or a tigerish Kali, whether God is love or tyranny, whether matter is embodied reason or embodied irrationality. This doubt is the mind's wonder whether the face it sees is that of its twin brother or its opposite. All externality breeds this ambiguity, for the ambiguity is the equivocation of error as such.

To see in a glass and to see darkly are the same. But in concrete knowledge the mind sees itself face to face, and knows even as it is known. Here the object is the subject, not in the sense of a *that is thou* which is the mere negation of individual distinction, but in the sense that the object finds its very life in being known by the subject, the subject in knowing the object. Of this experience it is said that *number* here in love is slain: not distinction, not individuality, but separateness, the externality of abstract units to one another. The whole objective world is concentrating its energies into the creation of this one act of consciousness, and this one act greets the whole world as its own world, not because it cannot see the difference between one thing and another, which is precisely the attitude of the abstract concept, but because it can see the identity which is the basis of this difference.

This absolute experience of concrete knowledge has nothing to do with any professional distinctions, any more than with distinctions of social class or physical race. The enjoyment of it has nothing to do with that "philosophy," a confused mixture of scientific abstractions and historical facts, which is professionally expounded by people called philosophers. It lives in a unity above all professional distinctions, and the philosopher may well achieve it in greater perfection when sailing a boat or telling stories to a child than when discoursing technicalities to a class. But it is not an intuitive or emotional experience, a mood whose precious visits illuminate the waste of life: it is just life itself in its infinite self-conscious development, a development which sees every detail of itself as organic to the whole.

This life has no map and no object other than itself: if it had such an object, that would be its map, for the features of the object would be its own features. Thus the external world, whose origin, growth, and structure we have been, throughout this book, investigating, is the Mirror of the Mind and the Map of Knowledge in one.

But to make such a cleavage as we have suggested between concrete and abstract knowledge, truth and error, is to commit another abstraction. Concrete knowledge is not generically different from abstract knowledge, it is abstract knowledge freed from its own abstractness by simply recognizing that abstractness. The mind is not one among a number of objects of knowledge, which possesses the peculiarity of being alone fully knowable: it is that which is really known in the ostensible knowing of any object whatever. In an immediate and direct way, the mind can never know itself: it can only know itself through the mediation of an external world, know that what it sees in the external world is its own reflection. Hence the construction of external worlds—works of art, religions, sciences, structures of historical fact, codes of law, systems of philosophy and so forth *ad infinitum*—is the only way by which the mind can possibly come to that self-knowledge which is its end.

Such a constructive process is one of abstraction and error so long as the external world in question is not realized to be the mind's own work. It is perhaps not possible to carry out this process in the full consciousness of what one is doing: the illusion of abstract objectivity is essential to it: it must be done in good faith, in the belief that one is now at last discovering the ultimate truth, coming into contact with a pre-existent and absolute reality. But when it is done, when the work of art or system of philosophy or what not is achieved, the mind, in so far as this exercise has really strengthened instead of exhausting it, realizes that it has not been exploring an external world but tracing its own lineaments in a mirror. In this realization it sees the abstraction of its previous work to be an abstraction and nothing more, and the abstraction, the error, is thus vanquished. The truth is not some perfect system of philosophy: it is simply the way in which all systems, however perfect, collapse into nothingness on the discovery that they are only systems, only external worlds over against the knowing mind and not that mind itself.

This process of the creation and destruction of external worlds might appear, to superficial criticism, a mere futile weaving and unweaving of Penelope's web, a declaration of the mind's inability to produce solid assets, and thus the bankruptcy of philosophy. And this it would be if knowledge were the same thing as information, something stored in encyclopedias and laid on like so much gas and water in schools and universities. But education does not mean stuffing a mind with information; it means helping a mind to create itself, to grow into an active and vigorous contributor to the life of the world. The information given in such a process is meant to be absorbed into the life of the mind itself, and a boy leaving school with a memory full of facts is thereby no more educated than one who leaves table with his hands full of food is thereby fed. At the completion of its education, if that event ever happened, a mind would step forth as naked as a new-born babe, knowing nothing, but having acquired the mastery over its own weaknesses, its own desires, its own ignorance, and able therefore to face any danger unarmed.

The collapse of a system of thought is therefore not equivalent to the cancellation of the process by which it came into being. It collapses, but it does not perish. In constructing and destroying it, the mind has learned a permanent lesson: it has triumphed over an error and so discovered a truth. The destroyed system collapses not into bare nothingness but into immediacy, into a characteristic or attribute of the mind itself, passes as it were into the muscle and bone of the mind, becomes an element in the point of view from which the mind raises its next problem.

For the life of the mind consists of raising and solving problems, problems in art, religion, science, commerce, politics, and so forth. The solution of the problems does not leave behind it a sediment of ascertained fact, which grows and solidifies as the mind's work goes on. Such a sediment is nothing but the externality of a half-solved problem: when the problem is fully solved the sediment of information disappears and the mind is left at liberty to go on. Philosophy, therefore, is not a prerogative kind of knowledge immune from this reabsorption into the mind's being: it is nothing but the recognition that this reabsorption is necessary and is indeed the end and crown of all knowledge, the self-recognition of the mind in its own mirror.

THE DRAMA OF ABSOLUTE MIND: THE REDEMPTION OF MAN AND GOD

To describe philosophy as the mind's knowledge of itself is only a formal or abstract description, and likely to cause misunderstanding. We shall not blame the reader if he sees a picture, first of a mind contemplating an entire universe, rich in detail of every kind —the picture being entitled "Realism"; secondly, the universe blotted ruthlessly out and the mind reflecting on its own forlorn condition, this picture bearing the title "Idealism." The mind, as conceived by the realist, seems to have lost everything that makes life worth living.

But the reader who feels this difficulty must not be offended if he is answered as people answer a child who says "When I am in heaven, I shall want a Rolls-Royce and a salmon-rod." The correct answer is, we understand, "If you want them when you get to heaven, you shall have them." If the mind feels cold without an object other than itself, nothing is simpler for it than to create a palace of art, a world of mythology, a cosmos of abstract conceptual machinery, and so forth. In fact that is precisely what it does when it cannot achieve what it really wants—self-knowledge—without the help of these things. But it is not these things that it wants: it is self-knowledge. For when it has its works of art, what it values in them is not themselves but the glimpses they give it of hidden and mysterious beauty. What it worships in the figures of its gods is not these figures themselves in their externality to itself but the revelation through them of something really divine, and so on. If then anyone feels that the ideal of knowledge, as we present it, is cold and unattractive, abstract and barren, we reply: How would you like to enjoy forever what in the highest art you glimpse, half-

Reprinted from *Speculum Mentis* (Oxford: Clarendon Press, 1924), pp. 291-303.

concealed in the torrent of sensation? How would you like to live face to face with that which now and then you have felt stir your heart in moments of worship and prayer? And if he is so simple as to believe that the very evanescence of these moments is what gives them their value, the answer is that to prefer them in the form of evanescent emotion is just to create the world of art and religion. To feel the need of an external world is already to possess such a world; for the error of thinking one needs it is the same as the error of thinking that it exists. This is parallel to the familiar truth that to look on virtue as cold and unattractive is not to wish one were vicious, but to be vicious.

Not that such creation of an external object is capricious. The mind cannot simply think whatever it pleases, or even imagine whatever it pleases. It is bound by the laws of its own nature to this extent, that even though it can deform its nature by misconceiving it, it can never deform it out of recognition, because misconceiving is after all a kind of conceiving. Its scientific concepts, its religious imagery, its aesthetic imaginings must grow out of the soil of fact, and that fact is just its own nature as that stands for the time being. This necessity of all its actions, ignored in the life of imagination, is though ignored not done away with. It is transformed, by being ignored, from a rational necessity to the blind necessity of instinct, obedient to a law which it does not understand. The discovery of necessity—not indeed an alien necessity, but the necessity of its own nature, which appears as external only so long as the figment of an external world remains—is the achievement of the religious consciousness; but this necessity is there from the first.

All externality is imaginary; for externality—a mutual outsideness in the abstract sense of the denial of a mutual insideness—is as such abstraction, and abstraction is always intuition or imagination. It is only to the imagination that the mind is *ever* outside its object; but to the imagination it is *always* outside its object, even when that object is itself, as in fact it always is. Therefore, since the externality of the object is only imaginary, the act by which we create the object is never capricious: we only imagine it to be capricious; in point of fact it is necessary and an integral part of the life of reason.

Philosophy therefore does not mean the negation of all other forms of experience and the reduction of all life to the dead-level of cold "thinking." That, no doubt, would "strike as chill as the coldest materialism"; in fact it would simply *be* materialism, for it would be the assertion of the abstract concept. The progressive reduction of art, religion, science, and history to philosophy means nothing but the exposition of the life of philosophy as the lives of art, religion, science, and history. In a sense, each one of these lives disappears; but philosophy itself disappears as completely as any. Certainly, it is not our doctrine that professional "philosophers" are the only people who are really alive!

Art has turned out to be philosophy; and concrete philosophy is therefore art. That beauty which is the fleeting quarry of the artist is no stranger to the philosopher. His thought must clothe itself in speech, and to him all the quire of heaven and the furniture of earth becomes a divine language, symbolizing in sensuous imagery the eternal truths of thought. Nor is this imagery to him mere art; for art in his mind is enriched and deepened into religion in the knowledge that what he was taught in his youth, and in his haste perhaps rejected as fable, is true: that God really lives and is his father, that the voice that speaks in nature is truly the voice of her creator, and that this very God became man to die for him and to atone by a full, perfect, and sufficient sacrifice for the sins of the whole world. And this knowledge is not, for him, in any conflict with the regularity and uniformity of nature, with the fact that he can and does abstract, generalize, conceive everything as matter and motion or in modern language as space-time; for this abstract conception of the world is to him only the schematic order which, without doing it violence, he detects in that infinite whole which is at once spirit and nature, the whole of which the starry heavens above him and the moral law within him are parts. And in learning to know this whole, a whole of truly objective fact in which art and religion and science all play their parts—so, and only so, he comes to know himself. Its true objectivity is not the abstract objectivity of a world in which the knower himself has no place, but the concrete objectivity which is only the correlative of his own subjectivity. It is *his* world that he knows in this way: if he were not, this world of reality as he sees it would not be. Other worlds would no doubt exist, and in their very difference these would be in a sense identical with his, versions of it; but they could never replace it.

This enjoyment of the entire world of fact, released alike from the intermittence of art and religion, the abstractness of science and the indifferent externality of history, is the life of philosophy. The philosopher can be a philosopher all his life, not only in his moments of inspiration. Everything, not merely the selected experiment, comes as grist to his mill, for his philosophical thought is infinite in its application. And he knows what the historian does not know, that his own knowledge of facts is organic to the facts themselves, that his mind is these facts knowing themselves and these facts are his mind knowing itself. Everybody enjoys this life, and enjoys it unceasingly; but those who do not know that they are doing so, and give a false account to themselves of their own experience, so deform that experience that it loses its highest qualities and actually becomes something not altogether unlike what they falsely think it.

This is called the life of absolute knowledge not because it is secure from error: that is impossible; but because in it there is no element of necessary and insurmountable error, as there is in the lives of art, religion, science, and history in the restrictive sense. In these lives the mind is by its very self-determination as aesthetic, religious, and so on, committed to certain errors and forced—always by its own act—to distort any truth it achieves, however great this truth may be, into conformity with them. In the life of philosophy such distorting media are done away with: the mind here says what it means, and therefore can for the first time say what is absolutely true. If it errs, the smallest error as to a matter of fact infects to some extent its whole life: to misjudge the tiniest fact is as if a cloud went over the sun and darkened the face of the world. And since every error is abstraction, this darkening of its world is the self-alienation of the philosophical mind, its degradation into the life of history or even lower. Consequently there is no such thing as a mere error of fact. Any such error distorts the whole mind and must be eradicated not by the correction of a detail but by the recovery of the balance of the whole.

It follows that the concrete life of philosophy is no mere haven of rest, but a ceaseless act of achieving this balance. The balance is achieved not by the static contemplation by mind of its own fixed given nature—mind has no fixed given nature—but by the self-creation of this nature in a perpetual discovery of fact which is at the same time the creation of fact: the creation of the fact of its discovery, which is only the indispensable subjective side of the fact itself. The life of absolute knowledge is thus the conscious self-creation of the mind, no mere discovery of what it is, but the making of itself what it is.

Now in error (and the same is true, of course, in wrongdoing) the mind also creates itself: determines itself in this way, just as in knowledge it determines itself in that. Whatever the mind does, therefore, it cannot escape that self-creation which is moral responsibility. But in error it creates in itself a nature which it conceals from itself: quite literally, error and evil are the mind knowing not what it does, creating itself in one shape while it thinks of itself in another. Thus it cannot be said that an idealistic view of mind finds no place for error and evil. On the contrary, it requires their continual presence in the form of that which, by conscious reflection, the mind in knowledge and in duty rejects; and inasmuch as its whole life is a process of self-determination, the past in any such process is the evil which is rejected, good when it was brought into being but now outworn and therefore evil if it had been retained.

But what is most fundamental is that the mind cannot only commit error but can redeem itself from error. This is because any error it makes concerning its own nature (and every error is that) creates two conflicting results: a new state of itself, and a new notion of itself. But because its own state is a state of consciousness, this new state, even though only implicitly, contradicts the newly formed notion. Thus there are two conflicting notions of itself in the mind, and this conflict is the mark of error and the signal that a return to the road of truth is required. Thus the equilibrium of thought is a stable equilibrium like that of a gyroscope; but it is only the energy of the gyroscope that keeps it upright.

It is customary to ask people who speak as we have been speaking about "the mind," what mind are you talking about?

It is no reply to say, that mind which is at once subject and object of the absolute experience. It remains to be asked what this mind is.

In the first place we may reasonably reply: We are speaking of any mind you please, mind in general. We are discussing the behavior of the mind as you might discuss the behavior of the trout or the potentilla. What we have said is true of every mind that exists, wherever and whenever you please, and by whatever name it is known.

That might stand as a provisional answer; but it evades the real problem. For it implies that we are discussing the abstract common nature of all minds as such, irrespective of the question what minds, if any, there are. And we may very well be asked, are there any minds in your sense of the word? And if so, where are they to be found? Thus our "theory of knowledge" is referred beyond itself to a "metaphysics," or statement as to the nature of real existence. But this is a flagrant collapse into the scientific fallacy and a fall from even the historical standard of truth. Mind in general is merely an abstract concept, and in appealing to it we are convicted of psychology.

The absolute mind, then, must be an historical fact, not a generalization. Is it the world-spirit, the mind whose life is gradually being developed as the universe evolves? Hardly, for the world-spirit is mere mythology. If there is such a thing, we know nothing of it. Moreover, a world-spirit embodied in the universe "whose body nature is, and God the soul" is a quite confused conception belonging to a primitive dualism of body and soul which history, and *a fortiori* philosophy, cannot for a moment tolerate.

The mind of which we are speaking is an absolute fact, one of which there can never in anybody's mind be any doubt. That is to say, it must at least be the mind of each one of us, for each his own particular mind. But if it is my own particular mind, it is not the same mind as yours; and hence my philosophy of it is a description not of mind as such but of my own individual mind, and all my knowledge is of my own mind and not of anything other than my own mind; and philosophy becomes mere autobiography.

This is solipsism, the answer to which is, from the idealistic point of view, easy. Realists are always afraid of solipsism, because it is a difficulty which they cannot answer except by an arbitrary refusal to listen to it. It alarms them because it contains two elements, a realistic background and an idealistic foreground, and these cannot be brought into focus together. The realist cannot explain away the idealistic element, but the idealist can point out that the realistic element is a false abstraction and so lay the specter. The background is the realistic separation of subject and object into two independent things; the foreground, the idealistic principle of self-knowledge. Put them together, and you get the disastrous consequence that the self-knowledge of the mind excludes all knowledge of anything else. The realist is helpless before this suggestion, and it drives him to all sorts of strange expedients such as denying the reality of self-knowledge; but the idealistic answer (as Kant once for all pointed out) is that the mind's knowledge of itself is its knowledge of everything else: in knowing itself it knows its world, and in knowing its world it knows itself. Thus solipsism, which is a disease endemic among realists—as is clear from their morbid interest in its symptoms—leaves our withers unwrung. In knowing my mind, I know yours and other people's: these reveal me to myself and I simultaneously explain them to myself. My mind is obviously a product of society, and conversely the society I know is the product of my mind, as thinking it according to its lights.

The absolute mind, then, unites the differences of my mind and other people's, but not as the abstract universal unites: rather as the concrete universal of history unites. The absolute mind is an historical whole of which mine is a part.

Yet the category of whole and part is false, for the part in its externality to other parts is but a reassertion of abstract difference. The absolute mind is not "one stupendous whole." It lives in its entirety in every individual and every act of every individual, yet not indifferently, as triangularity is indifferently present in every triangle, but expressing itself in every individual uniquely and irreplaceably. This is its necessary nature as concrete: it cares, so to speak, how many individual reduplications of itself there are, and will have so many as form a real organic whole in which every element is essential to the being of the whole.

To demonstrate in detail this necessity of every individual to the whole is precisely the work of history. It is in the nature of the case a work permanently incomplete; but that is only because it grows upon itself and every fresh thought is a fresh individual fact.

The philosophical concept of such an absolute mind requires that we should see it as concrete, that is, to banish solipsism and pantheism (abstract assertion and abstract denial of the individual), determinism and indeterminism (abstract assertion and abstract denial of the whole), and in general every form of the two complementary abstractions one of which denies the whole to assert the part, while the other denies the part to assert the whole. It requires us to conceive the whole as *totum in toto et totum in qualibet parte,* and the part as performing a function in the whole without which the whole would simply not exist. This is not a difficult feat, except to minds hidebound in the habits of abstract thought: it is simply thinking historically, and every historian enjoys it as the very breath of his life.

The absolute mind has nothing over against itself as a necessity by which it is bound; not even the laws of its own nature. These laws it creates by acting upon them, and this creation is not the arbitrary act of a divine tyrant who could make twice two into five if he pleased—as if that could mean anything—but the necessity of reason itself. The thoughts of this absolute mind, in so far as they are true, are known as true not by any so-called correspondence with fact but simply by being justifiable under criticism, which of course is always self-criticism, and from which there can be no appeal. Anything which is by definition non-mental is an object of this mind which it creates by lapsing into error concerning its own nature.

Thus, the reader may have imagined that when we spoke of the process of thought we were presupposing the reality of time, since every process is a process in time. Hence time would appear to be something external to the absolute mind, the necessity which stands over Zeus himself. But so to regard time is to forget that the process of which we are speaking is a process not of mechanical change but of thought: a self-knowing process. A mind which knows its own change is by that very knowledge lifted above change. History—and the same is true of memory and even perception—is the mind's triumph over time. It is a commonplace of philosophy that whereas sensation is temporal, thought is eternal or extra-temporal: sensation apprehends the here and now, thought apprehends the everywhere and the always. Hence the abstract psychology which splits the mind up into a sensitive and an intellectual faculty paradoxically presents us with a picture of man as standing with one foot in time and the other in eternity. This is mythology, but true mythology. All concrete thought is, in its immediacy, temporal, but in its mediation extra-temporal. The mind in its actual thinking at once recognizes and defies temporal (and spatial) limitations. The opposites, time and eternity, are necessary to one another. Time is not a mere appearance; it is perfectly real; but like all opposites it can be real only as the correlative of its equally real opposite, eternity. Time in fact is the abstraction of the externality to one another of the phases of a process: eternity is the opposite abstraction of the continuity of this process, the identity of the whole in its process. To describe the life of man as temporal or finite and the life of God as eternal or infinite is only a way of saying that time is not real in abstraction, but real only in relation to its opposite. In the absolute process of thought the past lives in the present, not as a mere "trace" or effect of itself in the physical or psychical organism, but as the object of the mind's historical knowledge of itself in an eternal present.

This is the solution of all those problems concerning finitude and infinity which have so vexed abstract thought. Man recognizes himself as finite and knows that, if he really is finite, he is thereby debarred from that infinity to which he aspires. But just as a being really limited in time could not know of its own limitation—for it could have no conception of a past and a future if it lived wholly in the present—so a being really finite could not know itself as finite. The self-knowledge of man as finite is already his assertion of himself as infinite. In the very act of abstraction by which psychology asserts the existence of finite centers of consciousness it is rising above its own theory and making a concrete act of thought which refutes its own ostensible content.

Religious imagery cannot prove the truth of any philosophy, because the interpretation put upon such imagery is already the work of philosophy; but it will illustrate, if it does not help to demonstrate, our conception of the absolute mind to point out the way in which one religion at least has expressed itself, when dealing with the ultimate questions which here concern us.

God is conceived as the absolute spirit, alpha and omega, the beginning and the end. Behind him, beyond him, apart from him, there is nothing: neither matter nor law, neither earth nor heaven, neither space nor time. In the beginning, by an absolute act which was not itself subject to any determination of time or space, God created the heavens and the earth: the visible world, with all its order and furniture, even the very space in which it floats and the time in which it endures and changes, is the work of this absolute act. But this world is no mere toy shaped by God and thrown off from himself in contemptuous alienation. His spirit moves upon the face of the waters, even the waters of chaos, and this same breath becomes the soul of life in the man whom he creates in his own image. Man is one with God, no mere part of a whole, but informed by the indwelling of the divine spirit. Now man, by his misguided thirst for knowledge, partakes of that knowledge which is forbidden, namely error, or the human wisdom which negates God's wisdom. This error deforms his own true, that is divine, nature, and the deformation takes the shape of banishment from the presence of God into the wilderness of the visible world. Having thus lost even the sight of God, the knowledge of what he himself ought to be, he cannot recover his lost perfection until he comes to know himself as he actually is. But not knowing himself as he ought to be, he cannot know himself as he is. His error is implicit just because it is complete. It can only become explicit if God reveals himself afresh, if the true ideal breaks in upon the soul clouded by error. This, in the fullness of time, is granted. Human nature sunk in error is confronted by the confutation of its own error, and thus, through a fresh dialectical process, redeemed.

Now in this imagery there is one flaw, namely the transcendence of God. God standing aloof from the drama of human sin and redemption, a mere stage manager, is no true symbol of the absolute mind in its concreteness. But this is exactly where the truth of our religious imagery shines most brilliantly. It is God who accepts the burden of error, takes upon himself the moral responsibility for the fall, and so redeems not his creature but himself.

The absolute mind, if our account of it is true, can never be more profoundly or impressively pictured than in this drama of the fall and redemption of man.

BIBLIOGRAPHY

1. THE WORKS OF R. G. COLLINGWOOD *

(a) *Philosophical Books and Articles*

1916 *Religion and Philosophy.* London: Macmillan & Co.

"The Devil," in B. H. Streeter and others, *Concerning Prayer.* London: Macmillan & Co.

1920 "What Is the Problem of Evil?", *Theology, I.*

Review of *King's College Lectures on Immortality,* edited by W. R. Mathews, *Theology,* I, No. 5 (November 1920), 299-300.

1921 "Croce's Philosophy of History," *Hibbert Journal,* XIX.

1922 "Are History and Science Different Kinds of Knowledge?", *Mind,* XXXI.

Ruskin's Philosophy, an Address Delivered at the Ruskin Centenary Conference, Coniston, August 8, 1919. Kendal: Titus Wilson & Son.

1923 "Sensation and Thought," *Proceedings of the Aristotelian Society,* XXIV (1923-1924).

"Can the New Idealism Dispense with Mysticism?", *Aristotelian Society, Supplementary Volume III.*

* Other bibliographies of Collingwood's philosophical works have been compiled by T. M. Knox, in *Proceedings of the British Academy,* XXIX (1943), 474-475 (and further amplified by Knox in *The Idea of History,* p. vii); Alan Donagan, in *The Later Philosophy of R. G. Collingwood,* pp. 308-310; and W. Debbins, in his edition of Collingwood's papers in the philosophy of history, pp. 141-148. Of these, the one by Debbins is the most complete. In particular it contains a valuable list of most of the reviews of Collingwood's philosophical books.

For a bibliography of Collingwood's writings in history and archaeology, see I. M. Richmond, in *Proceedings of the British Academy,* XXIX (1943), 481-485. Donagan has provided a valuable appendix in *The Later Philosophy,* pp. 311-313, which lists the dates on which Collingwood's philosophical books after *An Essay on Philosophical Method* were composed.

1924 *Speculum Mentis.* Oxford: Clarendon Press.

1925 *Outlines of a Philosophy of Art.* London: Oxford University Press.

"Plato's Philosophy of Art," *Mind,* XXXIV.

Review of H. Wildon Carr, *A Theory of Monads,* in *Hibbert Journal,* XXIII, No. 2 (January 1925), 380-382.

"The Nature and Aims of a Philosophy of History," *Proceedings of the Aristotelian Society,* XXV (1924-1925).

"Economics as a Philosophical Science," *International Journal of Ethics,* XXXVI.

1926 "Some Perplexities about Time: With an Attempted Solution," *Proceedings of the Aristotelian Society,* XXVI (1925-1926).

"The Place of Art in Education," *Hibbert Journal,* XXIV.

"Religion, Science, and Philosophy," *Truth and Freedom,* II, 7.

1927 "Aesthetic," in J. S. McDowall, ed., *The Mind.* London: Longmans.

"Reason Is Faith Cultivating Itself," *Hibbert Journal,* XXVI.

"Oswald Spengler and the Theory of Historical Cycles," in two parts, *Antiquity,* I.

1928 *Faith and Reason.* A pamphlet in the Affirmation Series. London: Ernest Benn. Reprinted in A. A. David, ed., *God and the Modern World.* New York: Dutton, 1929.

"The Limits of Historical Knowledge," *Journal of Philosophical Studies,* III.

"Political Action," *Proceedings of the Aristotelian Society,* XXIX (1928-1929).

1929 "Form and Content in Art," *Journal of Philosophical Studies,* IV.

"A Philosophy of Progress," *The Realist,* I.

1930 *The Philosophy of History.* Historical Association Leaflet No. 79. London: G. Bell & Sons.

1931 Review of Bishop Gore, *Philosophy of the Good Life,* in *The Criterion,* April 1931.

Review of M. C. D'Arcy, *The Nature of Belief*, in *Journal of Philosophical Studies,* IX (1931).

1933 *An Essay on Philosophical Method.* Oxford: Clarendon Press.

1934 "The Present Need of a Philosophy," *Philosophy,* IX (July 1934), 262-265.

1935 *The Historical Imagination.* An Inaugural Lecture. Oxford: Clarendon Press.

1936 "Human Nature and Human History," *Proceedings of the British Academy,* XXII. Reprinted, London: Humphrey Milford.

1938 *The Principles of Art.* Oxford: Clarendon Press.

"On the So-called Idea of Causation," *Proceedings of the Aristotelian Society,* XXXVIII (1937-1938).

1940 *An Essay on Metaphysics.* Oxford: Clarendon Press.

"Fascism and Nazism," *Philosophy,* XV.

1941 *The Three Laws of Politics.* L. T. Hobhouse Memorial Trust Lectures No. 11. London: Oxford University Press.

1942 *The New Leviathan.* Oxford: Clarendon Press.

1945 *The Idea of Nature,* edited by T. M. Knox. Oxford: Clarendon Press.

1946 *The Idea of History,* edited by T. M. Knox. Oxford: Clarendon Press.

(b) *Memoirs*

1939 *An Autobiography.* London: Oxford University Press. Reprinted, Penguin Books, 1944.

1940 *The First Mate's Log.* London: Oxford University Press.

(c) *Translations*

1913 B. Croce, *The Philosophy of Giambattista Vico.* London: Latimer. Reissued by Allen & Unwin in the Library of Philosophy Series.

1921 With A. H. Hannay and G. de Ruggiero, *Modern Philosophy.* London: Allen & Unwin.

1927 B. Croce, *An Autobiography.* Oxford: Clarendon Press.

G. de Ruggiero, *The History of European Liberalism.* Oxford: Clarendon Press.

1928 B. Croce, "Aesthetic," in *Encyclopaedia Britannica,* 14th edition.

(d) *Selected Bibliography of Historical Writings*

1923 *Roman Britain.* London: Oxford University Press. Revised edition, Oxford: Clarendon Press, 1934.

1936 *Roman Britain and the English Settlements* (with N. L. Myers). Oxford: Clarendon Press. 2nd edition. 1937.

(e) *Unpublished Manuscripts* **

1935 Correspondence with Gilbert Ryle. May 9 and June 6. Deposited in the Bodleian Library in 1964. ms. Eng. Lett. d. 194.

(f) *Editions of Collingwood's Writings*

W. Debbins, ed., *Essays in the Philosophy of History by R. G. Collingwood.* Austin: University of Texas Press, 1965.

A. Donagan, ed., *Essays in the Philosophy of Art by R. G. Collingwood.* Bloomington: Indiana University Press, 1964.

2. SELECTED BIBLIOGRAPHY OF LITERATURE ON COLLINGWOOD'S THOUGHT (INCLUDING REVIEWS)***

Anonymous, Review of *Concerning Prayer,* in *Holborn Review,* XLIX (1917), 136-137.

W. G. de Burgh, Review of *Human Nature and Human History,* in *Philosophy,* XII (April 1937), 233-236.

** In addition to the correspondence with Ryle, it is well known that there exist a number of other manuscripts which include, among other things, a draft of the incomplete and unpublished *Principles of History,* and a copy of Collingwood's own Cosmology. The latter was originally delivered as a set of lectures in 1934 and 1937, and was at one time intended as the concluding section of the *Idea of Nature.* In 1939, however, for reasons known only to himself, Collingwood replaced this section with another shorter piece. Except for T. M. Knox, no other scholar to my knowledge has examined any of these unpublished papers. At present the manuscripts are in the possession of Mrs. Collingwood, who has not yet, at least so far as I know, revealed her plans for their future.

*** For the purpose of this bibliography, only those works that were thought to be relevant to the materials included in this volume have been listed.

J. V. L. Casserley, *The Christian in Philosophy.* London: Faber and Faber, 1949.

A. Donagan, "Introduction" to *Essays in the Philosophy of Art. Op. cit.,* pp. x-xx.

———, *The Later Thought of R. G. Collingwood.* Oxford: Clarendon Press, 1962.

———, "Collingwood," article in *Encyclopedia of Philosophy.* New York: Macmillan & Free Press, 1967, II, 140-144.

J. Drummond, Review of *Concerning Prayer,* in *Hibbert Journal,* XV, No. 2 (1917), 327-331.

T. S. Eliot, Review of *Religion and Philosophy,* in *Journal of Ethics,* July 1917, p. 543.

G. Galloway, Review of *Religion and Philosophy,* in *Mind,* XXVIII (July 1919), 365-367.

E. E. Harris, "Mr. Collingwood and the Ontological Argument: Reply to G. Ryle," *Mind,* XLV (1936), 474-480.

H. S. Harris, "Introduction" to *Genesis and Structure of Society,* by G. Gentile. Urbana: University of Illinois Press, 1960, pp. 14-20.

J. N. Hartt, "Metaphysics, History, and Civilization: Collingwood's Account of Their Relationships," Journal of Religion, XXXIII (1953), 198-211.

Van A. Harvey, *The Historian and the Believer.* New York: Macmillan, 1966.

W. M. Johnston, "The Formative Years of R. G. Collingwood," Ph.D. Thesis, Harvard University, 1955.

T. M. Knox, "Notes on Collingwood's Philosophical Work," *Proceedings of the British Academy,* XXIX (1944), 469-475.

———, "Editor's Preface" to *The Idea of History. Op. cit.,* pp. x-xxiv.

D. Mathers, "Collingwood's Theory of History," Ph.D. Thesis, Columbia University, 1954.

A. J. M. Milne, *The Social Philosophy of English Idealism.* London: George Allen and Unwin, 1962.

J. Moffat, "Survey of Recent Theological Literature," *Hibbert Journal,* XV, No. 4 (1917), 678.

T. A. Roberts, *History and Christian Apologetic.* London: S. P. C. K., 1960.

N. Rotenstreich, "Historicism and Philosophy: Reflections on R. G. Colingwood," *Revue internationale philosophie,* XI (1957), 401-419.

———, "History and Time: A Critical Examination of R. G. Collingwood," *Scripta Hierosolymitana.* Jerusalem, 1960.

M. L. Rubinoff, "Collingwood and the Radical Conversion Hypothesis," *Dialogue: The Canadian Journal of Philosophy,* V, No. 1 (1966), 71-83.

———, "The Relation Between Philosophy and History in the Thought of R. G. Collingwood," Ph.D. Thesis, University of Toronto, 1964; to be published as *Phenomenology, Metaphysics, and Historicity: The Thought of R. G. Collingwood.*

G. Ryle, "Mr. Collingwood and the Ontological Argument," *Mind,* XLIV (1935), 137-151.

———, "Back to the Ontological Argument; Rejoinder," *Mind,* XLV (1937), 53-57.

L. Susan Stebbing, Review of *Speculum Mentis,* in *Hibbert Journal,* XXVIII, No. 3 (1925), 566-569.

H. F. Stewart, Review of *Concerning Prayer,* in *Journal of Theological Studies,* XVIII (1917), 79-80.

N. Sykes, "Some Current Conceptions of Historiography and Their Significance for Christian Apologetic," *Journal of Theological Studies,* L (January-April 1949), 24-37.

E. W. F. Tomlin, "R. G. Collingwood," *Writers and Their Works Series,* No. 42. London: Longmans, 1953.

———, "The Philosophy of R. G. Collingwood," *Ratio,* I (1958).

THE FOLLOWING BOOKS EDITED BY CANON B. F. STREETER WILL PROVIDE HELPFUL BACKGROUND MATERIAL FOR A STUDY OF THE INTELLECTUAL CLIMATE WITHIN WHICH COLLINGWOOD'S THOUGHT MATURED:

Foundations: A Statement of Christian Belief in Terms of Modern Thought, by seven Oxford men (especially the essays "The Atonement" and "God and the Absolute" by W. H. Moberly). London: Macmillan & Co., 1912.

The Spirit: God and His Relation to Man Considered from the Standpoint of Philosophy, Psychology, and Art (especially the essay "Immanence and Transcendence" by A. Seth Pringle-Pattison). London: Macmillan & Co., 1919.

INDEX